THE

HIDDEN DOOR

THE
HIDDEN DOOR

Understanding and
Controlling Dreams

Peter and Elizabeth Fenwick

BERKLEY BOOKS, NEW YORK

THE HIDDEN DOOR: UNDERSTANDING
AND CONTROLLING DREAMS

A Berkley Book / published by arrangement with
the authors

The Penguin Putnam Inc. World Wide Web site address is
http://www.penguinputnam.com

ISBN: 0-7394-0363-X

BERKLEY®
Berkley Books are published by The Berkley Publishing Group,
a member of Penguin Putnam Inc.,
375 Hudson Street, New York, New York 10014.
BERKLEY and the ''B'' design are trademarks
belonging to Berkley Publishing Corporation.

PRINTED IN THE UNITED STATES OF AMERICA

To everyone whose dreams contributed to the making of this book, with our thanks, and to Huw, Oliver and Sebastian in the hope that the best of their dreams will come true

Authors' Note

The authors wish to make clear that the use of the first person singular refers to Dr. Peter Fenwick only. Where "he" has been used in the abstract sense, it should be taken to mean "he/she."

Contents

Introduction

The dream is the hidden door in the deepest and most intimate sanctum of the soul.

Carl Jung

Accounts of dreams are as old as human history. People have always been fascinated by their own dreams, and have always looked for significance in them. From the most ancient civilisations of the Assyrians and Babylonians through to Biblical times it was believed that dreams brought messages from the gods in the form of warnings, omens and portents. In ancient Greece they were seen as prophecies, or instructions from Zeus.

Wherever dreams are taken seriously, regarded as meaningful and revelatory, interpreters of dreams are valued. In early cultures people relied on shamans, priests and wise men to tell them the meaning of their dreams. There are countless examples of dreams and dream interpretations in the Bible—in fact dreams seem to have been the preferred medium through which the Almighty conveyed his intentions, instructions or displeasure to his chosen people. In Biblical times the Jews were revered as dream interpreters by both the Egyptians and the Babylonians. Although Joseph's meteoric rise to power was clearly due not only to his talent for dream interpretation, but also the native wit that allowed him to turn matters to his own advantage ("Now therefore let Pharaoh look out for a man discreet and wise and set him over the land of

Egypt . . .''), he had already earned the respect of his peers as
a dream analyst.

Other notable Jewish dream analysts followed. When King
Nebuchadnezzar had a dream that troubled him, all the wise
men of Babylon—the magicians, the astrologers, the Chalde-
ans and the soothsayers—failed to interpret it. It was left to
the Israelite prophet Daniel to interpret the dream as predicting
the king's imminent seven years of madness: ''They shall
drive thee from men and thy dwelling shall be with the beasts
of the field; they shall make thee to eat grass as oxen and they
shall wet thee with the dew of heaven.'' A sense of delicacy
may have stopped him adding to the good news by pointing
out that the mad king was also to have, as it transpired, ''hairs
grown like eagles' feathers, and his nails like birds' claws.''

Throughout the ages certain places have been associated
with dreams that have special properties or give prophetic information. The Celtic seer would wrap himself in an animal
skin and sleep beside a waterfall in order to have a prophetic
dream. Dream oracles were used by the Greeks to facilitate
dream communication with the gods. ''Temple dreaming,'' or
incubation—the practice of sleeping at one of these holy places
in order to encourage significant dreams—was a well-
recognised and highly organised activity. Over 400 of these
temples existed in Ancient Greece, many dedicated to Aesculapius, the god of healing. Here the sick would come, first
of all to undergo rites of purification (including abstention
from eating meat or fish and having sex), then to sleep in a
special cell in the belief that Aesculapius himself might be
induced to visit them in their dreams and prescribe a treatment
or even perform a surgical operation upon their sleeping body.
The philosopher Aristides, seeking such a cure in the middle
of winter and in extremely cold weather, was told by the god
to bathe outdoors. He was, it is said, filled with well-being
after taking the advice.

It is possible that some of the dreams that were dreamed at
these sacred sites were drug-induced. It has been suggested
that during some of the religious ceremonies held at the sites,
psychedelic drugs might have been used to induce altered
states of consciousness as part of the ritual. Our current understanding of altered states of consciousness, particularly
from studying such drugs as LSD, psylocibin and mescalin,

shows that characteristic patterns are seen under the influence of such drugs, which take the form of circles, spirals and expanding geometric forms, and seem to be independent of culture and person. Freelance researcher and writer Paul Devereux and his colleagues have found that patterns carved on the walls of caves in sacred sites are very similar to the patterns induced by psychedelic drugs.

The Egyptians were probably the first to try to develop a system of dream interpretation and to incorporate individual dream symbols. They believed that dreams could be interpreted paradoxically: apparently happy dreams were omens of disaster; nightmares presaged good times to come. They also believed that dreams came from good and evil spirits, and used herbal remedies and spells to encourage the good and deter the bad.

With the Greeks a whole literature of dream interpretation developed, based on symbols and on the belief in the prophetic nature of dreams. The Greeks regarded as meaningless any dream that clearly had its origins in events or desires in the dreamer's daily life. However, some dreams that we would see as obvious candidates for psychological interpretation—for example, a dream (common, according to Sophocles) of sleeping with one's mother, the Greeks usually interpreted symbolically, and regarded as auspicious. Only Plato and Artemidorus anticipated the twentieth century and Freud by suggesting that wish-fulfilment might play a part in such dreams. Artemidorus, a soothsayer of Ephesus during the second century AD, deserves a special mention in the annals of dream research and interpretation. His four-volume work *Oneirocritica* ("The Interpretation of Dreams") is a compendium of ancient superstitions and draws together the works of earlier authors. He was one of the first to recognise the importance of the dreamer's personality in dream interpretation.

Early stirrings of scepticism about the divine nature of dreams are seen as early as the fifth century BC, when the first scientific theory of dreams proposed telepathy as a mechanism. Democritus suggested that dreams are images and thoughts emanating from distant people or objects, distorted in transmission before being received by the dreamer. Aristotle, a century later, proposed a modified version of this theory. He attributed clairvoyant powers to the soul, which he suggested was liberated from the body's constraints during sleep. He was also one of the first people to recognise that dreams can incorporate bodily sensations.

Whatever the doubts cast upon them by reason, logic or the inexorable march of science, dreams prophesying doom and disaster (or, less often, fame and fortune) continue to be dreamed, some by seemingly impeccable sources. A bishop, no less, dreamed of the assassination of Archduke Franz Ferdinand of Austria in Sarajevo, on the very morning it took place, and sent an account of the dream, together with a drawing of the assassination scene he had seen in it, to his brother, a Jesuit priest. Abraham Lincoln dreamed of his own assassination two weeks before it actually occurred.

The writer Mark Twain (who was, one has to remember, one of the world's greatest storytellers) had a remarkable premonitory dream of the death of his younger brother. At the time Twain, then still known by his real name, Sam Clemens, was working as an apprentice pilot on the steamboat the *Pennsylvania*, which plied the Mississippi river. His brother Henry worked as a clerk on the same boat. Sam's dream was that he saw a metal coffin resting on two chairs. In it was his brother and resting on his chest was a bunch of white flowers with a single red flower in the middle.

Some days later, Sam had an argument with the chief pilot and was transferred to another boat. The *Pennsylvania* continued down the river, but just outside Memphis it blew up with the loss of 150 lives. Henry was badly burned, and Sam sat with him for several days and nights until he died. Then, exhausted, he fell asleep. When he woke up, his brother's body had been taken from the room. He found it, as he had seen it in his dream, in a metal coffin resting on two chairs. And as he watched, a woman entered the room carrying a bunch of white flowers, at the centre of which was a single red rose.

When people allow their dreams to influence their actions, one has to suspect that an element of wish-fulfilment or self-justification may be involved. The conquest of Mecca and the spread of Islam were set in motion on the instructions of the Angel Gabriel, who appeared to Mohammed in a dream. Genghis Khan was told in a dream that he was destined to rule over the Mongols. Once he had conquered the Mongols, another dream gave him to understand that his destiny was to conquer yet more kingdoms. Bismarck is said to have made his final decision to invade Austria after a dream in which he had seen Prussian troops with banners moving forwards. Can we regard these as prophetic dreams? Or is it more likely that they are simply the product of a lust for power?

The most unexpected people have been influenced by their dreams. General George Patton, the brilliant military tactician and colourful World War II soldier known to his troops as "Old Blood and Guts," apparently regularly drew military inspiration from his dreams and was in the habit of summoning his personal secretary in the middle of the night to dictate dream-derived battle plans. It seems to be less common for a dream to initiate a search for peace, but a biography of Lyndon B. Johnson by Doris Kearns, an aide to whom the President was in the habit of recounting his dreams, claims that his decision to withdraw from the Vietnam War was influenced by a dream that clarified for him the impossible no-win situation he was in.

Dreams have influenced almost every culture and every age. Although "Dreamtime" is a modern European term to describe the creation of the world by the mythical giant ancestors of the Australian Aborigines, the Aborigines say it is a fair approximation of what the Dreaming means to them. For centuries the Aborigines have followed in the footsteps of their ancestors. As part of their seasonal tribal migration, or as a personal spiritual journey, they have traced the paths trodden by the giant beings who walked the flat, featureless land, creating the landscape as it is today. Every feature of the land, each rock or waterhole, has meaning for the Aboriginals, is the creation of their ancestors, marked by song and ritual and legend, and an essential part of their consciousness. Sometimes new information on dreaming tracks is given to a tribal member through the medium of a dream, resulting in new rituals and songs.

It is through some of the more extraordinary phenomena of dreams that myths and legends often arise: astral travel, the terror of night visitations by the legendary "Old Hag," even abductions by far-flung extra-terrestrial visitors may all be by-products of our sleep and dreams.

Dreams can be inspirational, a source of creativity, too. Plato describes Socrates, in prison and awaiting execution, composing poetry in obedience to a dream; tradition has it that Coleridge composed "Kubla Khan" as a result of a dream. The city of Puebla, in Mexico, was even founded on a dream—the dream of Julian Garces, Bishop of Tlaxcale. Garces dreamed of two angels descending from the heavens, each holding a measuring rod in one hand and a long tape measure between them. Gliding down into the valley between the volcanoes, they marked out an enormous square on the ground before dissolving in the haze. The day after his dream, a crowd accompanied the bishop in a search for the site the angels had indicated. When they came to an uninhabited area called Cuetlaxcuopen, which was intersected by three rivers, Garces ordered the procession to halt and said, "This is the place the Lord showed me and where He wants the new City to be built." And here indeed the city was immediately built and named Puebla de los Angeles after its heavenly town planners.

In more modern times, dreams have come to symbolise ideals ("I have a dream . . ."), to be the tool of the psychoanalyst, or the terror (according to Max Beerbohm) of the breakfast table. They have an established niche as a neat fictional device too. Dreams enable a writer to intertwine reality with illusion, as in *Alice in Wonderland*, or to overlay serious intent with fantasy, as in *The Wizard of Oz*. They may even serve as a lifeline to be grasped by a writer who has written himself into too tight a corner. "Bobby, I dreamed you were dead," gasped Pam Ewing, brought face to face with the husband too hastily written out by the *Dallas* scriptwriters several episodes earlier. Which (for older readers), as a fictional cop-out is on a par with Dick Barton's famed escape from the stake to which cannibals had bound him over a roasting fire: "With one bound, Dick was free. . . ."

We still look for meaning in our dreams, but when we manage to interpret their meaning correctly, we are likely to find that the messages they bring come not from the gods, nor indeed from any external source, but from ourselves. "If people would recount their dreams truthfully," Lichtenberg said, "one might divine character more correctly from dreams than from faces." In dreams our imagination is unfettered and anything is possible. But they can be unforgiving too, forcing self-knowledge upon us. We can ignore our dreams, or we can learn from them, choosing to go through Jung's "hidden door" and gain insights and resolutions which we might not have the courage to seek in waking life.

The writer and mystic P. D. Ouspensky regarded dreams as having different levels. The lowest category was the simple dream which took place on the same level as our ordinary waking life, and was of little significance. At a higher level were dreams which gave us insights and perceptions which we could not achieve in our ordinary waking life. In this category he included dreams of portents and predictions. His final category was of dreams which, in his words, "disclose to us the mysteries of being, show the laws governing life, bring us into contact with higher forces."

Once in a while, perhaps once in a lifetime, we may be given one of Ouspensky's "third-level" dreams, a dream that has the capacity to change our life. Jung called these "great dreams," and believed they could reveal some fundamental aspect of the dreamer and his life and spiritual development. Such dreams are remembered or recalled for years, and seem to extend our knowledge not only of ourselves, but of the very creation of which we are a part. These are the dreams which truly seem to be a gift, coming from some source beyond the boundaries of our limited selves and carrying a message that is revelatory.

1

The Dream World and the Real World

> *How troublesome is day!*
> *It calls us from our sleep away;*
> *It bids us from our pleasant dreams awake,*
> *And sends us forth to keep or break*
> *Our promises to pay.*
>
> Thomas Love Peacock (1785–1866)

This was a more acute observation on the nature of sleep than Thomas Peacock may have realised. Our instinct is to feel that the daytime world is the "real" world, and that sleep and dreams are quite separate processes, and merely an interruption of the daytime brain activity and mental state. But in fact it is just as logical—in many ways *more* logical—to look on dreaming as our "natural" state, and wakefulness as merely an interruption of the dreaming state.

We think of dreams as being different, something quite separate from our daily lives. Dreams seem to have their own life, independent of ours. They may be thought of as messengers (if we can interpret them—the message is often enigmatic), or as portents of joy or disaster. They may terrify us or sexually excite us to the point of orgasm (80 per cent of American high-school males say they have reached orgasm in dreams). However we think of them, the dream world seems to operate at a different level from the ordinary, waking world over which we have more control. But is this really true? Is the dream world really so very different from the real world?

Anyone who has ever driven on a motorway slightly farther

1

than they should have done without taking a break will have noticed the subtle changes that occur as you become drowsy. One of the main features of claims to insurance companies is the bewildering rapidity with which events apparently come to pass. "Suddenly this Volvo pulled out in front of me..." "Suddenly this white van appeared from nowhere..." Part of advanced driver training is to help the driver to eliminate the "suddenly" factor by making him give a running commentary on everything he can see. Precise, attentive driving requires the driver to be alert and living 100 per cent in the external world.

But as most of us are only too aware, what usually happens when we are driving long distances is that there is a gradual withdrawal into an internal world where thought images are pre-eminent and driving becomes automatic. Unchecked, the process would continue, and on the borderlands of sleep a wonderful world of images, colours, explosions into a different reality would occur. Is that our dream world? Does mental experience stop there? Or does it continue when we fall asleep?

The reality is that we have continuous mental experience through the twenty-four hours of the day. The brain never shuts down. All the time conscious processes are going on, some of which we remember very well—those that occur when we are awake—and others less well—those that occur on the borders of, and during, sleep. Hamlet said, "To sleep: perchance to dream." Our current understanding of sleep and dreams is that there is no "perchance" about it. We dream whether we like it or not. The brain goes on generating experience throughout the twenty-four hours. If Hamlet had said, "To sleep: perchance to *remember* our dreams," that would have been nearer the truth.

The idea of continual experience is counter-intuitive. If the primary purpose of sleep is restorative, surely that implies that the mind as well as the body must rest? A night filled with remembered dreams can leave us feeling as if we have not slept at all. What most of us mean by a "good night's sleep" is a night when we fall promptly asleep and know nothing at all until the first peal of the alarm next morning. A "good night," surely, is a mental blank, circuits switched off, brain inactive. Or is it?

Everything we now know about the brain tells us that this is not so. To begin with, let's look at the way conscious experience is generated.

Our current science regards the brain as a model-maker *par excellence*. It has a wonderfully discrete system of model-building functions, which combine to produce the self-conscious world which we see, hear, feel and move around in. Modern neuroimaging can produce very detailed visual images of the structure of the brain and of the brain at work, and shows that different aspects of these models are created in specific areas of the cerebral cortex. Visual images, for example, are created when impulses generated in the retina reach a primary receiving area in the visual cortex. They are refined and elaborated in other surrounding areas, whose function is very specific. There are special areas which deal with colour, shape, and even the recognition of words. If these areas are damaged, colours and shapes will be distorted, and the written word would be unrecognisable.

There is a similar localisation of function for sensation and the way this is integrated to make up our body image, and for speech and emotion. For example, speech in right-handed people is located on the left side of the brain. But it takes another area on the right side of the brain to add rhythm and melody to speech; without this, we would all talk like Daleks. The *understanding* of speech is located in a different area on the left side. To understand written words we need yet another area on the left. Movement calls into play a very widespread set of functions—joints must be stabilised; muscles prepared for movements. Each function has its own system.

An American neurophysiologist, R. R. Llinas, has shown, by implanting electrodes within the brain, that in dreaming sleep the firing patterns of the cells in the cortex of the brain are very similar to the firing patterns which are seen in the waking state. This is a powerful statement. It means that the model-building mechanism does not shut down as we start to dream. The brain goes on making models which come into conscious experience all the time, whether we are awake or asleep. It remains active in sleep, but its activity is modified. It has to base its models on the more limited data available to it.

We think of the objective external world which goes on

independently of us, and the subjective internal world which the brain creates, as two quite different states. A moment's thought shows that this cannot possibly be true, because the so-called objective external world—the "real" world—is also nothing more than a set of psychological constructs produced by the brain. What we see and what we feel depend on our emotional set and the state our brain is in. Any police constable will tell you that witnesses to the same accident will all remember it quite differently. There may be conflicting accounts of the speed of the cars, which direction they were travelling in, even what colour they were. Honestly remembered these accounts may be, but they seldom provide a truly objective picture of what actually happened.

The basic premise of Western science is that there is an independent external world which we can all accept and verify. This is only true to a limited degree. What we call an independent external world is only a set of psychological models held in common between people. What *is* true is that the day-time world seems to be closer to a common view and the sleeping world closer to a personal view. The more these psychological models depend on individual subjective experience, the less common ground there will be for science to explore, and the more hopeless will be the task of the scientist who tries to verify these experiences in a laboratory setting.

Can we find any objective evidence that the creative process of the brain continues throughout the twenty-four hours of the day? There is one simple way to find out. If you wake someone from *any* state of sleep and ask them, not if they are dreaming, but if there is anything going on in their mind, they will invariably say yes. At some times during the night they will come out with a flood of material, instantly recognisable as part of a dream. At other times what they report may tend to be rather confused, and they may have little memory of it, but still, they will be aware that there was *some* mental content. Never is the mental slate wiped clean. The brain never ceases to build its models, even if they are sometimes fragmentary and half-remembered. It only modifies them.

Llinas has suggested a neurophysiological theory of dreaming which starts by stressing how information comes up into the brain from all the major sensory organs, and passes through the thalamus (a major relay station) in a comparatively small number of channels, to the cortex (the part of the brain that analyses all incoming data and provides an output for action). Linking the cortex and the thalamus is a rich network of connections. This is the model-building mechanism of the brain. Activity from the cortex is integrated with activity from the thalamus, so that sensory information, information from memory, emotional content, are all synthesised together to create conscious experience at any moment. The richness of our conscious world, Llinas argues, is due *not* to the information that comes in from the outside world—there are rather few pathways for this, and a relative paucity of information—but to the multiplicity of the cortico-thalamic-cortico connections within the brain. It is as if, he suggests, the basic model that the brain builds is an internal one, and this is in some sense tailored or shaped by information from the outside.

During sleep the incoming flow of sense data to the cortex is restricted, allowing the basic, internal model freer rein. This puts quite a different complexion on the world of dreams. It suggests that the main difference between the dreaming and waking states is that the dreaming state is our basic model of the world, and when we are awake this basic model is continually modified and updated by a constant flow of incoming information to the brain from the outside world via the senses.

During dreaming, a control centre within the brain stem damps down a system (activated by a chemical messenger, noradrenaline) which has two functions: it allows information into the brain from the senses, and it enhances memory function. The effect of this damping-down is that the models the brain creates (dreams) are remembered less well; they are less dependent on information from the outside world, making use of emotion and memory from the internal world. Data from the outside world is sometimes incorporated in a dream, however—when our dreams involve travel to Antarctica, for example, we may well wake to find the duvet has fallen off. But the important point is that the centres creating this dreaming world are exactly the same as those that create the waking world. Dreams are not privileged: they use no special part of the brain circuitry. Dreams *are* reality, the substance of experience.

But if that is true, then why, when in our dreams we are at a dream disco, do we not get out of bed and dance around the room? In fact, as far as the brain is concerned, we do just that—the brain treats the dream body just the same as the real body. When we dream of dancing, the brain sends impulses from its movement centres to the motor nerve cells in the spinal cord, which would normally excite the muscles, inviting them to match the rhythmic movements of the dream dancer. The reason the muscles cannot respond is that within the brain stem there is also a centre which damps down the motor nerve cells in the spinal cord and prevents their full response. The dream dancer can dance in safety within his dream body because the real body is partially paralysed. It cannot respond.

If the same brain mechanism is used in both the dream world and the real world, then if this is damaged, both dreams and reality should be affected. And, indeed, this is what happens. If a stroke knocks out specific cognitive modules, the model the brain produces will have a specific defect not only in the waking, conscious state, but also in dreams. Llinas records the story of a woman who had a stroke which destroyed that part of the right hemisphere concerned with facial recognition. The woman lost her ability to recognise the faces of her friends, and in her dreams the people she saw were faceless.

It is as if the brain continually dreams, but there are times, when we are awake, when our dreams are constrained by the outside world. This is a rather different picture from the one we usually have—and may help us understand why it is something of a travesty to describe the picture we have of the outside world as "real," a faithful reproduction of whatever is out there, rather than a psychological model created by the brain.

If dreams are of the same substance as conscious experience and are created in the same brain structures as conscious experience, then it becomes increasingly difficult to draw a distinction between a dream model and a "real" model. Indeed, a number of studies have shown that if someone is lying in a warm bed, with eyes closed, low lighting and reduced sound, then even though they are awake their thought processes are similar to those of the dream state. Thoughts last about the same length of time as dream images. There are the same number of shifts from scene to scene, and scenes are linked in the same sort of way. In fact it is difficult to show any difference between these thought processes and those that occur when the brain is making dream models.

The story of Lakshmi is an Indian myth that suggests that the world is illusion. Lakshmi was walking along the banks of a river when a ring he was playing with fell into the water. He dived into the water in pursuit of the ring. There he met a charming girl with whom he fell in love. They married and lived together and raised a family. In the course of time Lakshmi became a grandfather, grew old, and died. As he died, his spirit came to the surface of the water, whereupon he got out of the river clasping the ring, which he had found at the bottom. The story illustrates the interconnectedness of the dream world and the illusion of the "real" world: the link is Lakshmi (the dreamer), who holds both within his consciousness.

Perhaps dreaming is the basis of what we call reality. Perhaps dreams are not modified reality, but reality only a modified dream. Maybe the Buddhists are right when they say the world is a dream. What Hamlet should really have said was: "To dream: perchance to wake."

2

What Happens When We Sleep

We spend a third of our lives asleep—much the same as the horse. Other species sleep less: ruminants such as the cow sleep away only 3 per cent of the twenty-four hours (continual grazing is necessary if they are to get enough energy to survive) and the elephant 19 per cent. Gorillas, on the other hand, sleep 70 per cent of the time; cats and bats even more (75 per cent and 83 per cent respectively). But until about fifty years ago, no one really understood what went on during sleep. It was thought that sleep was a passive process, and also a uniform state. You were either awake and conscious, or you were asleep and unconscious.

P. D. Ouspensky, in his book *A New Model of the Universe*, published in 1938, was one of the first people to suggest that sleep was a more complex and interesting state than that. His insights into the processes of sleep and dreaming, which came from direct observation, have since proved to be remarkably far-sighted and accurate. Ouspensky observed: "First it is necessary to understand clearly that sleep may be of different degrees and different depths. We can be more asleep or less asleep, nearer to the possibility of waking or further from the possibility of awaking."

The first great advance in the scientific understanding of sleep came when it became possible to use the then newly developed electroencephalogram (EEG) to monitor the "brain waves"—the electrical activity of the brain. This showed that sleep was not a continual or uniform process but was broken up into several distinct phases, each with a characteristic pattern of brain waves. Sleep did, as Ouspensky had suggested, have different levels, so that we are indeed either more asleep or less asleep, nearer to the possibility of waking or further from the possibility of awaking.

It used to be believed that the best sleep—quality-time sleep—was, in the words of the carol, "deep and dreamless." But we now know that there is no such thing as totally dreamless sleep. In the early 1950s, two scientists in the States, William Dement and Nathaniel Kleitman, found by looking at EEG recordings that there were periods during sleep when the brain waves were fast (almost as fast as they are in the waking state) and the eyes moved rapidly from side to side. If people were woken during these periods of rapid eye movement (REM) they reported that they were dreaming. On the other hand, if they were woken and asked if they were dreaming during periods when there was no rapid eye movement, and the brain waves were much slower, most people said no. However, if they were asked not if they were dreaming, but if anything was "going on in their minds," nearly three out of four adults said yes—about the same proportion as report ordinary dreams during REM sleep. But what they reported tended to be fragmentary impressions, thoughts, words, feelings and sensations.

THE CYCLE OF SLEEP

Nature loves a cycle. The seasons which come and go, the planets circling the sun, the movements of the moon and the tides, all are regular and predictable. In man every biological process has its own cycle too. Our body clock is governed by a pacemaker in the brain. It establishes the regular rise and fall of body temperature by about two degrees during each twenty-four hours, rising during the daylight hours, falling at night. Most people die at night because the hormone cortisol, which is secreted in response to stress, also follows a twenty-four-hour cycle and is at its lowest at about two a.m., and also because little water is drunk at night, so we tend to become dehydrated. We usually assume that the sleeping/waking cycle has the same twenty-four-hour circadian pattern as body temperature, but in fact although the two cycles usually synchronise so that we are awake and most active when body temperature is at its highest, and most deeply asleep when body temperature is at its lowest, the natural rhythm of the sleep/wake cycle is slightly longer, about twenty-five hours. This means that it can synchronise more easily with the changing light/dark cycles of nature.

It is in fact the light/dark cycle, mediated through a hormone, melatonin (secreted by the pineal gland), that sets the body clock. If you travel more than fifteen degrees east or west, your internal clock goes out of synch with the daylight cycle and this results in the feeling of jet lag. It is claimed that you can resynchronise your clock to a new night/day cycle by taking ½-3mg of melatonin before you go to bed. This fools the brain into thinking that it is night-time after all. Melatonin tablets are now such a fashionable way of reducing jet lag that they can be bought in every hotel gift shop in the Antipodes. Do they work? The only way to find out is to try them. In a small-scale clinical trial (one subject, one control) within our own family on a visit to California, the control partner who didn't take the melatonin observed that the subject who did became more edgy, irritable and intolerant than they ever were under the influence of jet lag alone. The most effective way to resynchronise your body clock is probably to spend as much time outside in the daylight as you can as soon as you reach a new time zone.

Synchronisation with nature isn't always easy for the body clock. A midsummer holiday in Reykjavik can cause real problems for someone from Ruislip. When night never seems to fall at all, the cues for sleeping are hard to come by. If you party till two a.m. and then retire to bed when all the noise has died down your body may be fooled into dropping off to sleep for a few hours. But there are some people who find it very difficult to resynchronise their clocks and get a good night's sleep in these conditions.

While it seems to be relatively easy to wind the body clock forward, it is almost impossible to wind it back. You can quite quickly adjust to going to bed much later than usual, at two or three a.m., and sleep for your usual seven hours or so. But if you then want to return to an earlier bedtime it may take several days to get back on schedule. This is why most people find it easier to deal with jet lag when they are travelling from

east to west. Shift workers and night workers face the same
sort of problems. If their sleep cycles become very much out
of synch, or even completely reversed, it is usually difficult to
change back to a different shift or working pattern unless they
are given two or three nights off duty in which they can rees-
tablish a normal cycle.

What happens to the body clock if all the normal cues for
sleeping and waking are removed, when there is no daylight,
no constraints and not even the cues normally gained from a
regular pattern of daily life? Experiments in which people have
spent long periods in caves have shown that the free-running
body clock runs slow to clock time above ground, with a
twenty-five-hour cycle. The longer they stay in the cave, the
more out of synch with "normal" time the body clock becomes. Some exceptional people developed sleep/wake cycles
of up to fifty hours, during which they would typically stay
awake for thirty to thirty-six hours, and sleep for fourteen to
twenty hours. They would still eat the conventional three meals
during the time they were awake (and consequently lost a considerable amount of weight during the experiment).

Sleep itself has its own cycle. As we fall asleep, the electrical activity of the brain starts to change, so that the frequency of the electrical brain waves becomes progressively
slower. Breathing and heart rates become slower too, and it
becomes gradually more and more difficult to wake us.

We define the depth of sleep by this progressive slowing,
from stage 1, just after the onset of sleep, to stage 4, the deepest phase of sleep, when the brain waves are at their slowest,
and we are most difficult to rouse. The deepest phase of sleep
occurs about ninety minutes after going to sleep. Just how
difficult it can be to rouse someone in stage 4 sleep many
people know from their own experience with young children.
You can pick a sleeping child in this phase of sleep out of a
car, carry him through a lighted house, up the stairs, and put
him into his bed without him stirring. But that isn't all. In this
deepest phase of sleep the brain switches vision off almost
completely, leaving us virtually blind. It is possible to hold
open the eyelids of a sleeping person, shine a lighted 60-watt
lamp twelve inches from his eyes, wave your hand in front of
him, and he still won't stir. You can poke him in the eyes,
squash his nose, rub his forehead and still he won't wake un-

less you continue for some time—maybe as long as ten or fifteen minutes. Someone in deep slow-wave sleep—stages 3 and 4—is not only difficult to rouse, but when he is woken he is confused and disorientated—it may take five or ten minutes for him to become fully awake.

Muscle tone decreases in slow-wave sleep, though it is never completely absent, so that the sleeper can—and does—move. In fact, slow-wave sleep can be a hive of activity. Video recordings made of sleepers show just how much tossing and turning goes on during the night—and insomniac partners of "restless" sleepers will confirm this. A host of other activities may take place in slow-wave sleep too, though these are not part of the normal pattern of sleep, but disturbances of it. Sleepwalking and talking, grinding one's teeth (bruxism), bed-wetting and night terrors all arise from slow-wave sleep; sleep-talking and bruxism during the lighter stages, sleepwalking, bed-wetting and night terrors during the periods of deepest sleep, stages 3 and 4.

DREAMING SLEEP

After about ninety minutes of deep slow-wave sleep, we enter a new and quite different phase of sleep—the stage of rapid eye movement sleep first described by Dement and Kleitman. The brain waves become faster again, heart and breathing rates increase and become irregular. If you watch the eyelids of someone in this stage of sleep you will be able to see the occasional bursts of flickering movement as the eyes move rapidly from side to side. REM sleep accounts for about a quarter of all sleep, and most adults have four or five periods of REM each night.

REM sleep is the sleep of dreams—or at least, it is the sleep of the dreams we remember. If someone is woken while in REM, they nearly always (about 74 per cent of the time) report that they have been dreaming, and "dreaming sleep" is the alternative name for REM. The first period of dreaming sleep during the night usually lasts from ten to fifteen minutes. The sleeper then falls back again into slow-wave sleep, but this time spends less time in stages 3 and 4, the deepest stages of sleep. Slow-wave sleep and REM sleep then succeed each other in approximately ninety-minute cycles throughout the night. Gradually, as the night progresses, we spend less time deeply asleep in each cycle, and more time in dreaming sleep. Towards the end of the night our dreams are more frequent and more intense, and when we wake naturally, it is usually from a period of dreaming sleep.

THE DREAMS OF SLOW-WAVE SLEEP

Because REM dreams are the only dreams that are easily remembered, for a long time it was thought that dreams *only* occurred in REM sleep. But since the early 1950s, and the advent of sleep laboratories, dream researchers have been able to look more closely at dreams and dreamers, and to study brain activity during sleep. Gradually it became clear that dreams were not limited to REM sleep, but occurred throughout the whole sleep cycle. However, the dreams that occurred during slow-wave sleep were very different from the ordinary dreams of REM sleep.

In the lighter stages of slow-wave sleep, stages 1 and 2, dreams are much more like the thoughts and imagery that we have when lying in a quietened room. In fact they are so similar that it is almost impossible to tell the difference between them. Not only is the imagery similar, but thoughts tend to last the same length of time, and there are shifts of scene at similar intervals.

However, in deep slow-wave sleep, stages 3 and 4, the mental imagery experienced is quite different. When someone is woken from deep sleep, they are confused. They also have much more difficulty remembering or recalling their mental content, because the thoughts and feelings have frequently disappeared before they can be recalled from memory. Although there are accounts of people in sleep laboratory experiments who have difficulty in distinguishing an awakening from REM sleep from an awakening from deep slow-wave sleep, for most people the experience is quite different. When people are woken from slow-wave sleep the most common reports are of thoughts and sensations. Occasionally (in a night terror, for example) they report feelings of being crushed or chased. One person described a feeling that the walls of the room were collapsing around him. Another remembered seeing a car crashing through the ceiling. But there is no real storyline, no characters, and no vivid visual images as there are in an REM dream.

This cycle of alternating periods of slow-wave sleep and REM continues throughout the night, though with each cycle the period of deep sleep becomes shallower and shorter, and time spent in REM sleep increases. Normally we wake from a period of REM sleep, and we wake quickly, alert and into full consciousness. However, if, instead of getting up at our normal waking time, we sleep in, the sleep cycle will start again, we will go into slow-wave sleep and may awaken from it feeling groggy and confused.

This ninety-minute cycle of sleep and dreaming may even provide some excuse for those of us who unaccountably lose concentration and find ourselves daydreaming at intervals during the day. Some scientists believe that the ninety-minute cycles continue during the day. During the dreaming phase of the cycle we are creative, laid-back and relaxed (morning coffee, lunch and afternoon tea). In the intervening times the slow-wave sleep cycle dominates and we are logical and incisive. The sleep cycle is part of a twenty-four-hour alertness cycle which is at its lowest at two a.m. and at its highest at nine p.m. Just after lunch, at one p.m., it takes a dip, which accounts for the post-prandial nap to which many of us succumb. It is well known on the conference circuit that it is disastrous to be given either the first slot of the conference (audience not present, still in sleep cycles) or the first one after lunch (audience returns to its sleep cycles).

WHY DON'T WE ACT OUT OUR DREAMS?

To anyone watching, the most obvious difference between REM sleep and slow-wave sleep is that in REM sleep the sleeper does not toss and turn. In fact he hardly moves at all. Occasionally he may make surprisingly large movements, but most of the time he simply twitches. Muscle tone disappears almost completely; the muscles are virtually paralysed.

It is not just a happy biological accident that we are paralysed during REM; it would be dangerous, possibly disastrous, if we were not. However vivid or violent our dreams are, we needn't worry that we will act them out. Watch a dog lying by the fire, whimpering and twitching in his sleep. We assume that he's dreaming—chasing rabbits perhaps, or fulfilling some other doggy wish. Fortunately, the dream remains a dream; the dog does not get up and create mayhem by rushing around the room in pursuit of his dream rabbit, simply because he cannot. During REM sleep the brain sends out the usual message to the muscles ("move it"), but instead of being relayed to the muscles from the spinal cord, the message is largely suppressed so that they don't respond. Part of the terror of a nightmare is often the feeling of helplessness, an inability to run away from some terrifying presence, and it's a feeling with a basis in reality, engendered by this muscular paralysis. In exceptional circumstances, if a small stroke damages the part of the brain stem which is involved in suppressing movement during dreaming, dreams may indeed be acted out. This can also happen in elderly people, because the activity of the mechanism to inhibit movement becomes less complete in old age. This is why some old people may tend to wander about at night.

There are other interesting differences between REM and slow-wave sleep. Myocardial infarcts (heart attacks) are more common during REM sleep, and the acid secretions of the stomach are increased too. In women, vaginal lubrication is increased during REM, and in men erections occur only during REM sleep; the reason men tend to have early-morning erections is that they usually wake from a period of REM. These erections are not necessarily associated with erotic dreams— they are simply an automatic response, and, incidentally, a good indication that the mechanism that causes genital arousal is in good order. When a man complains of erection difficulties, one of the first questions he will be asked is whether he ever has an erection on waking. If a man gets erections during sleep, or wakes with an erection, then it can usually be assumed that there is nothing wrong with the mechanics; any erection difficulties that he has with a partner probably have a psychological cause. If there is any doubt about this, he may be asked to sleep a night in a sleep laboratory, sleeping with a strain gauge which will monitor the state of his penis throughout the night. If no erections are detected, it is possible his erection difficulties have a physical cause.

SUDDEN AROUSALS FROM SLEEP

If you have ever shared a bed, or even a bedroom, with someone else, there may have been times when the other person has seemed suddenly to wake, usually in the first third of the night, when sleep is deepest. He will maybe open his eyes and stare blankly around, mumble something unintelligible and then go straight back to sleep. It's difficult to tell whether he is properly awake, or whether he is dreaming, and certainly if you refer to it in the morning he won't have any idea what you are talking about.

This usually happens at the end of the first or second period of deep slow-wave sleep, about ninety minutes after falling asleep. The sleeper is partially aroused, but before he can become fully awake he falls back to sleep again. These sudden arousals from slow-wave sleep are mostly just part of the normal pattern of the sleep cycle, occurring usually at the transition from one stage of sleep to the next, but sometimes they can be caused by a noise or some other external stimulus.

When children, especially young children, have these partial arousals from deep sleep, they are usually more intense, involve more confusion, and often last longer than in adults. When a child wakes crying in the night, the natural thing is to assume that he has had a "bad dream," even if he is too young to tell you about it, and too young for his memories to be harbouring those fearful images that are the stuff of nightmares. In fact, if the child is very young (under about fifteen months), it is more likely that he is experiencing one of these partial arousals from deep sleep.

The child may start to moan, and then cry, sit up and thrash about as though he is in pain. It is impossible to console him or even to get through to him—the child may seem to look right through you, may even call your name but be oblivious to your presence and seem not to hear you when you try to comfort him. If you try to hold him it will usually make matters worse; he may struggle to get free—parents often describe such a child as "possessed." We have no way of knowing what his imagery is, or indeed if there is any imagery at all. The episode may last several minutes, occasionally as long as an hour. But then the child will wake up properly, relax, and rapidly go back to sleep again as if nothing has happened. This is quite different from the child who has had an ordinary nightmare, who is clearly awake and wants to be held and tell you about the dream, and is probably reluctant to return to bed and to sleep.

These confused awakenings usually occur in the first half of the night, and although a few children may have several such episodes during the night, those that occur earlier are usually the most intense. They can start in infants as young as six months, or even younger, but they are usually gradually outgrown. They rarely occur in older children or adolescents. Young children seem to be more prone to these episodes when they are overtired or ill, or if their regular routine has been disrupted.

The true night terror is an even more intense but usually briefer version of a confusional arousal, and also begins in childhood, though usually in older children. The night terror is the "nightmare" of slow-wave sleep, and it is aptly named—at least as far as the onlooker is concerned. The good news is that the child (for children are the most frequent sufferers) who has a night terror usually remembers nothing of it. It is the parents, who have to witness their child's apparent abject terror and are unable to comfort him, who probably suffer most.

While a confusional arousal starts with moaning and gradually builds up to a dramatic climax, the night terror starts quite suddenly with a blood-curdling scream. When the parents rush into the room they usually find their child sitting up in bed, sweating, his eyes bulging, his heart pounding, his breathing rapid, and with a look of intense panic on his face. Occasionally the child may get up and run wildly around, seeming quite out of control. Usually the episode is very brief, lasting only a few seconds or minutes. The child may then wake up fully, but won't seem frightened, and will only want to go back to sleep. In the morning he will probably remember nothing of what happened, though occasionally he may have a vague memory of something frightening, almost always associated with a single scene: falling, being crushed, choking.

In older children and adolescents, night terrors, especially if they happen often, may have a psychological cause. This may not be obvious—indeed, typically these are young people who when they are angry or troubled *don't* behave badly, but bottle up their feelings. If night terrors are very frequent and distressing, medication such as a benzodiazepine (minor tranquilliser), which tends to suppress slow-wave sleep, can help, but it is more important to try and help the child acknowledge and deal with a possible emotional cause.

In a few people night terrors may persist into adulthood, especially if they begin after the age of ten. Like sleepwalking, night terrors run in families; indeed, the two are often linked, and a night terror may precipitate a sleepwalking episode.

WHY DO WE DREAM?

We know that sleep is necessary. We need to sleep. During non-dreaming sleep, growth hormone, which is responsible not only for growth but for the renewal and repair of body tissues, is secreted into the blood. So it is not surprising that the time we spend in non-dreaming sleep each night is at its height in childhood and adolescence—the time of maximum bodily growth. Elderly people have less non-dreaming sleep, and secrete less growth hormone, and athletes dream less on the nights after they have exercised heavily. If you are totally deprived of sleep, no growth hormone is secreted, and after a period of sleep deprivation you will tend to make up for this by dreaming less, spending more time in non-dreaming, growth-hormone-secreting sleep.

But what about dreams? Do we actually need to dream, or are dreams merely a by-product of sleep that don't in themselves serve any useful purpose? Countless theories have been put forward to explain why we dream, and whether dreams have a purpose. Some of these are more half-baked than others. It has been suggested that dreams are concerned with memory and learning; that they represent unfulfilled desires—usually sexual; that they are a way of dealing with anxiety; that they are a method of catharsis, a way of expressing and resolving some emotional crisis, or a method of synthesis, of integrating separate concepts so that they make a new whole.

Man may or may not be the only animal that dreams, but he is certainly not the only one who has REM sleep. Although reptiles and amphibians have no REM sleep, of all the species of mammals whose sleep has been studied, only duck-billed platypuses, spiny anteaters, dolphins and other members of the dolphin family lack REM sleep. Even the opossum, that most primitive of mammals, which has changed so little that it is virtually a living fossil, shows the unmistakable alternating pattern of REM and slow-wave sleep.

The fact that REM sleep is so universal makes it seem likely that it has some particular significance. It has even been suggested that we have a biological need to dream, that without the outlet of our dreams we would become insane. Certainly when we are deprived of dreaming sleep we tend to make up the loss by dreaming for longer periods, and after prolonged deprivation there is some evidence that dream imagery can break through into waking life. So this stage of sleep probably does have a biological function.

We know that REM sleep is associated with other things besides dreams. There is some evidence, for example, that it is concerned with memory and learning. Periods of REM sleep are longer in children, when learning is at its maximum. Newborn babies sleep more than older children and adults, and spend more time in REM sleep. Premature babies spend an even higher proportion of their time asleep in REM sleep, and the more premature they are, the greater the proportion of REM sleep. The amount of REM sleep decreases significantly with age. There is some evidence, too, that REM sleep seems to promote the storage of newly learned information and consolidates memory. Certainly people cramming for exams often feel that information seems to be retained most effectively if it is learned just before going to sleep. Rats who are given a "negative learning experience"—that is, taught to negotiate a maze by being given electric shocks at certain points in it—forget what they have learned more easily if they are deprived of REM sleep.

But is there any evidence that dreams themselves have a biological function? In 1923, well before the existence of REM sleep was recognised, the neurologist and ethnologist W. H. R. Rivers suggested that, in other animals if not in man, dreams might serve a "sentinel" purpose. Although sleep is necessary for recuperation, the sleeping animal is at an obvious disadvantage. The dream state, Dr. Rivers suggested, might be a mechanism which was activated in the presence of danger, and set the animal's "fight or flight" reaction in readiness even while the animal itself was still asleep. However, Dr. Rivers found it impossible to extend this ingenious theory to man: as he himself pointed out, the physiological reactions which accompany a nightmare—pallor, coldness and sweating—are more likely to inhibit the ability to flee from danger than facilitate it.

People who have worked with their own dreams and analysed other people's have claimed that they reveal aspects of the dreamer's personality and throw light on their emotional conflicts. It has even been claimed that they can provide information or insights that waking consciousness is unable to do. Are any, or all, of these claims founded in fact? Or is it more likely that *Träume sind Schäume*—dreams are froth—and entirely devoid of meaning?

The idea that dreams are meaningless rubbish is an old one. To illustrate the attitude of medical writers of his time, Freud, in *On Dreams*, quoted the German physician Strumpell as saying in 1874 that dreams had no more claim to sense and meaning than the sounds which would be produced if "the ten fingers of a man who knows nothing of music were wandering over the keys of a piano." In *The Interpretation of Dreams* Freud also quoted another early dream researcher, W. Robert, who, in 1886, described dreams as a "necessity of nature," and suggested that they were a form of mental excretion—"a great mass of uncompleted, unworked-out thoughts and superficial impressions" which, were they not released in dreaming, might accumulate in the brain and lead to madness. Confusingly, Robert also suggested that dreams had a second (and seemingly contradictory) function—to help fix other impressions lastingly in memory. We dream in order to forget, and in order to remember.

The waste-disposal theory of dreams was wheeled out again more recently, in 1983, by Nobel laureate Francis Crick, and Graeme Mitchison. They suggested that the brain uses dreams to "unlearn" (or "reverse learn," as they called it) "spurious memories"—disturbing thoughts or information it has received which might otherwise produce fantasies, hallucinations and obsessions. These "spurious memories" might overload the capacity of the brain if they were not discarded.

The theory does not stand up to much scrutiny. To begin with, it is difficult to understand why dreaming should help one to forget. Many dreams have a strong emotional content and it seems more likely that this would help fix the dream events in memory rather than facilitate forgetting. Crick and Mitchison did not define "spurious" memories, nor did they explain how the brain discriminated between memories that need to be discarded and useful memories that need to be retained. The concept of brain overload, too, is quaintly Victorian. The storage capacity of the brain is certainly more than adequate for one lifetime's impressions, even without "reverse learning" anything that is surplus to requirements.

What evidence there is seems to contradict Crick and Mitchison's theory. Several drugs inhibit REM sleep—most anti-depressants, for example, and clomipramine, a drug used to treat obsessional neurosis. People who take these drugs dream less, but this produces no apparent psychological ill-effects. Few brain scientists find this theory at all convincing, or even intuitively attractive. If it had been put forward by anyone but a Nobel laureate the peer-reviewing process would have ensured that it remained just a dream.

A more immediately attractive theory is that of the French physiologist, Jouvet, who suggested that dreams are a way of "rehearsing" biologically necessary behaviours. He argued that as the cortex became larger and animal behaviour more complex, instinctive patterns of behaviour such as fighting, mating, etc. became subordinated to learned behaviour. This carried a risk that, for example, when an animal's first opportunity to mate came along there was every chance they might muff it, with disastrous results for the species. Jouvet suggested that dreaming might therefore have an important biological function—to enable the animal to "rehearse" these genetically programmed essential patterns of behaviour during dreaming sleep when the muscles are paralysed.

To prove his theory, Jouvet altered the brain function of cats so that they were *not* paralysed during REM sleep. He suggested that if his theory was true, the cats would get up and act out these kinds of activities, and this indeed is exactly what happened. When Jouvet first proposed the theory, computers were not as widespread as they are now and so computer analogies were not as popular. We would now say that dreaming takes the computer off line by disconnecting its outputs and allowing it to work on material within it.

However, even if Jouvet's theory holds true for cats, it doesn't offer anything like an adequate explanation for dreams in humans, for whom complex learned behaviour patterns are probably more important for survival then genetic programming. The bulk of the content of most ordinary dreams consists of fragments of daytime experiences, few of which are significant, let alone relevant to personal survival. But there is an interesting echo of Jouvet's theory in a few dreams (described in more detail in chapter 7), in which the dreamer seems to practise some physical skill—such as learning to ride a bicycle, improving a golf stroke—in his dreams, and find that this helps him actually to acquire the necessary skill in real life.

J. Allan Hobson is a sleep researcher who has put forward one of the most convincing theories to explain why we dream. He suggests that dreams are formed by what he calls an "activation-synthesis." The brain responds to "signals" generated in sleep in the same way as it responds to signals in the waking state from the outside world. In dreaming sleep, the brain is activated, and generates quasi-sensory and quasi-motor information, which it then synthesises into the experience of a dream. When we "see" in dreams, it is because the visual brain circuits have been activated. When we feel emotion, it is because the emotional brain centres, probably in the limbic system, have been activated. The "dreaminess" of dreams, the bizarre happenings or distortions, occur because these internal signals are not quite the same as the signals we normally receive from the outside world.

Hobson suggests that the reason dreams are so often forgotten is that they are stored temporarily in the short-term memory system. It is probably just as well that dreams are not remembered as clearly as real-life events. If they were, it would be easy for the dreamer to become confused and unable to distinguish between a dream world and the real world. A few people do remember their dreams clearly, and do sometimes have genuine difficulty in deciding what is real and what was only a dream.

Hobson's theory fits very well with what we now know—

that the brain does not simply switch off in sleep, but remains active. Not only does it remain active, but its activity is very comparable to its activity in the normal, conscious, waking state. The dream world and the waking world are created by the same cognitive structures in the same parts of the brain. The main difference between the dreaming and waking states is that when we are awake there is a continual flow of incoming information to the brain from the outside world via the senses. During dreaming, this flow of incoming sense data is restricted. The brain continues to build models of the world, just as it does when we are awake, but they have to be created not by information direct from the outside world, but by drawing on emotion and memory from the internal world.

Our understanding of the brain has recently gone through a further revolution and it has now become clear that the brain's connections are ever-changing structures. We know now that it is a fundamental property of the brain—indeed, it is essential for its normal development—to respond to stimulation by growth. What this means is that the brain is actually modelled by its experience. And this in turn leads to a coherent dream theory.

Everyone is born with roughly the same number of brain cells—about 100 billion—and retains more or less the same number throughout life. What makes the brain grow and develop is not an increase in the number of cells, but the increasing complexity of the connections between these cells. Brain development starts even before birth. It is our genes which determine the basic pattern of the brain and the way the cells connect with each other. However, this is not a passive process directed only by the genes. By the second trimester of pregnancy the cells within the brain are beginning to fire and their activity becomes as important in establishing cell connections as does the push from the genes. By the final trimester of pregnancy the brain is beginning to respond to external stimuli—to pain, for example, and to sounds.

When the brain is stimulated it responds by a growth in the interconnections between its cells. From birth the central nervous system is flooded with stimuli from the outside world. These stimuli are relayed to the brain, and the pathways through which they travel become reinforced. If for any reason the brain does not receive the appropriate stimuli it will not set up the right connections. It has been known for a long time, for example, that it is by seeing that a child develops vision. A child who is born with cataracts won't develop proper vision unless they are operated on by the age of four.

To begin with there is much reduplication within the brain— it produces many more connections than it can ever use. It then undergoes a process of pruning. In fact this is a dual process: the neuronal connections that are most often stimulated and used grow strong, while those that are not used are weakened and eventually die away. There are thought to be two major periods of modelling, the first between three and ten months, the second starting around the age of ten and continuing through puberty until the age of eighteen. During these times the weak connections die away, leaving only the strong connections.

It is the strength and complexity of the interconnections between brain cells that influence an individual's mental capacity. There is evidence that rats brought up in a rich environment with toys which encourage their playful behaviour will have brains 25 per cent larger than those brought up in an equivalent deprived environment. This extra brain size is accounted for by a huge growth in the connections between individual cells. This seems to be true in humans too: children who are not given intellectual or emotional stimulation develop brains which are up to 30 per cent smaller for their age. Experience in the form of brain stimulation leads to sprouting and growth within the brain.

What seems clear is that inactivity is anathema to the brain. Use it or lose it seems to be the rule. And one can argue that without dreaming the brain would spend a third of its time inactive and unstimulated. We know now that the brain is never idle: even in deep sleep there is both neuronal and some kind of mental activity. When we dream, we reinforce those connections that we use during the day. That is why we dream about everyday events, and why the same brain systems and the same psychological models are used as during the waking state. It may be that in dreaming we have the perfect mechanism for keeping the brain in a constant state of stimulation, and maintaining the pathways within it.

3

The Stuff That Dreams Are Made Of

Most of our dreams reflect our waking lives and preoccupations. The dreams of REM sleep have a strong storyline and clear and recognisable visual images. But dreams are much more than a simple succession of visual images. In some respects the dream world is very like the real world. It looks much the same as the real world, we tend to behave in it much as we do in the real world. We can think and reason in dreams, and feel all the normal sensations and emotions of waking life—pleasure, pain, fear, intense happiness or sadness, guilt or jealousy, heat or cold. Even time is much the same in the dream world—it is a myth that time is telescoped in dreams. Work with lucid dreamers shows that dream time bears a close relationship to real time. And yet a dream remains indisputably "dreamy." When we wake we have no difficulty in recognising that it was, indeed, a dream.

Most dreams are visually very vivid, and most people dream in colour. Even if you think your dreams are usually monotone, it may simply be that you don't remember. Before the days of sleep laboratories, less than a third of people who were asked to recall their dreams said that they dreamed in colour. But in a sleep laboratory, when people are actually woken from dreaming sleep, more than three-quarters report that they were dreaming in colour when they were woken.

Although vision is the most commonly experienced dream sensation, every other sense is represented in the dream world too. Sound and sexual sensations are common, taste and smell less common—probably because even in waking consciousness most of us don't find it as easy to summon up the memories of tastes and smells as of sights and sounds. The experience of pain in dreams is always said to be unusual, but I have certainly felt pain in dreams and have come across many other people who have experienced it too.

Do blind people "see" in their dreams? That depends entirely on how long the person had normal sight before he became blind. People who are born congenitally blind, or who have become totally blind before the age of five, do not have visual dreams. Seven seems to be the crucial age at which "dream sight" is fully retained, though some people who become blind between the ages of five and seven do have dreams with visual images. But the lack of visual imagery does not make dream life any less fascinating. The dreams of people who have been congenitally blind from birth are no less vivid and complex than the dreams of sighted people, even though they see nothing.

What happens to the dream body image when the real body is damaged? How quickly does the dreaming mind adapt and modify its own reality? Oliver Sacks has described in his book *A Leg to Stand On*, a dream he had two days after an operation to repair ruptured tendons in his left leg, which had been badly damaged in a climbing accident in Norway. That day Dr. Sacks had discovered that despite the operation his leg was still totally unresponsive and lifeless, the muscles "horribly and unnaturally limp . . . like some soft inanimate jelly or cheese." He had, he says, a qualm of absolute horror, and then immediately repressed the emotion, and dismissed his apprehension about the leg as something "silly," some kind of "mistake." By the end of the day

> I had indeed "forgotten" it, forgotten all about it; but down in the depths it had not been forgotten . . . In the night . . . I had a dream of peculiar horror . . . I was on the Mountain again, impotently struggling to move my leg and stand up. But—and this, at least, was a dream-like conflation—there was a peculiar confusion of past and present. I had just had my fall, and yet the leg was sewn up . . . "Splendid!" I thought . . . "I'm all reconnected, I'm ready to go!" But the leg, for some reason, didn't budge in the least, even though it was so neatly and nicely

sewn up . . . I put my hand down and felt the muscle—it felt soft and pulpy, without tone or life. "Heavens above!" I said in my dream. "There's something the matter—quite dreadfully the matter. The muscle's been *denervated* . . . It's not just the tendon—the nerve-supply's gone." I strained and strained, but it was no use at all. The leg lay motionless, and inert, as if dead.

He woke terrified, trying to tense the flaccid muscle. But, as in the dream, it didn't work. Dr. Sacks's dream was a faithful reflection of both his anxiety about the leg, and the state of the leg itself. It replayed the horror of feeling the "soft and pulpy" muscle and the realisation that the leg was totally useless and lifeless.

A colleague of mine was an avid yoga enthusiast at one time in his career and worked with a famous hatha yoga teacher. On one occasion the yoga teacher put the class into a pose which involved holding the hands up and pushed back from the shoulders behind the head. My colleague noticed after only two minutes that his left arm was going dead and mentioned it to the teacher, who told him to continue. After a further two minutes his hand suddenly dropped and hung by his side, quite useless. Compression of the nerves in the plexus leaving the spine had induced a severe nerve palsy. The teacher rather unsympathetically said he had seen this sort of thing before, and there was no need to worry, it would recover. Indeed it did, but what his teacher didn't tell him was that it would take nearly two years to do so. My colleague noticed that his dreams changed immediately after the injury. To begin with he continually dreamed that his arm was trapped under a large stone and he couldn't move it; or he would be lying on the grass and find that his arm was lying underneath him, useless; or he would try to use his arm and discover that it was quite paralysed and dead. Just as in the case of Oliver Sacks's dream leg, there was little difference between dream imagery and the real body image. And this is not surprising, because in each case the brain was receiving distorted signals from the partially damaged sensory nerve indicating that the arm was paralysed and didn't respond when motor impulses were sent to it.

It may seem obvious that the dream should reflect reality in this way. Isn't it just that the dream mind "remembers" the injury, "remembers" the consequences? Well, no, it isn't quite as simple as that. In certain circumstances a limb may be even more severely damaged, and yet the dream limb may be unaffected. Motorbike accidents are, unfortunately, very common, and what often happens is that the rider comes off his bike and falls on his shoulder so that the nerves leading to the arm are completely torn away, severing all nervous connection between arm and brain. But surprisingly, the dreams of the injured biker are unchanged. He can move his dream arm normally, even though his real arm is totally flaccid and useless. Why? Possibly because the nerve pathways to the arm *are* completely severed, not just damaged as they are in the case of the injured yoga student. There is no way messages can be sent to the central mechanism of arm movement in the brain to indicate that the arm is damaged. So when a dream arm is constructed, it is a perfectly normally moving dream arm. It is only if the nerve pathways are damaged but not completely severed that the brain receives the distorted signals about the arm which enable it to construct an abnormal dream image.

When a limb is either amputated or its nerve supply is completely severed from the spine, the part of the brain which controls movement and sensation for that limb begins to contract. Gradually healthy neighbouring cells take over the space left as this area of the brain dies back. It is this that causes the sensations of a "phantom limb" when an arm is no longer there, or at least no longer has any nervous connection to the rest of the body. The phantom limb then also appears in dreams, again suggesting that movement and feeling in both the dream and the real arm are controlled by the same part of the brain.

Two American dream researchers, Dr. Calvin Hall and Professor Robert van de Castle, have analysed the dream content of large numbers of dreams of American college students and children aged 4–16, and also dreams of people of other cultural groups, such as Australian Aborigines and Hopi Indians. They found that the sex differences in dreams mirror pretty accurately the differences between men and women. We know how closely allied are the dream mind and the waking mind, and how accurately our dreams reflect our waking lives, so perhaps this isn't too surprising. More people appear in women's dreams, and they report more emotions, and more conversations, mostly with other women. Men's dreams are centred much more on outdoor and physical activities and unfamiliar settings, and involve success or failure more often. The people men meet tend to be groups of strangers.

Hall and van de Castle found that their male dreamers reported more sex dreams, and that these tended to revolve around unknown females somewhat resembling *Playboy* centrefolds. Our dreams are proof, if proof were needed, that sexual preoccupation knows no age bounds. Erotic dreams persist well into old age, and many men in their seventies still have wet dreams.

Hall and van de Castle found that although men have aggressive dreams only slightly more often than women, their aggressive dreams contain much more physical aggression— dream scenarios in which a character is chased, hit or killed by another character. The good news, though, is that the aggression is directed mostly towards other males and towards strangers. Men are also attacked more often in their dreams— again, by unfamiliar characters. When women have dreams involving physical aggression they tend to be spectators rather than participants. Hall and van de Castle also found interesting changes in physical aggression with age. It is children between the ages of two and twelve whose dreams contain most physical aggression and it is usually the child himself who is the target of it. Even at this age, the level of physical aggression is much higher for boys than for girls. During adolescence this sex difference levels out, but after the age of eighteen the level of physical aggression in the dreams of males goes up, while for women it goes down.

Children's dreams as well as adults' reflect their waking lives and preoccupations. The predominant characters in children's dreams are parents and other family members, and their dreams contain significantly fewer strangers and significantly more animal characters. The dreams of children seem to increase in length and complexity as they grow older. A three- or four-year-old who is woken during a period of dreaming sleep and asked to tell their dream will generally say only a few words. This may be at least partly due to the fact that a young child simply does not have the language to do justice to his dreams, although this is probably not the complete explanation. At five or six the child's dream reports double in length, and the child starts to become a gradually more active participant in his dreams. In late childhood friends rather than family start to emerge as the central characters of the child's dreams, reflecting the increasing importance of peer relationships and the decreasing dependence on the family in his waking life.

REMEMBERING YOUR DREAMS

Everyone dreams, though not everyone remembers their dreams. The dreams that we have during the night aren't usually remembered unless we happen to wake up soon after them. Most dreams occur in the last half of the night, and when we awaken naturally, it is usually from a dream. It is the dreams we have just before awakening that are remembered most easily, though even these quickly fade unless we write them down or make a positive effort to remember them. The ability to remember dreams seems to be distributed in the population rather like height, intelligence and most other characteristics, with a "normal distribution" curve. Most of us remember some of our dreams some of the time, and then forget them pretty quickly. A few people (those whom Max Beerbohm listed as being among the terrors of the breakfast table) seem able to remember every last particular of every dream with the clarity and detail usually encountered only in a large-scale Ordnance Survey map. Others confidently assert each morning that they have not dreamed, even though, like everybody else, they have spent 25 per cent of the night dreaming.

If you have a good visual memory you will probably remember your dreams more easily than people who have a poor visual memory. Depression seems to affect your ability to remember your dreams—in fact, people who suffer recurrent depression may recognise the onset of a depressive episode because they notice that they seem to be dreaming less. When a dream has a very strong emotional content or seems particularly significant, it is more likely to be remembered. Nightmares, for example, tend not only to be remembered on waking, but to persist and to remain vivid in the dreamer's mind for a considerable time.

There are mornings when we wake with the feeling that we have been dreaming all night but have hardly slept at all. When we're ill or anxious we may sleep more lightly than usual, and wake up more often. Because when we wake it is usually from a period of dreaming sleep, we'll tend to catch more dreams than usual. It may feel as though we have been dreaming all night, but really we are just *remembering* more dreams than we usually do.

There are good reasons why we should forget our dreams. If dreams were remembered as clearly and seemed as real as events in the everyday world, we would quickly be thrown into a state of confusion, unable to distinguish with certainty dream life from real life. One can sometimes observe this in people who have frequent lucid dreams (see chapter 13), which are remembered much more easily and much more vividly than ordinary dreams. One lucid dreamer told us:

> Sometimes my dreams seem so real that I don't know whether I'm awake or asleep and I have to do something to test it out—say, drive my car across the pavement and into the house next door. This can be a problem the day after a night when I have been dreaming a lot. I suddenly find myself unsure, during the day, whether or not I'm really awake, and there have been times when I feel compelled to test reality, though so far it's always been in a rather more harmless way—maybe knocking on a door to check that my fist doesn't go through it, rather than driving the car at it.

NIGHTMARES

One of the advantages of sleeping with another person is that there is someone to wake you from your nightmares. It would be a terrible act of marital vengeance to let the moaning, twitching person lying beside you whimper on without prodding them insistently out of the stuff of their nightmare into a safer, waking world.

Anxiety is one of the most common dream emotions, and

the nightmare is simply an anxiety-laden dream from which the dreamer awakens spontaneously and which they remember, at least for a short time, vividly. But there are degrees of fear in the nightmare world, from mild panic to sheer terror, and these tend to mirror the degree of anxiety which triggers them. In its extreme form you awaken from the nightmare in terror, sweating, your heart pounding, pupils dilated, breathing rapidly, with the dream's terrifying imagery still vivid in your memory.

But more often anxiety shows up in our dreams in a less melodramatic guise—the discovery that thirty people have come for supper and the only food in the house is a tin of baked beans, for example; the realisation that you are running naked through the streets; the feeling that you are trying to run but that your mind cannot force your legs to move, so that you run as if in slow motion, each step a mighty struggle, while others rush past you effortlessly. The most common nightmare theme is of being chased. In children's dreams the pursuer is often a frightening animal or monster; in later life the nightmare threat is more likely to be of human origin. Feelings of helplessness and of being threatened are also common nightmare themes, especially for women.

For most people nightmares are no real problem. But if they occur very frequently and are very intense, they can be disruptive of sleep and may be distressing enough to drive people to their doctor for treatment. The anguish that nightmares can cause is described very clearly in this letter written by Samuel Taylor Coleridge to his friend Robert Southey in September 1803.

> . . . my last night was just such a noisy night of horrors as 3 nights out of 4 are, with me. O God! When a man blesses the loud Scream of Agony that awakes him, night after night; night after night; & when a man's repeated Night-screams have made him a nuisance in his own House, it is better to die than to live.

In fact the dreadful dreams Coleridge started to record in his notebooks around 1803 may have been due more to his increasing opium addiction than to a natural predisposition to nightmares, but there is evidence in some of his letters and in the images of many of his poems that he had been continually haunted by bad dreams ever since his childhood.

Why is it that some people are seldom bothered by bad dreams, while others, like Coleridge, may come to dread sleep because of the terrors it brings? An American psychiatrist, Ernest Hartmann, who has made a special study of nightmares, has classified people who seem to be particularly nightmare-prone as "thin-skinned"—they are people who seem to be particularly sensitive and neurotic in their waking lives, and who have suffered from chronic nightmares since childhood or adolescence. They seem to show more fear of death than people who have fewer nightmares. When life is going well for them they will have rather fewer nightmares, but bad dreams will probably continue to plague them regularly throughout their lives. Women have been found to be more nightmare-prone than men, and there also seems to be a relationship between personality and the type of nightmare that you have. Type A people—ambitious, driving achievers, are said to be more likely to report fantastic and post-traumatic nightmares.

It started quite simply. I was walking along a cliff pathway and I then heard a noise behind me. I knew someone was stalking me—I didn't know who they were, but I knew they had a knife. As I looked I heard a clatter of stones but still saw nobody so I ran to the cliff edge and looked over. There was a ledge about six feet below; if I could stand on that I would be hidden. Below the ledge was a two- or three-hundred-foot drop—there were rocks below, pounded by the waves. I jumped down and cowered against the cliff face. Almost immediately someone threw a rock over the cliff, but a little way along from my ledge. Thank God, I've got away, I thought, clinging to the cliff face for dear life. But just then another rock landed close by me and I knew I'd been discovered. Terrified, I looked for somewhere to jump to. As I looked about me I saw a huge rock falling towards me. I slipped over the edge, holding on with my fingertips; I was slowly losing my grip, I knew I was going to fall to my death. I remember trying to shout help, help as my fingers slipped. Then I woke, sweating with fear.

If you are prone to nightmares there are a few obvious ways to protect yourself—avoid watching horror videos and films before you go to sleep, for example. Certain drugs, for example the beta blockers prescribed for some heart patients, may increase the frequency of nightmares. People with Parkinson's disease, too, tend to have frequent nightmares and vivid dreams, probably due to the drug, L-Dopa, which is used to treat the disease. But by far the most common and most potent triggers of nightmares are psychological factors—anxiety, mental stress and major life events. When we are distressed our dreams become traumatic—we dream more often of death, separation and mutilation. So close is the link between life traumas and nightmares that it has even been suggested that the detailed and copious dream diaries which were quite commonly kept in the seventeenth and eighteenth centuries might serve as a useful tool for historical research: when traumatic dreams are recorded, a researcher might well look for parallel personal distress in the dreamer's life.

It has been suggested that the function of nightmares might be to reduce anxiety, but this is certainly not always the case. Dreams can be helpful in integrating stressful events, but they are not helpful to someone who is dealing with stress by walling it off or keeping it out of their conscious awareness. Probably the most stressful situation human beings are called upon to face is active combat, when they may be under constant threat of sudden death or mutilation for long periods of time. During the First World War, W.H.R. Rivers analysed the battle dreams of soldiers, including the war poet Siegfried Sassoon, who had been invalided to the Craiglockart War Hospital for Officers from the front. He was treating them for "war neurosis" which we would now call post-traumatic stress disorder, and he found that the terrifying nightmares they suffered were usually a faithful replaying of some horrific event they had witnessed or been a part of. Often the dream would recur in the same form night after night, sometimes several times a night, and each time the sufferer would wake in a state of such profound terror that he would try to prevent himself sleeping again because he dreaded a repetition.

Like most dream analysts at that time, Rivers was influenced by the Freudian theory of interpretation of dreams, and certainly some of the simple dreams his patients told him confirmed Freud's view that dreams were concerned with wish-fulfilment—one soldier, for example, dreamt that he was sent back to the front, but directly he landed in France, peace was declared. But Rivers found that the idea that these awful nightmare experiences could owe anything to wish-fulfilment was absurd. He believed that the dreams occurred not because the dreamer wished to repeat the experience—far from it—but because of his strong desire that he should *not* have to go through it again. As long as the dreamer was awake, he could try to repress the terrible memories, to banish them from consciousness. But in sleep the repressed experience was able to surface and recreate itself in all its horror.

It was only when the dreamer learned to stop trying to repress these memories in waking life that they surfaced less often in his dreams. Dr. Rivers observed that the first sign of recovery was that the nightmares would undergo a transformation, become more grotesque or fanciful, less a faithful reflection of grim reality. Although the dreams still had their origins in the traumatic experiences of trench warfare, this transformation distanced them a little from the sufferer and made their emotional impact less painful.

Subsequent studies of veterans of other wars have shown the same phenomena. Soldiers who have actually been involved in fighting have more nightmares than non-combat military personnel, and their nightmares are more likely to be recurrent and to reflect actual events. The nightmares of even the most nightmare-prone civilians do not usually show this quality. By and large most people's lives are fairly uneventful; our nightmares are more likely to mirror emotional trauma, and to be represented by fearful situations that have no basis in reality. But when people really are faced with life-threatening situations, they react in precisely the same way as soldiers who have been in combat. Survivors of disasters— earthquakes or hurricanes, or tragedies such as the sinking of the Zeebrugge ferry—may in the immediate aftermath relive the disaster in their nightmares in all its horror. But gradually the dream content changes. Nightmares may still recur, but they are less likely to be reruns of the nightmare events that form their mainspring.

COPING WITH NIGHTMARES

Obviously if stress is causing frequent nightmares the best so-lution is to reduce the stress. But psychological treatments can often help to reduce both the frequency and the intensity of nightmares. Learning a relaxation technique and practising this before going to sleep can help. Hypnosis is sometimes suc-cessful too. An alternative is to try to develop strategies for coping with the nightmare as it happens.

The essence of most such strategies is to learn to face the dream fears by rehearsing the nightmare in waking life. This is a technique that anyone can try for themselves. A friend of ours, for example, had been plagued by a terrifying dream for as long as he could remember. In the dream he is walking alone through a dark forest and suddenly hears a rustling, scuf-fling sound in the bushes. He sees nothing. Frightened, he looks again to see the bushes quivering. Terrified, he watches and then, rushing headlong towards him down the forest path, he sees a huge wild boar, eyes glittering, mouth slavering as it charges furiously towards him. He tries to run for his life, but his feet are glued to the path. A split second before the boar reaches him, in panic and utter terror, he wakes up.

When he told me about this I suggested that he try this "treatment." When the boar started to chase him, he should not run away but turn around in his dream and face it, telling himself it was only a dream. He looked doubtful. If he had that much control over his dream imagery, he said, then he wouldn't be walking down the forest path in the first place. It took some time to persuade him that we have more control over our dreams than we realise. What he had to do was to set up the memory that if he did meet the boar in his dream he was to turn and face it. When he did eventually meet the boar in his dream, then the memory of what he had to do might be triggered. I didn't set up any expectations by telling him what would happen if he managed to do this, simply asked him to try and do it, and let me know what happened.

For some time our friend practised, several times a day, turning to face an imaginary boar, and telling himself it was only a dream. At first nothing happened. A number of times he had the nightmare without remembering what he was meant to do, and on each occasion, as before, he woke terrified and sweating. Then one night the dream recurred, but this time, as he was walking down the forest path, a memory stirred and he remembered that he had to turn and face the boar. There was a rustle in the bushes on the far side of the clearing and he knew the boar was about to come. The feelings of panic mounted as usual, but this time he stood his ground. Nearer and nearer came the boar—and suddenly, almost at his feet, it turned into a little sucking piglet which ran round him and then disappeared off into the undergrowth. The feeling of panic receded, supervened by a satisfying feeling of sheer mastery. Since then he hasn't had the dream—but he feels confident he would be able to do the same thing if it did happen again.

Some dream therapists advocate a more aggressive approach to a nightmare threat, not simply turning to face it, but fighting back against the dream adversary with verbal abuse or even physical violence. This dreamer learned to deal with a recurrent nightmare in an intriguing way.

> In my childhood for some unknown reason I continually dreamed about *snakes*. In these dreams, which were numerous, I was always hovering in mid-air, floating down towards a pit containing snakes. But by shutting my eyes and exercising extreme will power I was always able to rise up away from them, and *always* ended up floating above the rooftops. These particular dreams lasted into my early and late teens.

People who regularly have lucid dreams, and are used to having some degree of control over their dream scenario, can sometimes develop even more sophisticated strategies to deal with their nightmares, not only levitating to rooftop level, but flying over (or passing through) a brick wall to escape potential danger (see p. 238).

Professor Isaac Marks of London's Institute of Psychiatry has devised a form of nightmare therapy which is cheap, successful and easy—anyone who has the time and the inclination can do it themselves at home. He treats nightmares by using the familiar psychological principle that if you are continually exposed to a fear, it attenuates. In other words, you get used to it. Nightmare sufferers were sent a diary and a list of instructions. They were asked to either write down or tape-record their nightmares and then spend at least an hour a day either rewriting, or listening to, or simply rereading their nightmare accounts. The results were dramatic. Those who exposed themselves to their nightmares in this way showed a much greater improvement than those who simply listened to relaxation tapes before going to bed, or who received no treatment at all.

"BAD DREAMS"

Some dream researchers have claimed that children's dreams are not particularly frightening. Many others disagree. Certainly anyone who has children themselves, or remembers their own childhood dreams, believes that children, especially young children, do have more bad dreams than adults.

Bad dreams are most frequent and most frightening between the ages of five and seven. Frightening figures like monsters appear in children's nightmares, and fear and helplessness are always present. An American researcher, Patricia Garfield, collected dreams from 109 American schoolchildren, and eleven children from India, most aged between five and eight years old. Of the collected dreams, she classified 158 as "bad"— dreams in which the child was being chased or attacked, or sensed danger from some threatening presence, or dreams in which some other character was accidentally killed or injured. Far fewer dreams—eighty-nine—she classified as "good." But bad dreams become much less frequent, and may cease altogether, during adolescence.

Children who wake frightened by a bad dream need comfort and reassurance—a parent to stay with them for a while, or permission to come into the parents' bed. This is no time to worry about the child getting into "bad habits"—if the child knows the parents will always give this kind of support when he needs it, he will be less afraid to go to sleep by himself.

SUDDEN AWAKENING FROM SLOW-WAVE SLEEP

When someone wakes, or is woken, from REM sleep it takes them only a few seconds to orientate themselves and become alert. If they are suddenly aroused from deep sleep, however, they may be very confused and disorientated for several minutes before fully awakening. It is quite usual for anyone roused from stage 3 or 4 sleep to wake into a confusional state—it is something that most of us have probably experienced at some time. Not only do you feel confused when you are aroused from this level of sleep, but because memory is also affected—particularly when you are extremely tired—you may remember nothing the next morning. It is not at all unusual for an exhausted junior houseman in hospital who has finally got to bed and been asleep for about an hour to roll out of bed again in response to a telephone call, go to the ward, put up a drip, and next morning remember nothing of the night's events at all. When he appears on the ward, Sister may say, "You were surprisingly polite when I rang you at two a.m." and the patient may thank him profusely for replacing the drip. But the doctor will have no memory of any of this. Loss of memory and confusion are part of a slow-wave-sleep awakening, and they may be prolonged in severe tiredness.

That these sudden night-time arousals so seldom end in disaster is probably often due to the vigilance of the more widely awake ward staff. But the confusion which can suffuse a sudden awakening from slow-wave sleep can have serious, even devastating, results. Of such cases, one of the earliest recorded is that of a knight, Gutlingen, who, in the year 1600, was aroused from sleep by a companion in arms. In the confusion of awakening, he attacked his friend and stabbed him to death. Gutlingen was tried and found guilty of murder.

Gutlingen's case would have had a happier outcome (at least for Gutlingen) had he been tried today. Compare his fate with that of an insurance clerk who was recently on trial on a very similar charge. This young man had been travelling home after a night out. He carried with him, as he usually did, a knife which he used at work to cut the string of the bundles of letters which were delivered to his office. As the train left the station he relaxed into his seat and was soon fast asleep. At the next station some rowdy adolescents got on and for the next twenty minutes were larking about in the carriage. One of them picked up a cushion and threw it at a friend, who ducked. The cushion struck the sleeping clerk on the head. The clerk jumped up and rushed into the middle gangway, taking the knife out of his pocket and opening it. With one quick movement he slashed the neck of the boy nearest to him and then went and stood by the door of the train in a confused and disorientated way. A fellow passenger came up and admonished him, saying, "You shouldn't have done that." "Done what?" asked the clerk. He remained confused for several minutes, and when the train drew into the next station the guard reported that he still seemed to be unaware of where he was and what had happened.

When the case came to trial it was accepted that the attack had occurred during a sudden arousal from slow-wave sleep. The victim was left with an ugly scar on his neck, and the clerk was set free.

One of the most famous cases of a crime committed during a sudden arousal from slow-wave sleep happened in Switzerland. A barrister, tired after a hard day's work in court, arrived at the railway station to find that his train was running about an hour late. He decided to find a comfortable corner in the waiting room and have a nap, and asked the station master to wake him when the train was due.

He settled down, relaxed, and soon fell asleep. After about an hour the station master went in to tell him his train was approaching. The barrister was sound asleep, and the station master tried to shake him awake, shouting, *"Monsieur, votre train est arrivé."* The barrister, roused and confused, reached into his brief case, pulled out a pistol, and shot the station master dead.

It was unfortunate that the barrister had been asleep for about an hour, just the right length of time to ensure that he was in the deepest stage, stage 4, of slow-wave sleep. When he was shaken by the station master he was aroused from deep sleep into a dense confusional episode. In his confused state he did not know what was happening, but assumed he was being attacked, reached for his pistol and shot his "assailant," the innocent station master.

Dreaming, it has been said, permits each and every one of us to be quietly and safely insane every night of our lives. But ordinary dreaming cannot give rise to this kind of violence. Although feelings of aggression are common in dreams, in ordinary dreaming sleep—REM sleep—however wild, violent or promiscuous your dreams, you cannot act them out. During

the waking stages of a dream the paralysis starts to wear off
and the dreamer may start to move a little, but clear consciousness returns too quickly for him actually to perform any coordinated act before he is fully awake. But when we look at
the dreams and night terrors of slow-wave sleep, we find a
quite different picture, and one that is not so reassuring.

The most significant difference between an ordinary dream
or nightmare and the dreams and night terrors of slow-wave
sleep is that in slow-wave sleep, the muscles are not paralysed.
And it is in slow-wave sleep that sleepwalking occurs. Theoretically, at least, it is perfectly possible for the feelings and
emotions of slow-wave-sleep dreams to be translated into action.

4

The Darker Side of Dreaming

Doctor of Physic: *When was it she last walked?*
Gentlewoman: *Since his majesty went into the field, I have seen her rise from her bed, throw her nightgown upon her, unlock her closet, take forth paper, fold it, write upon it, read it, afterward seal it, and again return to bed; yet all this while in a most fast sleep.*
Doctor of Physic: *A great perturbation in nature! To receive at once the benefits of sleep, and do the effects of watching. In this slumbery agitation ... what have you heard her say?*
Enter Lady Macbeth, with a taper.
Gentlewoman: *Lo, you, here she comes! This is her very guise; and, upon my life, fast asleep. Observe her; stand close.*
Doctor of Physic: *How came she by that light?*
Gentlewoman: *Why, it stood by her; she has light by her continually; 'tis her command.*
Doctor of Physic: *You see her eyes are open.*
Gentlewoman: *Ay, but their sense is shut.*

Even in Shakespeare's time, the "slumbery agitation" of sleepwalking captured the imagination. Shakespeare's description of Lady Macbeth's night-time activities was nearer to the truth, too, than the stereotyped picture of the sleepwalker, arms outstretched, eyes closed, walking round the house and bumping into furniture, which most of us have. Sleepwalking is much more complex, and much more interesting, than that, and it is very far from being a music-hall joke. It is no joke to waken, as one sleepwalker did, to find himself thirty feet up the hundred-foot cliffs near Torquay, the waves crashing on the rocks below him. He had sleepwalked for about half a mile from his home to the foot of the cliffs, and his last memory was of dreaming that he was lying on a tiny ledge. That story has a happy ending (he was rescued by the Torbay Coast Guard), but it could as easily have ended in disaster.

Sleepwalking is what is called a "sleep transition disorder." It happens at the end of a period of deep slow-wave sleep, usually the first and deepest period, about ninety minutes after falling asleep, but it can, and frequently does, also occur in stage 2 sleep towards the end of the night. Normally the sleeper passes quickly from slow-wave to REM sleep, but in a few people the transition does not occur so smoothly and rapidly. They remain for a little while in an odd state, partially awake and yet still asleep, able to move around and perform quite complicated acts, and yet quite unconscious that they are doing so.

Usually sleepwalkers perform mechanical stereotyped actions, such as sitting up in bed, or getting up and walking around the room. They may get dressed, open and shut doors, urinate in wardrobes, go downstairs, raid the fridge. Their eyes are open and searching and they seem to respond to what is going on around them; they will, for example, negotiate their way safely around obstacles. In fact, it may only be when you look at them closely that you can tell that they are partially out of touch and asleep. Like Lady Macbeth, their "eyes are open but their sense is shut." Episodes of sleepwalking may be very brief, lasting only for a few minutes, or go on for half an hour or even occasionally longer. Often, left alone, the sleepwalker will return peacefully to bed, with no harm done.

Although at first the sleepwalker tends to move around in a confused and clumsy way, he gradually becomes more coordinated, and may, like Lady Macbeth, carry out complex, purposeful and often highly inappropriate actions. One sleepwalker was found to have collected all her shoes and lined them up on the windowsill. She had no clear memory of doing this, but when she saw them in the morning, it stirred a vague recollection. Another telephoned her sister during a sleepwalking episode. Shortly afterwards her sister called her back, and she dimly remembered having telephoned her. One sleep-walker was discovered fiddling under a sofa in her bedroom while sleepwalking. When she was woken and asked what she was doing, she said that she was potting roses.

It isn't always easy to find out what is going on in the sleepwalker's mind. It is difficult to waken a sleepwalker; he will wake only gradually, and be very confused and disorientated. By the time he is fully awake he will have difficulty in remembering anything much about his dream and what he can recall will probably consist of fragments of thoughts, words, feelings and sensations—there is seldom any narrative story, as there is in an ordinary dream.

It isn't true that it is dangerous to wake someone who is sleepwalking. This is a myth which probably arose simply be-cause at the beginning of a sleepwalking episode the sleep-walker is so difficult to wake, and when he is woken he is so confused and disorientated. If he is not woken, he will usually simply return to bed, and next morning will remember nothing of the episode at all.

Sleepwalking nearly always starts in childhood or adoles-cence. It is very unusual for it to start out of the blue in adult-hood, although it may do so after a head injury, and occasionally someone may have a single episode of sleep-walking induced by drugs or alcohol and severe anxiety. Sleepwalking runs in families. The American psychiatrist Wil-liam Dement tells the story of one of his patients who claimed that his entire family—aunts, uncles, parents, siblings—were all sleepwalkers. His patient described how at a Christmas family reunion he awoke one night to find himself surrounded by all his sleeping relatives gathered in his grandfather's din-ing room.

There are plenty of accounts of sleepwalkers who have climbed out of windows, walked out on to fire escapes, fired guns, driven cars and put themselves, not to mention other people, at considerable risk. Sleepwalking is taken seriously by the medical profession and in the armed forces. Intractable sleepwalkers can face honourable discharge from the services because of the danger they are to themselves or to others—sleepwalking sailors might wander overboard; land-based per-sonnel might, it's been suggested, frighten the sentries.

Habitual sleepwalkers can sometimes be helped by hypnotherapy, which may involve a combination of learning a relaxation technique, hypnotic suggestion and learning to put themselves into a light trance. Waking the sleepwalker before the usual time of a sleepwalking episode is effective in the short term as it breaks up the sleep cycles and makes sleepwalking less likely. All sleepwalkers need to learn to recognise and avoid, or at least minimise, the triggers that usually precipitate a sleepwalking episode—tiredness, stress or too much alcohol, for example.

It is also sensible for those prone to sleepwalking to take other precautions. They should keep their windows closed at night, for example, and lock their bedroom door. They would be well advised to wear pyjamas too, as this salutary tale goes to show.

Alec was a thirty-six-year-old sales manager who had been a sleepwalker since childhood. He had been sent by his company on a refresher course which was being held in a hotel near the centre of a large town. Alec arrived tired after a long car journey, had a couple of drinks, and went straight to bed. At about eleven p.m. he arose, opened the bedroom window and jumped out, fortunately on to the low roof of an outbuilding. He jumped off the outbuilding, landing amongst the dustbins, and then walked out of the back entrance of the hotel into the main street of the town, quite naked.

Alec's memory of events begins around this point. He had a confused feeling that he had somehow become involved with aliens who had landed beside him in a spacecraft with a blue flashing light. Fortunately the police who picked him up and took him to the police station were sympathetic. After he had convinced them that he was a sleepwalker and that the last thing he remembered was tucking himself safely up in bed, they lent him a pair of boxer shorts and drove him back to his hotel.

Not so lucky was another sleepwalker who, after a night out during which he had drunk twelve single whiskies, retired to bed in the flat which he shared with his mother. About an hour later a neighbour spotted him walking naked up and down the common balcony of their neighbouring flats. The neighbour called the police, who arrived, found the poor fellow asleep in bed, and arrested him. He was convicted of indecent exposure and bound over to keep the peace.

It's not unusual for a sleepwalker's partner to say how amorous he or she can be at night. A man may grope his partner's genital area or rub her breasts and indicate to her that he would like to have sexual intercourse. There is something about these episodes that allows the partner to recognise that they are part of a sleepwalking episode and not a conscious sexual approach. Even so, this kind of sexual behaviour in sleep can be misinterpreted, and there have been cases in which a man accused of rape or sexual assault claims that the woman in question was consenting, while she maintains that she gave no consent and was, in fact, asleep; or in which a woman claims to have been sexually assaulted by a man who has no recollection of such behaviour because he was, he maintains, asleep. I know of no instance in which a man has complained of being sexually assaulted by a sleeping woman (perhaps they seldom complain), but there are instances of allegations of homosexual assault during sleep. The following case illustrated how easily a sleepwalker may run the risk of being, in this respect at least, misunderstood.

Homosexual behaviour has traditionally been regarded very seriously in the armed forces. One young officer, A, on training manoeuvres in a foreign country, had had a very hard day and was extremely tired. That evening he decided to go to bed early and his room mate, B, said he would come up later when he had finished his drink. About an hour later B went upstairs to bed, and quickly fell asleep. He was soon awakened by feeling a hand groping at his genitals. Alarmed, he turned over on to his side and the hand withdrew. A minute or two later it was back again, and this time he seized it and pulled it towards him, to find it attached to A, whom he had pulled out of bed and who was now lying naked on the floor. Not surprisingly, B was very upset and informed his room mate that he was going to tell their commanding officer. While he was dressing, A was clearly confused and kept saying, "What is happening, what are you on about, what have I done?"

When B returned with the commanding officer they found A fast asleep in bed. When he was woken he denied any knowledge of what had happened. Unfortunately, now that the complaint of homosexual assault had been made, it was difficult to stop, and a court martial followed. In court it was agreed by the prosecution that the defendant had declared his sleepwalking on entry into the services, but the case turned on whether or not the defendant was sexually aroused at the time of the assault. The court felt that in a milieu in which there were such severe penalties for homosexual behaviour, no man would have carried out such an overt sexual assault unless he had been sexually aroused, with an erection. However, if the defendant had been sleepwalking, he would, in this phase of sleep, have been highly unlikely to have had an erection. When asked, the victim agreed that the defendant had not had an erection and so the case was dismissed.

In this type of sleepwalking the person's behaviour is generally passive, and the sleepwalker shows no signs of fear. But if the sleepwalking has been triggered by a night terror they will behave quite differently.

NIGHT TERRORS

Night terrors are closely allied to sleepwalking. We've already discussed night terrors in children and mentioned that in a small number of people they continue into adulthood. Night terrors, like sleepwalking, run in families, and probably have a genetic basis. They too are a sleep transition disorder, and like sleepwalking occur because, as the brain switches over from slow-wave to dreaming sleep, the process does not go to completion. But in a night terror the sleepwalker is highly aroused, his heart is racing, his pupils are dilated, his breathing becomes fast and laboured and he may feel panic-stricken and threatened. In this state of terror he is much more likely to rush wildly around and injure himself, and if he feels under threat he may become violent in response.

Sometimes the episode is heralded, as in children, with a blood-curdling yell. The person jumps out of bed, and may rush headlong through the house as though pursued by the furies, as if his life depends on it. He may jump downstairs, even run through plate-glass doors. Sometimes he will call out something like "Let me go!" or "Leave me alone!"

As the episode passes he gradually quietens down. Although next day he doesn't usually recall anything of the night before, if awoken he may report fragmentary dreams, which consist mainly of feelings ranging from mild anxiety, or shame, or guilt, to a terrifying nameless dread, a black hole into which he is falling, composed of total fear. The feelings most frequently recalled are of being chased or crushed. In one research study, one man described feeling that the walls of the room were collapsing around him. Another remembered an image of a car crashing through the ceiling.

Sometimes the awakening is suffused with intense feelings of anxiety or guilt, a feeling that the person has done something terribly wrong or committed some awful social misdemeanour. One man described how he had woken in a confused state realising that he had invited his company chairman and every member of the board to dinner; he could hear the cars coming up the gravel drive and knew that nothing was ready. On another occasion he woke knowing that he was responsible for erecting a marquee for the village cricket match and had forgotten all about it. He was certain that the mayor and other civic dignitaries were standing in an open field waiting for him and it was about to rain. In his state of confusion, his wife couldn't get through to him to convince him that it was two a.m. and this wasn't actually happening. He insisted that he had to go out, and it was ten to fifteen minutes before he returned.

The sheer intensity of these episodes, especially if they are associated with strong feelings of fear, or shame, or guilt, sometimes means that they are treated as psychological problems rather than physiological disturbances of sleep, which is what they truly are. I was once consulted by a colleague who said he was very puzzled about a patient whom he was unable to help. Marina was a twelve-year-old girl who was suffering the results of psychological trauma. During the night of the Great British Hurricane, in October 1987, a tree had fallen on Marina's home, crushing the roof and bringing beams and ceiling down. Fortunately no one was injured and the rest of the family all managed to get out of the damaged building. However, Marina had been asleep when a beam crashed down upon her, trapping her in her bed. As the beam fell, some of its force was absorbed by the duvet covering her, and it then came to rest across the bed, pressing her down into the mattress, but with the metal bedstead taking the full weight of the beam.

Marina wasn't hurt, but she was, not surprisingly, terrified.

Some weeks later Marina's parents took her to their GP. Shortly after the night of the storm, they said, Marina had started suffering terrible nightmares. About an hour and a half after falling asleep she would sit up in bed, give a blood-curdling scream, rush out of her room and headlong down the stairs. Several times she had slipped and hurt herself. Marina's GP referred her to my psychotherapist colleague who, assuming quite rightly that her experience on the day of the storm had precipitated these episodes, tried to explore the nature of Marina's "nightmares" with her. He asked her to draw a picture of what was in her "nightmare." All Marina could draw was a round circle, which she coloured in black. There must be more to your nightmare than that, said the puzzled psychotherapist. Draw it again. Marina's response was to draw another circle and colour that black. Clearly this form of dream therapy was going nowhere.

When Marina's behaviour was described to me, it sounded very like a night terror. The reason she couldn't adequately describe the "nightmares" she had been having was that there was no visual dream content, only fear, as she was suffering from a night terror and not an REM nightmare. The treatment was not analysis, but to sort out her sleep physiology. I suggested to her mother that she should wake her daughter about three-quarters of an hour after she had gone to sleep, before the night terror began. This would break up her sleep cycles and stop the night terror arising. I also gave her a small dose of a minor tranquilliser which is known, when first given, to reduce the occurrence of night terrors. Her night terrors settled down; soon she didn't need the tranquilliser and eventually didn't need to be woken.

It is easy to see how this kind of sudden awakening, where utter confusion is mingled with an overwhelming conviction of imminent danger or disaster, can sometimes result in tragedy. There are several such cases on record. In 1791 a Silesian woodcutter, Bernard Schedmaizig, woke suddenly after only a few hours of sleep. In a confused state, he thought he saw an intruder at the foot of his bed, picked up his axe and killed his wife who was sleeping beside him. Equally tragic was the case of Esther Griggs who, in 1859, dreamed that her son was shouting that the house was on fire. On awakening from a deep sleep she threw her baby out of a window to its death.

Murderous aggression may be part of the content of a night terror, but the terror is usually focused on the dreamer, associated with a feeling that the dreamer's own life is being threatened. Sometimes, though, it is turned outwards, against some other person or presence. And even though the imagery is seldom as detailed as that in an REM dream, it is sometimes quite elaborate. In one study of adults who suffered night terrors, one person described being attacked by Indians, and pulling arrows from his wounded friend. Another, imagining that his father was being electrocuted, rushed into his father's room and dragged him from his bed. On another occasion this same man, in bed with his partner, beat her with his fists because he believed she was being attacked by an intruder.

The night life of anyone who is subject to night terrors, or to sleepwalking, can clearly be an adventurous one. Sleepwalking is a risky business. And unfortunately it isn't always just the sleepwalker him or herself who is at risk. Although it is rare for people to act violently, or even to kill, during slow-wave sleep, it is by no means unknown.

MURDERING WHILST ASLEEP

A famous French detective, overworked and exhausted, was told to take a week's holiday. He left Paris for a week at a seaside hotel. When dressing one morning he found that his socks were wet. Thinking little of it, he went out for a walk. On the beach he saw a crowd of policemen standing around a corpse. The local police chief, recognising him, asked him to help solve the case. Studying footprints in the sand around the body, the detective noticed that one of the toes of the prints was misshapen. On examining the body he found that the man had been shot; the bullet was found in the sand some distance away and sent for forensic analysis.

The detective walked back to his hotel deep in thought. He packed his clothes, spending some time contemplating his wet socks. On his way back to Paris he picked up the forensic report on the bullet, then went to see his chief. He put his own gun on to the table, saying, "This is the murder weapon, and ballistic tests confirm it." "If that is the weapon," said his chief, "who is the murderer?" "Why, I am," replied the detective. "When I awoke the morning after the murder my socks were wet and I have a misshapen toe which matches the prints which were found beside the body."

The detective had undoubtedly killed the victim. But was he guilty of murder? For a person to be found guilty of murder, it must be proved that there was an intent to kill, and it is generally accepted that someone who is sleepwalking is in an automatic state, unaware of his behaviour, unable to control it and certainly unable to form an intent. At the detective's trial, his plea of sleepwalking was accepted by the jury, and he was released, a free man.

Until quite recently our understanding of sleep was only fragmentary. It is probable that many of the earlier reported cases of sleep-related murders took place, like the ones described in the previous chapter, not during an episode of sleepwalking, but in a confused state following partial arousal from slow-wave sleep. One of the earliest recorded cases of someone using sleepwalking as a successful defence against a charge of murder is that of Colonel Culpepper who, in 1686, shot a guardsman and his horse on night patrol. At his trial he pleaded, successfully, that he committed the crime when asleep, and was convicted of manslaughter while insane.

A very similar case is that of Simon Fraser, who in 1878 was tried for the murder of his baby son, whom he had thrown against a wall, thinking he saw a wild beast attacking the child. Evidence was given that he suffered from night terrors and was a sleepwalker, and that he had frequently dangerously assaulted others—his father, wife, half-sister, fellow lodgers, a fellow prisoner in jail—while sleepwalking. A vivid account of what happened was given in court.

> Having fallen asleep, great terror suddenly seizures him, and he starts out of bed under a vivid feeling that some dreadful evil is impending, that the house is on fire, that its walls are about to crush them, or that a wild beast has got into the room and is about to attack them. Roaring inarticulately . . . he tears his wife and child out of bed to save them from death . . . or he suddenly seizures his companion by the throat under the idea that he is struggling with the beast . . . his wife is in the habit, before

going to bed, of hiding the knives, and putting the poker out of the way, lest her husband would readily find a dangerous weapon.

Simon Fraser was set at liberty, but had to give an undertaking that he would henceforth sleep in a separate room, alone, an arrangement which must, one imagines, have come as a great relief to his wife.

Partners of sleepwalkers often complain of being kicked, punched and occasionally even partially throttled by their sleeping partner, although they seldom feel they have to go to the lengths of Simon Fraser's wife and hide any potentially offensive weapon before going to bed. In fact, it is rare for partners of sleepwalkers to come to any serious harm, as they can usually manage to rouse the sleeping spouse if there is a threat of real violence. Two British psychiatrists, Professor Ian Oswald and Dr. John Evans described the case of a twenty-two-year-old man who had had vivid dreams since he was a child, sitting up and shouting in his sleep. Several times in the eighteen months of their marriage he had lashed out at his wife in his sleep, but it was when she was woken at one o'clock one morning to find him attempting to strangle her that she finally decided action had to be taken and insisted he seek medical advice. Luckily her struggles woke her husband, who was horrified at what he had done.

Others have not been so lucky. In one case on record a schizophrenic woman killed her daughter during a sleepwalking episode precipitated by the drugs she was taking. In another, a young American girl felt, in a dream, that she was being pursued by a band of robbers. While still asleep she got out of bed, took her gun from its holster and ran through the house firing shots at random. Unfortunately, some of these pierced the ceiling and killed several members of the family. At her trial she pleaded sleepwalking. This was accepted by the jury and she was freed. Then there was the case of the man who partially awoke from sleep during a night terror, picked up a knife which lay beside the bed and gave himself a fatal stab wound. His wife awoke at this point and asked what was happening. As he lay dying, he told her that he felt himself to be surrounded by devils, who had told him that unless he killed himself he would be destroyed.

In recent times, two people have stood trial for murder, made somnambulism (sleepwalking) their defence, and been acquitted. The first of these was Colin Kemp. One morning in August 1985 the body of his wife Ellen was found at the bottom of the stairs of their home. She had bruising on her cheek and a cut over her left eye. A post-mortem showed that she had been strangled in her sleep. Mr. Kemp told the court that the night before, he had "crashed out" after they had made love. He had had a nightmare in which he was fighting two Japanese soldiers, strangling one of them, kicking the other. Eventually the second soldier rolled away and shot him. He woke up to find Ellen lying on his right arm. He was unable to wake her, and afraid no one would believe that he had strangled her in his sleep, dragged her to the bottom of the stairs.

The defence claimed that Mr. Kemp had strangled his wife during a night terror. He described his dream graphically—so vividly, in fact, that the prosecution suggested that it was more like a nightmare than a night terror, a point crucial to the case. Had his "dream" been an ordinary nightmare he could not have acted it out in the way that he claimed. It would have been an REM dream and he would have been paralysed: the killing would have to have taken place *after* he had woken up. And if he had woken from REM sleep, not from the deep stages of slow-wave sleep in which night terrors arise, he would not have been confused or unaware of what he was doing. The jury, however, accepted his story and he was acquitted.

Even more intriguing is the case of Kenneth Parks, a twenty-three-year-old Canadian electronics technician living in Toronto. Ken had had a troubled childhood and from the age of fifteen had lived with his grandparents. When, at the age of twenty-one, he married, he became closer to his parents-in-law, particularly his mother-in-law, than to his own parents.

After the couple had been married about a year, Ken began to gamble. He got deeper and deeper into debt, and to cover his losses, started first to take money from the family savings, and then, disastrously, to embezzle at work. Hiding these problems from his wife and covering up the thefts at work placed even more strain on him and, predictably, on his marriage. He began to sleep badly and on occasion to lie awake all night thinking about his problems.

Some months later the embezzlement was discovered and Ken was fired and charged with theft. His house was put up for sale to cover the debt, and Ken gradually became more withdrawn and uncommunicative. He felt unable to explain or justify himself to his wife, too guilty and embarrassed to meet his in-laws, who now hardly ever saw him.

For several weeks Ken gave up gambling, but then started again. Twice he forged his wife's signature to get funds. Finally he decided to confront his problem and went to his first Gamblers Anonymous meeting. It was agreed that he should discuss his problems with his family, and he arranged to tell his grandmother first, and then meet his parents-in-law the following day and tell them everything.

The night before he was due to meet his grandmother, Ken did not sleep at all. In the morning he announced that he had decided to put off telling his grandmother till the next day, and to play rugby with his mates instead. Not surprisingly, his wife was incensed at what she regarded as backsliding. When he came home after the game they had a blazing row. His wife then went to work and Ken had supper, put the baby to bed, and started to watch TV. Around ten p.m. his wife returned from work. They watched TV together till midnight, when she went to bed. About half past one Ken finally fell asleep on the sofa, with the next day's visits to his grandmother and his parents-in-law very much on his mind. The show he had been watching just before he fell asleep showed several violent scenes.

The next thing Ken said that he remembers was looking down at his mother-in-law's face. Her mouth and eyes were open and she had what he described as a frightened "help me" look. After this he had a patchy memory of going downstairs, getting into his car, realising that he had a knife in his hands and driving to the police station for help. He remembers saying, "I think I have killed some people . . . my hands." It was only then that he felt any pain in his hand and realised it was badly cut.

The police deduced that during the period for which he had no memory he had got up off the couch at home, put on his shoes and jacket, and left the house (without locking the door, something which he never normally failed to do). He then drove his car some twenty-three kilometres through three sets of traffic lights, and entered his parents-in-law's home. He struggled with his father-in-law, who was strangled unconscious, stabbed his mother-in-law five times in the chest and neck, and beat her about the head with a blunt instrument.

Ken was perplexed, horrified and very remorseful about what had happened. There seemed to be no motive, no personal gain, and Ken strongly denied that he had had any intention of killing his wife's parents. He had never done anything violent before. There was no medical problem which might have caused either the violence or the amnesia. He hadn't been drinking and there was no evidence that he had taken any drugs. The possibility that he might have been sleepwalking was raised by the team of medical experts examining him. At first the sleep specialist who was consulted, Professor Roger Broughton, was sceptical. It seemed impossible that such a complex series of events, carried out over a relatively long stretch of time, could have occurred during an episode of sleepwalking. But the more he found out about Ken's "sleep history" the more convinced he became that it was indeed a possibility. There was a strong family record of sleep disorders—sleepwalking and talking, bed-wetting and night terrors. Ken had been a severe bed-wetter until early adolescence. He was a deep sleeper who was very hard to waken and had poor dream recall. He talked in his sleep and since early childhood had been an occasional sleepwalker. On one occasion his brother had caught him by the leg as he was about to climb out of a window while sleepwalking.

While he was in prison, Ken's cell mates had on several occasions seen him sit up in bed with his eyes open, mumble and then lie down again. He didn't seem to be awake, and didn't respond when spoken to. Ken would also sometimes wake at night, frightened, with palpitations and a feeling of heaviness in the chest, as though he was having an incomplete night terror. In addition, he had been under considerable stress, he had been sleeping very badly and was seriously sleep-deprived, which meant that when he did fall asleep he was likely to sleep more deeply.

Two questions remain. First, why did Ken go to his parents-in-law's house that night? His doctors believed that the most likely explanation was that he was very anxious about his planned visit next day, and this stressful event was probably on his mind as he was falling asleep. Secondly, why should he have behaved so violently and aggressively? The explanation put forward is that he was accosted by one of his parents-in-law while wandering round their house, that they tried to impede him in some way and that his aggression was an automatic response to this.

There is no evidence that a sleepwalker can act from a conscious intent formed during wakefulness, or that he can create such an intent. So what drives the somnambulist? Ken's actions that night were not random. He went to a place he knew and his aggression was directed towards people he knew. We know the highly emotional state he must have been in when he went to sleep. Sleepwalking is often preceded by a night terror, and it may be that the impulses which drove Ken that night arose from the feelings evoked in a slow-wave dream or night terror, a dream that will remain forever beyond his recall.

Both dreams and sleepwalking behaviour are certainly strongly influenced by daytime emotions. Very often, when violence has occurred during a sleepwalking episode, the person is under stress, or has gone to bed feeling depressed or angry. But it is too simple to say that violent feelings are being "acted out" in sleepwalking. Someone's emotional state may influence their dream content, and their sleepwalking behaviour, but any actual violence may be quite randomly directed. Oswald and Evans describe a tragic case which seems to illustrate this very well. It concerns a fourteen-year-old boy, who rose at two a.m. and stabbed and severely injured his five-year-old cousin with a bread knife. He denied any memory of stabbing her and was described by everyone who knew him as an unaggressive, healthy boy for whom such an act was completely out of character.

However, he did talk a lot in his sleep, and on one occasion, when camping, had apparently got out of his sleeping bag in the night, stood up and shouted, "Here, Davie! Catch!" and hit the tent violently. On the day of the stabbing he had had a quarrel with some friends, and when he went to bed he was feeling angry and depressed. He had also had some sort of disagreement with his father. The boy's defence lawyers, however, didn't consider offering a plea of not guilty due to a sleepwalking automatism. Instead, the boy pleaded guilty to attempted murder. And yet, as Professor Oswald suggests, "when a healthy youth rises from his bed at two a.m. and does something quite inexplicable, the first interpretation should be that he was sleepwalking."

Amongst doctors who have made a study of sleepwalking there is even some controversy about whether sleepwalkers are indeed truly asleep, or whether they are conscious, or whether they are in some other state of mind altogether. One suggestion is that sleepwalking is a "dissociated state"—that is, a state in which some mental processes become separated off from normal consciousness and function independently. Some sleep-research workers believe that sleepwalkers are often people who like to be the centre of attention, and who tend to dissociate easily.

Dr. P. Roper, of McGill University, has suggested that it is even possible to "premeditate" actions during sleepwalking. He cites the case of a sleepwalking woman who used to raid the refrigerator every night during her sleep. In an attempt to stop her nocturnal feasts her husband, knowing she was afraid of snakes, put a toy snake on the kitchen table every night before going to bed. No more raids occurred—except on the nights she knew her husband had forgotten to put the snake out. Does this mean that someone can "intend" to commit an act when they are awake, and then carry it out while they are asleep? Or might it simply indicate that slow-wave dreams, like REM dreams, incorporate daytime memories and feelings? If this is indeed so, can we be held responsible for actions carried out under the influence of a dream?

British law recognises that a man can only be held responsible for a criminal act if he is aware of his actions, and understands the impact they may have. If it can be shown that someone who commits a crime was acting in an automatic state, perhaps because of a disease such as a brain tumour, or in the aftermath of an epileptic fit, the defence of automatism is open to him. There are exceptions to this—drunkenness is no defence in law, for example, because someone who drinks can be expected to know the consequences of his actions.

Sleepwalking would seem to fit the automatism defence perfectly. Can a man be held responsible if he is unfortunate enough to break the law while he is to all intents and purposes fast asleep? Common sense, that stalwart backbone of the English law, would say not. And yet as a defence, sleepwalking has been described by Lord Justice Lawton as "a quagmire of the law, seldom entered save by those in desperate need of some sort of a defence." It is an area which leaves many of the doctors and lawyers who have to contemplate it with a slight feeling of unease. The following story may indicate why.

There is a psychiatrist who perhaps we should call Dr. X, whose reputation is of a man who is prepared to say more or less anything a defence counsel would like him to say. On this occasion he was called upon to defend a man on a charge of shoplifting. The defendant had been observed throughout on video. He had been recorded replacing the labels on various products with other labels that indicated a considerably lower price. He had been recorded stuffing articles into the recesses of garments about his person. Finally he had been recorded attempting to leave the shop without even paying for those relabelled articles for which he had fabricated a hefty discount. The defence was that he had acted in a state, hitherto unknown to medical science, of "dream fugue automatism."

Counsel for the prosecution expected to have a field day. "Am I to understand, Dr. X," his cross-examination of this expert witness began, "that it was in a state of *dream fugue automatism* that the defendant entered the shop?" "Indeed it was." "And was it in a state of *dream fugue automatism* that he removed the labels on the goods in question, as we clearly saw him do on the video?" "That is so." "And was it also in a state of *dream fugue automatism* that he then marked these same goods with labels indicating a lower price?" "I believe that to be the case." "And was it, Dr. X, in a state of *dream fugue automatism* that he secreted, as the video clearly showed, several articles that were found on him when he was subsequently arrested?" "That is my view." "Tell me then, Dr. X, how do you know that I, too, standing here before you, am not also in a state of *dream fugue automatism?*" "Without having had the opportunity to examine you," Dr. X replied smoothly, "I could not possibly come to a reliable conclusion."

There has been a growing suspicion among lawyers that sleepwalking might come to be looked on as an easy option of a defence. It is not always easy to be absolutely certain whether someone was or was not sleepwalking when they committed a crime: "proof," in this grey area, is hard to come by. And in any case, if someone is a habitual sleepwalker and they have committed some offence during a sleepwalking episode, might they not do so again?

Until the late 1980s in this country, sleepwalkers could enter a plea of not guilty due to automatism, and if the jury agreed, the judge had no option but to let the defendant go free. However, if the jury did not accept that he was sleepwalking, then the defendant would have to go to a hospital, and quite often was threatened with a secure hospital, such as Broadmoor. The law did have disadvantages in that defendants who were swinging the sleepwalking lead might go free, or that a jury having a bad day might send a genuine sleepwalker to Broadmoor, which is clearly unfair. The case of Regina v. Burgess provided an opportunity for a much-needed review of the law.

Barry Burgess was a car-park attendant who set up a friendship with a woman who lived in a flat above his. Each week, he would go up there for supper, taking his video recorder, and they would watch videos together. Unfortunately for Mr. Burgess, his feelings for the woman began to deepen, while she wanted their relationship to remain platonic. One evening he went upstairs determined to resolve matters. They had a meal together as usual, and then the story becomes difficult to follow. The woman's account is that she went to sleep on the sofa and was rudely awakened some minutes later when a bottle of wine was broken over her head by Mr. Burgess. She was temporarily stunned, and the next thing she knew was that Mr. Burgess had picked up the video recorder and hit her over the head with it—such a severe blow that the machine was significantly dented. She tried desperately to escape by crawling across the floor, but was pursued by Mr. Burgess, who then tried to hold her down with his knees and throttle her. She managed to grab hold of one of his hands, and the struggle continued for a short while until she said, with great presence of mind, "I love you, Bar," whereupon he stopped trying to throttle her and let her go. He went downstairs, and called an ambulance, then got into his car and drove around in a distraught state until the police finally caught up with him. He said he had intended to commit suicide but was arrested before he could do so.

The defence claimed that Mr. Burgess was sleepwalking when he broke the bottle of wine over his friend's head, stunned her with the video machine and tried to throttle her. For the prosecution I suggested that the episode was too soon after sleep onset to be a true sleepwalking episode and it was either a deliberate attack or occurred when Mr. Burgess was in a dissociated state, that is, he was not fully in control of his actions, though not sleepwalking.

The jury agreed that he should be found not guilty due to automatism, but they could not say whether he was sleepwalking (as the defence suggested) or in a dissociated state (as the prosecution alleged). As the law then stood, if it was decided that Burgess was in a dissociated state he would have to go to hospital, but if he was sleepwalking he could go free. The judge, however, ruled that even if Burgess *had* been sleepwalking he was to be sent to hospital and not set free. The defence claimed that this was unfair, and appealed, but the court of appeal upheld the trial judge's ruling.

All this has led lawyers in this country to decide that sleepwalking should be considered an "insane" automatism. This means that although it is accepted that a sleepwalker acts automatically, and is not responsible for what he does, it's also recognised that it may be dangerous simply to acquit him. Following an Act of Parliament in 1991, sleepwalkers no longer *have* to be sent to hospital, but the judge is given the powers to decide what is appropriate. He may recommend hospital treatment, or even detention in a special hospital such as Broadmoor if he thinks this is appropriate. Faced with Broadmoor as a possible outcome, a potential flood of sleepwalking pleas is dwindling to a trickle.

The situation in Canada is very different. Following the case of Parks, the Canadians had an opportunity to change their law in line with the British law following Burgess. But they chose not to do this. You can still, in Canada, kill, claim sleepwalking, and if this is accepted by the jury, walk out of court free. The Canadians argue that sleep is a natural function, and even though sleepwalking is abnormal, because it arises from normal sleep it is not insanity or an illness, and therefore sleepwalkers should not be penalised for acts carried out during a sleepwalking episode.

We are now waiting for the first murder story in which a

British husband wishing to get rid of his wife reads a few medico-legal textbooks, takes a holiday in Canada, murders his wife in a "sleepwalking episode," and walks out of court free to claim the insurance money.

5

The Meaning of Dreams

*If we meditate on a dream sufficiently long and thoroughly,
if we carry it around with us and turn it over and over,
something always comes of it.*

Carl Jung, *The Practice of Psychotherapy*

Just as every culture in every age has done, we look for meaning in our dreams. Our ancestors believed that dreams came
from some external source, and carried a meaning beyond the
merely personal. It was those modern seers and dream interpreters of the nineteenth and twentieth centuries, the psychoanalysts, who dramatically altered our perspective on dreams
with the revelation that both the source and the meaning of
dreams are to be found within us.

At the turn of the century, theories of sleep and dreaming
were dominated by the numerous analytical schools. The belief
was that unfulfilled wishes were held at bay in the unconscious
by the ego censor, and only allowed to come into consciousness in the dream. Even then they were disguised so that dangerous wishes would not wake the sleeper. It was the duty of
the same censor to keep motor impulses away from the
dreamer's psyche, for if they broke through and passed the
censor, then sleepwalking, or somnambulism, would occur.
Dreams were thought to be elaborated throughout the night by
the dreamer, and then like a firecracker, to be released with
explosive force in the seconds before waking.

Dream analysis still plays an important part in all schools
of psychoanalysis, even though there is no real evidence that

analysis of dreams can lead to a more useful understanding of personality than analysis of waking behaviour. But even when interpreters agree that dreams have meaning, they may not agree on exactly what they mean. Freud was concerned primarily with the hidden traumas that dreams conceal, Jung with the insights that they may reveal into the future direction of the person's life. Freud would explain a dream of walking up a staircase or climbing a ladder in sexual terms, interpreting the climb as a series of rhythmical movements with increasing breathlessness. Jung would interpret the same dream in quite a different way, as about ambition, growing up, achievement in a career. But where most dream analysts and interpreters agree is that dreams represent wishes about which the dreamer may be in conflict. They also agree that dreams are enigmatic—the wishes they represent are disguised, hidden beneath the surface, manifest layers of the dream. What dream analysis can do is to bring to the surface or highlight anxieties or concerns that the dreamer may not have fully acknowledged, and show him or her how significant they are.

Dream interpretation can often help someone face emotions or conflicts they have repressed. But the analyst has to choose the right time to encourage the patient to see that he has put up these defences, and suggest an underlying meaning of his dreams. If this is done too early the patient may reject the suggestion. A skilful therapist judges the time right—usually just as the patient is on the verge of making the same insight himself. When the patient feels the interpretation is his own, he is more likely to accept it readily, and derive more benefit from it than if he sees it as only the analyst's suggestion.

SIGMUND FREUD

Sigmund Freud began his career as a neurologist, specialising in the treatment of nervous disorders. His interest in dreams was aroused when he noticed how often patients who were talking to him about their symptoms referred to their dreams. The idea came to him that there might be a link between dreams and neurotic symptoms, and that both had their origins in early sexual conflicts. He decided that the new method of psychological investigation, psychoanalysis, which he believed was an effective treatment for many mental problems in waking life, might also be used to throw light upon dreams.

It was the emphasis which Freud put on sexuality which led to his gradual alienation from many of his colleagues. Carl Jung, Alfred Adler and Wilhelm Stekel were among his early associates who broke away and developed their own, less sexually orientated, approaches to psychoanalysis. The bedrock of Freud's theory of psychoanalysis was that much of human behaviour is determined by experiences in early childhood, especially sexual experiences. If these experiences are painful, or interfere with our need for other people's approval—especially parental approval—they may be repressed, buried in the unconscious mind and inaccessible to our waking, conscious mind. It was his belief that the unconscious mind holds the key to why people behave in the way they do, and he believed, too, that dreams are one way of gaining access to the suppressed experiences it contains.

Much of this repressed material, Freud believed, arises from (in his terms) the ''id''—that primary part of the mind which is concerned only with our most basic and primitive instincts for survival and which dominates the unconscious mind. Waking life is dominated by the ''ego,'' the conscious, rational and moral aspect of the mind which keeps these primitive instincts under control and out of conscious awareness by various defence mechanisms: repressing them, denying them or projecting them—that is, not recognising the feelings in yourself, but attributing them outside yourself, to someone else. Freud assumed that in sleep, however, the ego's defences are relaxed so that all this dangerous material which is normally repressed can enter the sleeper's consciousness.

Freud believed that all the dreams of children are simple and undisguised wish-fulfilment. The wishes fulfilled in the dream are usually carried over from the day before, and in waking life have been accompanied by intense emotion. He quotes, for example, the dream of a small boy who, on the previous day, had been made to give his uncle a basket of cherries of which he himself had been allowed only one. He awoke, said Freud, with the cheerful news: ''Hermann eaten all the chewwies!''

In adults, according to Freud, the function of dreams is still to represent the dreamer's longings and desires, but the dream seldom expresses these longings so straightforwardly. The dream has to be interpreted before the wish can be recognised, except under unusual conditions: the dreams of polar explorers wintering in the icefield, for example, do not, even for Freud, demand much subtle interpretation. They regularly dream of large meals, mountains of tobacco, and of being back home.

Much more commonly, Freud believed, the dreams of adults represent irrational, usually sexual, infantile wishes and desires. However, often these are so threatening or abhorrent that the conscious ego has to be protected from their true significance. They can only be allowed to enter consciousness in a heavily disguised and symbolic form. In sleep, the watchdog that polices our consciousness (the "superego," in Freud's terms) is inactive and dozing, allowing these inhabitants of our psychic underworld (the id) free play. But when we wake, the superego takes up its role as a watchdog again and immediately wipes out everything that it let slip through during its unguarded moments. This, he maintained, is why dreams are so quickly forgotten after waking. Freud attached particular importance to the fragments of dreams which seem to have been forgotten but emerge when the dream is being discussed or analysed. Such fragments, he suggested, are forgotten because they are so firmly suppressed, and the fact that they are so well suppressed is because they offer the most direct access to the meaning of the dream.

The story of a dream as told by the dreamer on waking is not the full story, or the real story. For Freud, a dream always has two layers of meaning. The most obvious, manifest or surface content may appear trivial, or even nonsensical. But it represents the heavily disguised and nefarious impulses which have emerged from the subconscious, and which form the "latent" content of the dream. In Freudian dream analysis, the "disguise" of the manifest content must be penetrated to get at the latent content, which contains the true motivation of the dream, and which is the message which the unconscious is trying to convey to the conscious mind.

Often, Freud believed, the meaning of a dream is concealed by what he referred to as "displacement"—the transferring of emphasis so that what appears to be the most important element in a dream actually, on analysis, turns out to be insignificant, while the truly essential content of the dream seems at first sight to be inconsequential.

Eventually Freud modified his view of dreams, and made a distinction between those dreams which are drawn purely from the unconscious, and those in which a large part of the content is drawn from ordinary events of daily life—though this might still be influenced by "repressed" desires from the unconscious mind.

When analysing and interpreting a patient's dreams, Freud used the technique of free association, encouraging the patient to let his or her thoughts "free-wheel" from the starting point of a dream image. The chain of association might lead back to the source of the unconscious problem or, alternatively, it might suddenly stop, revealing a resistance that Freud believed would reveal the nature of this same problem. Freud also believed that he could gain this information by seeing the ways in which people revised their dreams when they remembered them or recounted them to other people.

Most people now believe that one of the main weaknesses of Freud's technique of dream analysis is that he attributed a fixed meaning to various dream images, and assumed that the vast majority of these stereotyped symbols were expressions of childish sexuality—particularly likely to be suppressed, Freud thought, because their manifestation usually provoked strong parental reactions of shock or disapproval. Any phallic or womb-like object—snakes, steeples, tunnels, caves—was assigned a sexual meaning, whatever the context, and taking no account of whether or not the dream involved any sexual feelings or sensations.

It may be difficult for the client in Freudian analysis to avoid being seduced by the analyst's interpretation. When a client denies an interpretation, the analyst may interpret the denial as confirmation that he is right in making it—the client is simply determined to avoid the issue, which "proves" how significant it is. By the time he has worked through these conflicts again and again the patient may finally come to accept the analyst's interpretation.

CARL JUNG

Although Jung worked closely with Freud for five years, between 1909 and 1913, their approaches to dream analysis, and indeed their entire attitude to dreams, were very different, and eventually resulted in a rift between them in 1913. Freud was later to voice criticisms of Jung and minimise Jung's contribution to psychoanalysis, but Jung, even though he disagreed with many of Freud's ideas about dream analysis, remained generous in his appraisal and acknowledgement of Freud's achievements.

Dreams were central not only to Jung's work as a psychiatrist but to his own philosophy of life. Jung never published a systematic theory of dream analysis—indeed, he *had* no theory, but believed that every dream carried its own significance and meaning and must be interpreted individually. It was his belief that the dreaming mind possesses insights and abilities which are often superior to those of the waking mind, and whose source must lie somehow outside the mind as they cannot be explained in terms of memory. Throughout his life he was interested in psychic phenomena, and maintained that he had found by experience that telepathy can influence dreams. He also believed strongly in the creative power of dreams to throw up ideas and images that are not merely fragments of memory but insights that have not yet reached the threshold of consciousness.

All his life Jung had vivid recall of his dreams, and often relied on them to help him make decisions or resolve uncertainties. For Jung, dreams carried messages that led to the path of self-realisation, and shortly before he died, he had a dream which seemed to confirm this belief. In this dream he saw "high up in a high place" a boulder illuminated by very bright light. Carved on it were the words, "Take this as a sign of the wholeness you have achieved and the singleness you have become."

Jung, like Freud, believed that dreams could help to reveal the source of unconscious problems. However, unlike Freud, he did not believe that all the dreams his patients had stemmed from their personal unconscious conflicts, nor that most such conflicts were primarily sexual. Jung's approach to symbols in dreams was also less rigid than Freud's. He regarded them not as signs with fixed interpretations, but as symbols which could be interpreted with much more flexibility: the same dream image (of a mother, for example), might have a different personal meaning for different dreamers. While for Freud a snake symbolised only a penis, for Jung it might have "seven thousand meanings," sometimes favourable, sometimes unfavourable. A dream symbol can have a variety of meanings and be interpreted on a variety of levels.

Neither did Jung make use of the method of free association used by Freud in dream analysis. He accepted that free association might give valuable psychoanalytical insights, but not that these might have much relevance to the meaning of the dream itself. It was more likely, he believed, that free association would lead away from the dream altogether. Instead, Jung employed a method of amplification or direct association, focusing on one image from the dream, and making the dreamer explore all his associations with that particular image, returning to it again and again. He encouraged his patients to keep a dream diary, and to make drawings or paintings of their dreams.

One of the functions of dreams, according to Jung, is compensation—the correction of a conscious attitude in the dreamer. He quotes a young man who had an excellent relationship with his father, a man seen by his son as an "ideal" father—someone in fact who the son found it hard to live up to. One night the young man dreamt that his father was behaving in a drunken and disorderly manner quite out of character for him. The dream, Jung said, was showing the young man that there was no need for him to feel inferior—his father was not as marvellous as all that. His idealistic view of his father was preventing him from having confidence in himself and developing his own personality.

Many dreams, Jung believed, have much more than personal significance. These dreams are often vivid and make use of symbols which seem to be meaningless to the dreamer and have no personal significance for him. Jung believed that they stem from some common source—the "collective unconscious," through which we have access to mythological images which have meaning for everyone, in all ages and all cultures. These universal symbols he called archetypes. Jung believed that dreams which contain these symbols can only be interpreted by using historical and mythological analogies to discover what these symbols may have meant to other men in other ages. A "collective" dream has significance for others as well as the dreamer. When a dream has no apparent personal relationship to the dreamer or meaningful associations for him, these mythological parallels can throw light on the collective meaning of the dream and it may then be possible to work out its relevance to the dreamer. Jung gives an example of mythological imagery which cannot be accounted for by an individual's own experience in a patient of his, insane and in a mental hospital. Although very disturbed most of the time, in his quiet periods this patient would occasionally have peculiar visions containing strange symbolic images and ideas which he would be able to describe very clearly. One day in 1906 this patient called Jung over to the window to show him the tubes of energy hanging down from the sun. He described them so carefully and in such detail that Jung immediately remembered the episode when, four years later, he saw the same image recounted in a newspaper. It was a translation of an Egyptian hieroglyphic text recently excavated from four thousand years of oblivion beneath the sand. The four tubes from the sun, as the patient described, turned to each of the four directions, and their energy was the source of the north, south, east and west winds.

Perhaps the best-known example of a collective dream (as well as being one of the most successful examples of dream interpretation) is Pharaoh's dream, described in Genesis 41, and interpreted by Joseph.

And it came to pass at the end of two full years, that Pharaoh dreamed; and, behold, he stood by the river.

And, behold, there came up out of the river seven well-favoured kine and fatfleshed; and they fed in a meadow.

And, behold, seven other kine came up after them out of the river, ill-favoured and leanfleshed; and stood by the other kine upon the brink of the river.

And the ill-favoured and leanfleshed kine did eat up the seven well-favoured and fat kine. So Pharaoh awoke.

And he slept and dreamed the second time; and, behold, seven ears of corn came up on one stalk, rank and good.

And, behold, seven thin ears and blasted with the east
wind sprung up after them.

And the seven thin ears devoured the seven rank and
full ears. And Pharaoh woke, and, behold, it was a dream.

Corn and kine both had tremendous significance for the Egyptians. They figured in their myths and religious ceremonies, and in Jungian terms were archetypal symbols which had meanings beyond the everyday one of food: of death, rebirth and creation.

Jung saw dream analysis much more as a vehicle for discovery and personal self-realisation than as a therapeutic trowel to dig out past traumas. Archetypal dreams, for example, may centre on a journey or a quest, interpreted as a search for some aspect of ourselves, and are most likely to occur at significant transitional points from childhood to old age, and at times of spiritual upheaval. The purpose of analysis is to help a person to become whole, and to help resolve any conflicts between the conscious and unconscious mind, so that all aspects of the personality are reconciled. Dreams are of value because they give a picture not only of forgotten memories and present problems, but with a forward-looking aspect too, revealing goals of which, again, the dreamer might be unaware. Ideally, interpretation of a dream should be the result of its mutual exploration by the analyst and the patient, but Jung would never try to impose an interpretation on a patient. It was, he believed, more important for the patient to understand his own dream than for the analyst to do so.

GESTALT ANALYSIS OF DREAMS

Gestalt therapy is one of the most popular modern ways of using dreams to treat psychological problems. The method was first developed by Fritz Perls at the Esalen Institute in California. Perls trained as a Freudian analyst, but eventually came to the conclusion that more insights could be gained when problems were worked on in a group setting.

Gestalt analysis does not have a theory of dreams—rather, it concerns itself with dream *work*, the analysis of dreams by the client, with support from the therapist. Dreams are regarded as unfinished emotional business—"a message of yourself to yourself," in Perls's words. Gestalt theory presupposes that people have an innate goodness and that psychological problems originate in frustrations and denials of this goodness.

Gestalt analysis stresses the importance of symbols in dreams, but sees them as stemming from the dreamer's personal experience, without shared meaning or roots in the collective unconscious. In a Gestalt session the dreamer is helped to see the message the dream is trying to convey by acting out every image in the dream in turn, role-playing even inanimate dream objects and taking up the physical positions in which they were seen in the dream. These images are seen as alienated fragments of the dreamer's self. By telling and retelling the dream over and over again in the present tense from the standpoint of each image, the patient can begin to reintegrate these alienated fragments and accept them.

A woman in Gestalt therapy who dreamt of climbing up a rugged mountain path bordered by tall, straight pine trees was asked by the therapist to become one of the trees. She described how serene she felt, and how her roots stretched down, anchoring her securely in the ground. This made her feel aware of her own desire for such security. When she was asked to become the steep mountain path, she wept as she acknowledged the uphill struggle she felt her life to be at the moment and her inability to overcome her difficulties. The therapist used the dream to get the client to express feelings which she usually avoided so that she could become aware of them, acknowledge them and perhaps decide that she wanted to change them.

The Gestalt therapist takes care not to impose any idea of his own about the meaning of a dream, but encourages the client to say what the dream means to him at that very moment, and to recognise the emotion it evokes. It is made quite clear that the dream is the dreamer's dream, and that its only significance is the meaning it holds for the dreamer when discussing it in the session.

OTHER APPROACHES TO DREAM ANALYSIS

Although Freud and Jung were the founding fathers of the psychoanalytic approach to dreams, many other twentieth-century psychiatrists have developed their own methods of using dreams to provide psychological help to their patients. Alfred Adler was an early associate of Freud's whose approach was to treat the whole dream as a symbol rather than to focus on any particular element of it. In fact, he regarded an absence of dreams as a sign of good mental health, on the grounds that someone who deals adequately with his problems during the day has no need to dream. Neither did he hold much with the notion of the "unconscious" mind; for him, personality was unitary, the same in dreaming as in waking life—an idea that equates very comfortably with much of what we know about dreams today.

Wilhelm Stekel was another early associate of Freud's, but parted company with him in 1912. He believed that dreams show the struggles between good and evil that exist for everyone. Like Jung, Stekel believed firmly that telepathy could occur in dreams; he maintained, too, that people sleeping in the same room could influence each other's dreams. Stekel also had the insight to realise that one of the most potent influences on the dreams of someone in analysis was the analyst himself. He pointed out that dreams were often "made to order" to please the analyst—and that therefore an analyst could never use a patient's dreams as proof that his own particular theories were correct.

Medard Boss was a Swiss psychiatrist who worked largely on the manifest level of dreams. He concentrated on the "story" of the dream, and believed that in looking for a deeper, symbolic interpretation, one was in danger of missing the message of the dream altogether. It was Boss's belief that a dream simply reflects the dreamer's feelings about his life and relationships with others at the time of the dream. By drawing the client's attention to these dream feelings and encouraging him to recall the real-life situations in which the same feelings arose, Boss would help him see how he might change his attitude or respond in a different way in these situations.

Dr. W.H.R. Rivers, neurologist, ethnologist and anthropologist, was one of the first people to study the dreams of soldiers suffering "battle neurosis"—what we would now call post-traumatic stress syndrome. In July 1915, Rivers joined the staff of a military hospital for private soldiers at Maghull. Here, he says, "the idea had got about that dreams were used by the medical officers as means of testing whether their patients were to be sent back to France, and it was only rarely that one was able to obtain more than the merest fragments of a dream." The emphasis was very much on the Freudian interpretation of dreams; and, perhaps not surprisingly given the circumstances, when a soldier could be persuaded to release a fragment of a dream, it usually tended to confirm Freud's views that dreams represented wish-fulfilment.

In October 1916 Rivers was transferred to Craiglockhart War Hospital for officers, where he was responsible for treating officers, including the poet Siegfried Sassoon, who had been invalided back from the front. Many of them were suffering the most appalling nightmares, and in an effort to understand more about dream interpretation, Rivers began to study Freud's theory in more detail. He found it unsatisfactory, partly because the notion that the nightmare battle dreams these soldiers suffered represented wish-fulfilment seemed ridiculous, and partly because of the arbitrariness of some of Freud's ideas—the suggestion, for example, that every element of a dream may mean either one thing or its opposite.

However, working with these war-shattered soldiers convinced Rivers that their dreams were prominent symptoms of nervous disorder, and could be the means of learning the real nature of the mental states underlying war neurosis. He believed that these nightmares were the expression of memories which were so terrible that they were repressed during wakefulness. Only in sleep did these banished memories resurface in all their horror. And only when the dreamer learned to stop trying to repress the memories in waking life did the nightmare experiences start to fade.

Interpretation of dreams is a tricky business. First of all it is vital that a dream should be fully recorded before analysis begins, so that there is no danger of its contamination by the analysis itself. There is also some evidence that people tend to dream the dreams their analysts expect of them. Clients of Freudian analysts dream Freudian dreams. Jungian clients have

Jungian dreams. Dr. Montagu Ullman, a leading dream re-searcher in the States, has pointed out that dreams are a highly creative art form and that often we put too much emphasis on trying to interpret our dreams, when what is simpler, and often more revealing, is to learn how to appreciate them.

APPRECIATING YOUR OWN DREAMS

Do we need a dream analyst to help us to work out what our own dreams are trying to tell us? The truth is that you are the only person who can really appreciate and interpret your dreams. Other people can comment or suggest interpretations, ask questions about aspects of the dream that puzzle or interest them. But because they don't know you and every aspect of your life as well as you know it yourself, they cannot have your insights, or hope to understand every nuance of your dreams, or make the associations that you might make—if you are prepared to look hard and honestly.

Usually we dream about the people we are most involved with, the events that most concern us, and our dreams are set in the landscapes that are most familiar to us. Very often, though, our dreams take an unexpected turn, or seem to offer us a fresh viewpoint and often a new insight. A dream won't necessarily tell us anything we did not know before, but it can help us look at things in a new way. It may not solve a problem, but it can force you to pay attention to it.

Our own dreams are fascinating—always, every one of them. Other people's dreams, let's not mince words here, can be tedious beyond belief. If you like to start the day listening to nothing more demanding than the crackle of cornflakes or the crunch of toast and marmalade, it can be hard to live with someone who not only has total dream-recall, but for whom no day has properly begun until they have shared with you the previous night's experiences.

We can regard dreams as messages, just as the ancients did, but as coded messages we have sent ourselves, which only we can truly read. Sometimes a dream message can even change the course of a life. Psychiatrist Marta Elian has experienced two such dreams.

Marta was brought up in a puritanical family with a strong

work ethic and firm moral values. Her parents were very happily married; divorce was unthinkable. So it was very difficult for Marta to come to terms with the fact that, after fifteen years and two children, her own marriage was so unhappy that it could not be sustained. Leaving her husband seemed impossible because of the distress she believed this would cause her family. Unhappy though she was, she stayed in the marriage for several more years, until finally one night she had a dream. In the dream she was about twelve years old, and being taken by her mother to a swimming pool in Budapest, her childhood home. While Marta was swimming, her mother was talking to a woman at the poolside. On their way home, Marta's mother explained that this woman had been telling her that she was divorced and living on her own with two children. It was very sad, Marta's mother said, and life was very difficult for her, but she quite understood that it had been necessary for the woman to leave her marriage.

Marta understood her dream to mean that her mother, in spite of her own happy marriage, wouldn't expect Marta to stay in a relationship which had become intolerable. The dream released Marta, gave her the "permission" she needed to leave her own marriage. And in fact, when she did tell her family of her decision, her mother's reaction was simply "Thank God you've come to your senses!"

The second dream also marked a change of direction in Marta's life. At the time of this dream she was a single parent, working as a doctor in a psychiatric hospital in Switzerland. It was, she says, more like a prison than a hospital. She loathed both the job and the work environment and was determined to leave. However, the hospital would only accept resignations from its staff between the twentieth of one month and the first day of the next. On the nineteenth of the month Marta began to feel ill and panicky. For some reason she felt quite unable to hand in her resignation. These feelings lasted for the next ten days—until the time to give in her notice had safely passed. Exactly the same thing happened the following month, and the next, and the next. Each month Marta was determined to leave, and could not understand why she couldn't bring herself to resign from a job she hated. Then one night she had a dream, in which her father, who had died some time before, came and stood silently beside her bed. He said nothing, sim-

ply looked at her benevolently and smiled. When she awoke
Marta realised for the first time exactly what was stopping her
handing in her resignation. One of her father's rules in life,
which Marta had often heard him repeat during her childhood,
was that "one doesn't give up a secure job without having
another one to go to." Although she hadn't consciously remembered this, it was clearly what had been holding her back.
Marta's interpretation of her father's benevolent smile in the
dream was that, had he still been alive, he wouldn't have condemned her but would have acknowledged that there are exceptions to every rule. Again, the dream gave her
"permission" to make the decision she wanted to make and
that month she felt no reluctance when the time came to give
in her notice. She left Switzerland, came to England, and built
a new life for herself—all consequent upon a dream.

You can think of your dream as having a surface level,
composed of the sounds, sights, events and characters that
make up the dream, and an underlying level, which holds the
meaning or message that the dream is trying to express. In the
surface level you will nearly always recognise fragments of
events that have happened to you during the day, or people
you have met or thought about, or issues you've been thinking
or worrying about. Sometimes though, there may be no such
obvious links with your waking life; the dream may seem to
make no sense at all. But remember that the surface, manifest
content of a dream is a pretty good guide to the deeper, hidden
meaning.

However, it is also worth remembering that not all dreams
are meaningful. Dr. Anne Mathieson is a hypnotherapist who
uses hypnosis to help patients sift those dreams which might
be relevant to their problem from dreams which are simply the
equivalent of "doodling." In a state of light or medium hypnotic trance the hidden truths of a dream may be more accessible; the patient often finds it easier to remember details of a
dream and to explore different levels of meaning within it. She
also suggests to patients under hypnosis that perhaps they will
have a dream which will help to clarify or solve their problem.

When you are trying to interpret a dream, remember that
dreams are often about conflict, and the conflict is one which
affects you. A dream often brings us face to face with problems or issues that we may have tried to ignore or suppress in

our everyday life. You can be fairly sure that your dreams reflect self-interest. You don't dream about other people's problems, unless the other person is someone with whom you are so involved that their problem is, in a sense, your own.

One of the most fascinating aspects of dreams is not their ability to present insights or to solve problems, but the way they translate these problems into "dream language," showing them to us in the form of symbol, metaphor and analogy. Why do we dream in symbols? If our dreams are indeed messages from our unconscious, why can't they tell us what we need to know in a more straightforward way? Why do we need all the bizarre images that so often appear in our dreams, that seem to act as a bridge between the conscious and unconscious minds?

One explanation is that if the dream message is something we may not be ready to hear, symbolism gives us the opportunity to ignore it as just another weird and inexplicable dream. On the other hand, the very obscurity of our dreams, the sheer oddity of the symbolism, may so intrigue us that we pay more attention to the dream and think about it more deeply than we might otherwise have done. Solving the metaphor may make us feel that we are "seeing" the problem more clearly, and perhaps even solving it.

Another reason that has been suggested is that during sleep we can only handle limited quantities of data. Symbolism is a very economical way of presenting information: the maximum amount of information is available in the fewest data units. Dream symbols are chosen to convey the message and so make sense only to the dreamer. But when you are looking for meaning in your dreams, remember that it is the emotion attached to the particular symbol that gives the real clue, more than the actual symbol itself.

Sometimes the symbolism is so obvious that it needs little analysis. R. D. Laing, for example, quotes a dream by a nineteen-year-old girl who was fast approaching a marriage which, for various reasons, she had come to dread. She dreamed that she was in the back seat of a car, which was driving itself. Another similar example is this dream, recounted by a woman who, although happily married, felt very attracted to someone she had just met.

We were in a garden, both naked and lying on the grass, facing each other but at arm's length. Both our arms were outstretched so that our hands were clasped. There was no sexual contact, except just this clasping of our hands, but a very powerful sexual feeling about the whole dream. When I thought about the dream the next day I thought how neatly it had summed the whole thing up—the acknowledgement of the powerful attraction, plus the realisation that I had no intention of doing anything about it that might damage my marriage. I appreciated the way my dream-mind had decided this other man had to be kept, literally, at arm's length.

Laing regards this type of dream as dissociative, in which a normal individual, in a situation which he realises is threatening to his being and from which he can't seem to escape, becomes a mental observer, looking on detachedly at what his body is doing, or what is being done to his body.

Dreams do sometimes seem to suggest solutions to our problems. But a problem seldom has one and only one correct solution. If it does, it is usually so blindingly obvious that we don't need a dream to show us. However, if there are several possible options, a dream may highlight the option we really wanted all along, or perhaps one we hadn't thought about seriously, but realised at some level was worth further consideration. Quite often dreams produce solutions which are so wrapped up in imagery that the waking mind can interpret them in a number of different ways. One woman who was undergoing a traumatic time in her marriage had this dream.

I dreamed I was walking down a road and went into a slaughterhouse. I disliked this intensely, felt extremely unhappy there and desperately wanted to get out. I searched everywhere for a door and finally I found one but I couldn't open it. I looked all round the place for a key and there was none. Then finally I felt in my pocket and there was the key. So I opened the door, and went out into the fresh air breathing a sigh of relief. The door banged shut behind me, and I knew it was locked, so that I couldn't get back in there again.

She immediately saw this as a suggestion that the key to her marital discord was within herself, that the only way forward was to leave the marriage, and that if she did this, there could be no going back. This was the course she finally took, and she feels now, ten years later, that it was absolutely the right decision; the slaughterhouse was not for her.

However, she could equally well have interpreted the dream quite differently. She might have taken the key to mean that she herself held the solution to the carnage within her marriage; that it was in her power to change the situation. She could have interpreted the feeling that there was no turning back to mean that to return to her previous behaviour was inappropriate and the way forward was a change in attitude. Or, of course, she could have taken the dream entirely at face value as a drama taking place in a slaughterhouse. The dream itself was not important; it was her interpretation of it which mattered. She chose the interpretation which pointed to divorce because she felt this to be the right meaning for her.

The woman who described the following dream told us that it had an enormous impact on her at a very difficult time of her life:

The background to this dream was that I had recently separated from my ex-husband, who was a person who needed to control and take over. I obviously went along with this for a long time (being married for twenty-two years) and let him make all the decisions. Perhaps I was not confident enough to make them for myself.

I was in a very long dark tunnel, although I could just see the light as a small spot in the distance. I wanted to leave the tunnel and get out into the light, but then became aware that lying on the ground between me and the end of the tunnel were hundreds of dead, mutilated bodies and to get out I would have to climb over them. My first emotion was one of complete panic as the thought of actually going near these dead bodies was just too awful to contemplate. I then pulled myself together and thought that if that was what I had to do to get out then I would steel myself and do it. My overwhelming feeling was then one of determination, and no matter what, I would get to the end of the tunnel.

After trying to analyse the dream I took it to mean that at least I was taking control of my own life, and although I found the task quite daunting I knew I could do it. In the dream I had felt such determination to get there on my own, without anyone's help.

WORKING WITH YOUR DREAMS

If you are interested in studying your own dreams, the first step is to train yourself to remember them.

- Keep a "dream journal" so that you can record your dreams. If you are serious about this, you should keep a notepad and pencil by your bed so that you can scribble down at least an outline of the dream as soon as you wake from it. It's especially important to do this if you wake from a dream in the middle of the night. However vivid it seems to be at the time, however sure you are that you will remember it in the morning, unless you record it before you go back to sleep it will almost certainly be beyond recall next day.
- Where dreams are concerned, first impressions often count for most. If you do nothing else, write down what immediate association the dream had for you, or what was the first thing that came into your mind when you thought about it.
- As you lie in bed before you go to sleep, relax and think about your day, and in particular about any areas in which you feel a little "dream enlightenment" might be helpful— emotional conflicts that you haven't managed to resolve, problems whose solutions are eluding you.
- If you wake up during the night, and when you wake in the morning, keep your eyes closed and try to hold on to the images that were in your mind as you woke. Maybe you can remember where the dream was taking place, or who else was with you, or what you were doing or how you felt Then see if you can remember what led up to this image. Dreams are often a sequence of images, which seem disjointed, with no connecting thread, and this backtracking process may help you work your way back through them.
- When you feel you have recalled as much as you can, write

down the dream in as much detail as possible. Don't try to "edit" it at all.

- Think especially about the emotions you felt in the dream, and the feelings that you are left with when you wake. The feelings a dream evokes in you are more important than the actual images.

ANALYSING THE DREAM

When you come to analyse your dreams in more detail, remember that they are primarily about you—what is happening in your mental, physical and emotional life, your relationships with people around you. Even when a dream seems to tell you something very clearly about somebody else—a precognition of someone else's death, or a disaster, for example—there is almost certainly a link with your own thoughts or feelings. Try to find these dream associations if you can. If in your dream you felt insecure, or jealous, or frustrated, try to identify relationships or situations in your life in which you've felt the same way. They may not be the same situations—in fact it's very likely that they won't be, because your dream mind likes to communicate obscurely. The imagery in our dreams is often symbolic.

Soon after her husband had left, at a time when she was still trying to come to terms with the end of a marriage she had greatly valued and a husband she had loved, a friend had the following dream.

I dreamed that in my garden was a pure white marble statue. It was a figure, quite beautiful, and I loved it. Then I saw that dark green ivy was growing from its side, twisting around the body of the statue, gradually covering it. Friends kept telling me I had to get rid of the ivy but I didn't want to—I felt it would spoil the statue. But finally I did, stripping the ivy from it. And where the ivy had sprouted there was a wound, a scar in the side of the statue. But even so I realised in my dream that the ivy had to go, that otherwise it would gradually have destroyed the statue. When I woke I realised for the first time that even though I still grieved for our marriage, it had been the right decision for my husband to leave. It had the most powerful effect on me, that dream, and I can still remember it so well, all these years later.

Sometimes a dream can help us see ourselves as others see us, tell us things about ourselves that we find it hard to acknowledge and would rather not know. One man described a particularly vivid dream in which he was in a cave and saw, sitting on a high ledge, "an 'Alice in Wonderland'-type slothful creature. Its face had human characteristics. It disgusted me to the core . . . I had awoken thinking of it . . . I am convinced that I was shown 'sloth personified' as a warning to me of what I was in grave danger of becoming."

Monica Jackson described two profound and rather frightening experiences which were each triggered by powerful, and very negative, emotions.

The first occurred at a time when I had been very angry, for some time, over family matters. I woke up one night coughing and choking and sat up in bed feeling as if something like hot smoke was coming out of my throat. It came to me that this was anger, and shortly after I felt spent and empty but aware that there was a huge cloud of undirected anger at the foot of my bed. I was frightened but because the anger *was* undirected, not very frightened. I seized a rosary I kept on my bedside table, put it under my pillow, pulled the bedclothes over my head and promptly went to sleep. In the morning my throat still felt faintly scorched and I felt totally exhausted all day, but all my anger had disappeared and I was at peace with the world, a state which lasted about a month.

On the second occasion, I woke from a nightmare in which I had killed my beloved old dog who had recently been put down on compassionate grounds. I was sitting up in bed crying, "I've killed her," when suddenly I was caught up in what seemed just like the "review" some respondents report in their NDEs [Near Death Experiences]. That is, I went through, very fast, all the wrongs I had done to others in the past, feeling all their pain—it was terrible. I was arched backward in physical as well as mental agony, and thought it would kill me, until the

words came into my head. "I accept." I said it aloud—
screamed it—and the experience stopped. I was exhausted, tearful and deeply depressed for about three
weeks. Very salutary.

It is interesting to compare these experiences, which seem to
have had quite different, though in each case very powerful,
effects. In the first case the experience was cathartic and healing. It enabled Monica to get rid of her anger, which was made
concrete, no longer inside her but at the foot of her bed, and
left her feeling at peace. The second experience was a nightmare which triggered guilt feelings which persisted when
Monica woke, reminding her of all the wrongs she had ever
done in the past, and leaving her exhausted and depressed.
However, she described this as "very salutary," so perhaps
for her it was a useful, if not a happy experience.

We can look at and learn from a dream in two ways. One
way is to see how the emotions and difficulties we have in our
lives may be translated into dream language. The other is to
look at the dream images and symbols themselves, and see
how far we can use these to explain what is going on in our
lives.

It is usually easiest to start with the first kind of dream
analysis, because there is usually no mistaking the emotional
quality of a dream. Anxiety is probably the most common
emotion expressed in dreams, and anxiety dreams are troubled,
unsettled dreams filled with uneasiness. If too much is going
on in our lives, and we're finding it impossible to meet dead-
lines or fulfil obligations, our dreams will reflect this. We'll
be faced with impossible tasks to carry out, we'll be late for
a train or an appointment, and events at every turn will tran-
spire to make us even later; although mentally urging ourselves
on we can move only in slow motion. If shyness or social
inadequacy are making us anxious, our dream situations may
involve embarrassment or social humiliation. If you are anxious about failure in real life, you will probably fail in your
dreams too. The dream of having to take an examination for
which you are unprepared, perhaps even in a subject you have
never studied, is a classic failure dream which haunts many
people long after they have taken their final examinations in
real life.

The following dream shows very well how these two aspects—the dream emotions and the dream symbolism—blended in a dream which had a very clear message for the dreamer. For two years Mary and her husband had belonged to a semi-religious organisation, which they had originally joined out of interest and to make friends. But gradually Mary had come to feel that it was demanding more of her than she wanted to give, and that she was being sucked in far deeper than she wanted to be. One night she had this dream.

I dreamed I was on a square platform, raised up, rather like a boxing ring, in the middle of a forest, except that there were no ropes around it. There were a lot of other people around and we were all wearing the same uniform, like a school uniform. I hated being there and I wanted desperately to get away. But although there were no ropes around the platform, nothing to keep me there, somehow I couldn't get off.

This dream didn't tell me anything I didn't consciously know. I knew that I disliked the rigidity of the organisation we were in, that it felt like a school, beset with rules and demanding uniformity even if it didn't go so far as to make us wear uniform, and that I resented having to conform. But it did bring my feelings to the fore and make me realise how strong they were, what a disproportionate part they were playing in my life. It also made me see very clearly that I wasn't actually trapped at all—maybe I felt that way, but in fact, there were no ropes around the ring, nothing to stop me getting off if I really wanted to. The day after my dream we made the decision to leave the organisation.

Is there a dream language, common to everyone? In a very general sense, there probably is. Dreams of being trapped or in captivity, like Mary's dream, for example, may mean that you are unable to express something that is important to you, or that there is something you want to be free of, a relationship perhaps, or a work or social commitment.

If we feel that our lives lack direction, we may feel lost or disorientated in our dreams. Loss of a sense of personal identity may mean that in our dreams we are wandering in a strange town unable to find where we live. The classic identity-crisis dream is of looking into a mirror and seeing someone else's face reflected there.

In dream analysis, symbols that often appear in dreams are sometimes allotted standard meanings. These can be useful as a starting point when you are trying to analyse your own dreams, so long as you remember that your own dreaming mind may not be using this particular symbol in this particular way. It can be interesting to use these as guidelines, to see if this particular meaning seems to be relevant to you, but they are not to be taken too seriously.

Fire, for example, is said to symbolise anger. Climbing dreams are said to symbolise ambition (or, to Freud, a desire for sexual fulfilment). Dreams of falling from a great height may signify failure, or that the dreamer has lost control, that he has reached a position in his professional or personal life that he cannot maintain—that he is, in fact, heading for a fall. Drowning suggests a fear of being engulfed by some unexpressed subconscious need. But, equally, if you have a phobia about fire, a fear of heights, a terror of deep water, whatever anxiety you have may well be expressed by this particular dream metaphor.

Dreams may express a need for change (redecorating or moving house, for example), or a fear of it (finding oneself lost and bewildered in unfamiliar surroundings). A bridge in a dream is a classic symbol of change, but the dreamer may feel dread and apprehension when he approaches, or excitement and optimism at the possibilities of what lies on the other side. Dreaming of a church symbolises the spiritual nature of the dreamer.

In classical dream analysis, the dreamer himself is often represented by a house. The front of the house may represent the face the dreamer presents to the world, the back his more hidden or guarded aspects. When the dreamer comes across a hidden or secret room it may signify some aspect of himself that he has ignored, or needs to explore or develop. These hidden rooms are usually "special" places, and there is usually a feeling of excitement about discovering them. One woman described her room as "full of bits and pieces. I get very excited about it and keep discovering things and thinking,

I can use this for something and that for something else.''
Another said,

> When I find my room it's always a very exciting discov-
> ery. It's always a room I need for something, it's hidden
> away but just off another room, or up a little staircase
> that I know and recognise because I've been there often
> in my dream. When I find it I'm always pleased and think
> it is just what I was looking for.

Masks are symbols of the image we present to the outside
world. A mask that can't be removed or that the dreamer is
forced to wear may indicate that the dreamer feels his ''real''
self is being eroded or obscured.

Animals are common dream symbols, especially in the
dreams of children, but whether they are fierce or frightening
or playful and friendly will depend on the dreamer's state of
mind. Birds are said to symbolise the higher self; the lion is a
symbol of power. In Freudian terms, the lion may represent
the powerful, benevolent aspects of the father, a wild horse his
frightening threatening aspect. Fish, usually considered a lowly
form of life, are high in the hierarchy of dream significance,
used to symbolise divinity, spiritual abundance and insights
into the unconscious.

Dreams of travel are often rich with symbols. For Freud *any*
travel dream involved a suppressed desire for sexual intercourse, the quintessential Freudian travel dream, of course, being the train going into a tunnel. Flying dreams are nearly
always pleasant, and often exhilarating, with a wonderful sensation of freedom. Dreamers seldom fall out of the air, but
float gently to earth. Sometimes the dreamer's bed may take
off, or he may take flight in an armchair; this may well suggest
a longing for adventure, combined with a reluctance to take
too many risks.

Dreams which are concerned with religion or spirituality
often contain light—usually a white or golden light, bright,
but not dazzling to the eyes. Light in a dream, according to
Jung, always refers to consciousness. The being of light is an
image that symbolises a universal spiritual principle, common
to all cultures and religions. Dreams in which the dreamer goes
towards a light, or meets the being of light, have a special

mystical or religious quality and are discussed in more detail in chapter 15. The Virgin Mary is a symbol of purity, of self-less love and compassion.

A recurrent dream may be showing us that some problem or conflict is unresolved—when we resolve the problem, the dream may disappear. Children's recurrent dreams are often frightening or disturbing, embodying some nameless undefin-able childish fear. One little girl dreamed several times a year, from the age of about four, of a vast room, quite empty except for a raised throne, behind which hung purple curtains. On the throne sat a large wolf. The wolf never moved, she said, never even bared its teeth, and yet it filled her with terror. As often happens, the dream recurred over a period of several years, and then finally vanished, never to trouble her again.

Recurrent dreams can often show us something about our emotional or spiritual life. They don't always recur in exactly the same way, and the way the dream changes may reflect changes in our emotional state. Averil Meallen, a physiother-apist, has two recurrent dreams which have changed in quality over the years in a way which she feels reflects changes in her own life. In the first a tidal wave would sweep over her, and the dream was very frightening. But now she says she is often able to get on top of the wave and ride it. The dream is no longer frightening, in fact she now quite enjoys it. And her mastery of the wave, her ability to ride it, she feels reflects the degree of mastery she has managed to achieve in her own life.

Averil also has a recurrent flying dream. This she has always enjoyed, but when she first had it she had to make a huge effort to get off the ground. Now she can do it easily—she just flaps her arms and off she goes. For Averil, the dream seems to mirror her personal quest for self-realisation. She meditates, and says she can relive the dream when she does so.

Dreams often show us our emotional needs. But sometimes they fulfil them too. MW describes a dream which he had a few nights after the death of his father.

I went to bed that night, and as far as I know went to sleep. All of a sudden I found myself in the air and float-ing above Wordsley Church which is about a mile and a half from the house where we lived. I floated down and ended up somehow inside the church. At this point I must say that to my knowledge I had not been inside that church since I was very small.

I was aware of the church organ on the left-hand side of the aisle. As I looked down the aisle of the church, what I can only describe as a panel slid open behind the organ and my father appeared. He was wearing the clothes that he had worn in his occupation as a top-class mechanic and lorry driver. My father saw me and spoke to me and said that he was all right and very happy, and told me not to worry. He then went back inside the organ panel and it slid shut again.

Wordsley Church is the church where my mother and father were married in 1937. Could it be that my father's spirit had returned to the place where he experienced one of the happiest days of his life, and why was I there? Was I privileged on that night? I wish there was a logical explanation.

Such dreams are common after a bereavement, and they can have a cathartic, healing quality. This dream meeting with his father was clearly enormously important to MW, reassuring him that his father was happy, and that he had no need to worry. The dream gave him permission to move on in his own life. If he had any sense of unfinished business with his father, the dream would almost certainly have helped him resolve this too. In that sense, he surely was privileged on that night.

MW himself feels that he did truly meet his father at the church, and rejects the explanation that it was "just a dream" precipitated by his father's death. The fact that he recognised the church even though he hadn't been there since he was a child is easily explained: even childhood experiences are retained in memory and may be re-created long after they have been consciously forgotten. If MW really *did* meet his father on that night, then there *is* no logical explanation: we would have to accept that our current scientific concept of consciousness is too narrow to encompass this kind of experience. In practical terms it really matters very little. Marta Elian too had a dream in which she "met" her father (see p. 75). She has no doubt that it *was* just a dream. But this did not lessen its impact, or the positive and very timely purpose it served. She was "released" by her father just as effectively as if he *had* appeared to her in person. The dream simply displays the power we exercise over ourselves, and our ability to free ourselves from imaginary shackles.

6

On the Borders of Sleep

I am falling asleep. Golden dots, sparks and tiny stars appear and disappear before my eyes. These sparks and stars gradually merge into a golden net with diagonal meshes, which moves slowly and regularly in rhythm with the beating of my heart which I feel quite distinctly. The next moment the golden net is transformed into rows of brass helmets belonging to Roman soldiers marching along the street below. I hear their measured tread and watch them from the window of a high house in Galata, in Constantinople, in a narrow lane, one end of which leads to the old wharf and the Golden Horn with its shops and steamers and the minarets of Stamboul behind them. The Roman soldiers march on and on in close ranks along the lane. I hear their heavy measured tread and see the sun shining on their helmets. Then suddenly I detach myself from the windowsill on which I am lying and in the same reclining position fly slowly over the lane, over the houses, and then over the Golden Horn in the direction of Stamboul. I smell the sea, feel the wind, the warm sun. This flying gives me a wonderfully pleasant sensation, and I cannot help opening my eyes.

P. D. Ouspensky's vision, described above, was dream-like, but not a dream. He describes it as taking place in a "half dream state," that fascinating twilight zone that you enter just as you are dropping off to sleep, or in the first moments of waking. Pictures appear and are transformed one into another. The "golden net" is transformed into the helmets of the Roman soldiers, the regular rhythm of a heartbeat into their "measured tread."

If these dream-like visions occur as you are falling asleep they are known as "hypnagogic." If they occur as you are awakening they are sometimes known as "hypnapompic," but essentially the experiences are the same. Hypnapompic visions can be more frightening, because they sometimes persist into full consciousness as you wake. In fact the state of hypnagogia can occur not only when you are dropping off to sleep, but in any situation where your level of consciousness falls through boredom—motorway driving, for example.

Hypnagogic experiences have a hallucinatory, sometimes almost a magical, quality, but they are not true dreams, and don't have the narrative quality of most sleeping dreams. A medley of pictures may seem to dance before your eyes, rapidly changing and merging into one another. More often they consist of a series of shifting images, changing before your eyes and transforming into another image. These images may be formless, barely perceptible, or concrete hallucinations seen in minute and vivid detail. Usually they are visual—brief glimpses of animals, objects, faces or figures, swirling clouds of colours, patterns or moving lights. Sometimes landscapes are seen, or natural phenomena such as rivers or waterfalls. In fact, there is an infinite variety, and they simply appear, without being imagined, willed or consciously visualised. Although often they are pleasant, they can be terrifying, though usually a frightening hallucination jerks the person into a full awakening.

It happens virtually every night and has done most of my life. Nearly always it's at the same time—about a quarter to twelve. I'll see snakes on top of the wardrobe, water coming up through a hole in the bedroom floor, a wolf eating the curtains. The dressing gowns hanging on the back of the door become two people and I wonder what they're doing, standing there, looking at me. Once I got out of bed and hustled my wife into the wardrobe, telling her that we had to get into the lifeboat because the ship was sinking. Whatever I see it is always bizarre, but not necessarily frightening in the way that a nightmare is frightening. After half a lifetime I've learned how to deal with them. I know that if I sit up, then sit on the edge of the bed with my feet on the floor, everything will vanish. Then I may get up and make myself a cup of tea, or read for a bit and go back to sleep again.

Although hypnagogic experiences are usually visual, the other senses may be involved as well. Some people hear noises— bangs, crashes, bells—as they fall asleep; others hear voices— often their own name being called or snatches of (usually non- sensical) conversation. A few people experience hypnagogic smells, sometimes disgusting, sometimes delightful, and hyp- nagogic taste experiences have also been reported. There may be feelings of being touched, sensations of heat or cold, dis- orientation and distortions of body image, or feelings of weightlessness.

Is there any essential difference between hypnagogic expe- riences and "real" sleep-dreams? Some people maintain that there is no difference between the two; others that hypnagogia are merely the "elements" of dreams, too fragmented to be truly dreams. Probably the borderline between the two is blurred. Like true sleep, there seem to be varying depths of hypnagogia, from light experiences in which the person has some awareness, feeling detached, as though he is watching the whole thing but not participating in it, gradually deepening so that the hypnagogic imagery comes to dominate his private world and the outside world is totally lost.

Stanley Melling is now over eighty. In about 1981 he began to have hypnagogic experiences like the one he describes be- low, either as he was going to sleep at night, or in the morning when he was coming to. They seemed very real and, because he did not understand what was happening, rather frightening. In the experience he describes below, you can see the hyp- nagogic images gradually merging into a true dream.

I had experienced a small pale blue light in front of my head before going to sleep for a few weeks before this happened, then in front of my face, although my eyes were closed, came a full moon with dark clouds passing in front . . . I started to rise head first and go through the dark centre; this formed a tunnel and as I looked back I could see an eye and part of a face. I descended down the tunnel at a terrific rate, then I was travelling in the darkness of the night. I could see small flickers of light passing me as you would if they were coal fires on a tip, then as I came to the ending of my journey the most beautiful light and scenery you could imagine . . . I am in some sort of a transparent vehicle, which is slowly coming to a halt. I see a man in a white robe come in front of me, we do not speak, he has dark curly hair and beard. We have some kind of rapport through the eyes, and then I return to my bed . . . As all these things are happening you are aware, not through words, that someone has prepared the way and no harm will come to you . . .

Some years ago some colleagues and I carried out experiments to look at the effects of meditation on the electrical activity of the brain. What we found was that meditation appears to be an excellent method for holding the meditator in a prolonged state of sleep onset, halfway between waking and stage 1 sleep. Ordinary relaxation did not have the same effect at all—when we simply asked people to relax they usually passed rapidly through this twilight zone and fell asleep. Recent evidence suggests that brain activity may be different at this level of consciousness, making it in some way an especially creative zone of experience.

In some ways, the hypnagogic state is very comparable to the experience of entering a flotation tank. This is a dark, sound-proof chamber partially filled with salt water at body temperature. Buoyant in the warm salty water, the body is in a state of sensory deprivation as complete as is possible. In this state the mind, with virtually no input from the outside world, withdraws into its own imagery, and becomes footloose and fancy-free. With no restraints, the brain models expand and intertwine to form a kaleidoscope of images, brightly coloured, with wonderful stories, and at times these may become so profound that the floater finds himself drawn into a totally new reality. He may experience mystical union and be privy to the secrets of the universe.

Seekers after ecstasy have discovered that the flotation tank may be a short cut to Nirvana—they say they are different when they emerge, much more relaxed and tranquil. In fact there is some scientific evidence that the brain does actually work differently after the experience, and that the right hemisphere becomes much more active than it was previously. An object put into the left hand (from which sensation goes to the right half of the brain) can be detected and its shape remembered more easily than before the float. Just being quiet does not seem to achieve the same degree of altered function.

Something very similar happens when we go to sleep. Normal bedtime rituals are simply attempts to cut out all sensory stimulation. The curtains are drawn so that the room is dark. We make sure everything is quiet (some people even have to remove a ticking clock from the room if they want to fall asleep). We get into a soft bed, which quickly takes on our body temperature, so stimulation to the skin is reduced to a minimum. We make sure that the room is neither too hot nor too cold, and if we are in any pain we take an aspirin.

In effect, what all this does is to put us into a state of sensory deprivation. The amount of information coming into the brain from the outside world is cut to a minimum. The brain, no longer constrained by input from the outside world, starts to generate its own world and runs much more freely. Thoughts and images come into the conscious mind and these bear no close relationship to the outside world. It is this that makes this borderland, where the mind roams free without constraint, a particularly creative state, and one which sometimes leads to insights inaccessible to the waking mind.

These "waking dreams" have provided inspiration for numerous creative artists. Charles Dickens is said to have had the inspiration for many of his characters and stories in a state of hypnagogia. Max Ernst and Salvador Dali both used hypnagogic imagery in their paintings. Andreas Mavrotamis, in his book *Hypnagogia*, describes how Dali is said to have trained himself to doze in a chair with his elbow propped on a table and his chin resting on a spoon which was held in one hand. As he was on the verge of falling asleep, his chin would drop, dislodging the spoon and waking him, often in the middle of a hypnagogic dream, whose imagery he would then paint. Edison used a similar strategy—whenever he had reached an impasse in his work he would take a cat-nap, holding steel balls in his hands. As he dozed, the balls would clatter into metal pans on the floor, waking him—often with the way forward clear in his mind.

It is this suspension of the logical mind that lies at the heart of what Robert Graves has described as the "poetic trance."

> The nucleus of every poem worthy of the name is rhythmically formed in the poet's mind, during a trancelike suspension of his normal habits of thought, by the supralogical reconciliation of conflicting emotional ideas. The poet learns to induce the trance in self-protection whenever he feels unable to resolve an emotional conflict by simple logic. If interrupted during this preliminary process of composition he will experience the disagreeable sensations of a sleepwalker disturbed; and if able to continue until the draft is completed will presently come to himself and wonder; was the writer really he?
>
> As soon as he has thus dissociated himself from the poem, the secondary phase of composition begins; that of testing and correcting on commonsense principles, so as to satisfy public scrutiny ... The amount of revision needed depends largely on the strength and scope of the emotional disturbance and the degree of trance. In a light trance, the critical sense is not completely suspended; but there is a trance that comes so close to sleep that what is written in it can hardly be distinguished from ordinary dream-poetry: the rhymes are inaccurate, the phrasing eccentric, the texture clumsy, the syntax rudimentary, the thought-connexions ruled by free-association, the atmosphere charged with unexplained emotion.

The German organic chemist F. A. Kekulé seems to have had a particular facility for making notable scientific discoveries in this half-awake, half-asleep hypnagogic state. This is how he describes the events that led to one of the most important discoveries in the history of organic chemistry, the prediction of the ring structure of the benzene molecule.

> I was sitting, writing at my textbook, but the work did not progress; my thoughts were elsewhere. I turned my chair to the fire and dozed. Again the atoms were gambolling before my eyes. This time the smaller groups kept

modestly in the background. My mental eyes, rendered more acute by repeated visions of the kind, could now distinguish larger structures, of manifold conformation: long rows, sometimes more closely fitted together; all twining and twisting in snakelike motion. But look! What was that? One of the snakes has seized hold of its own tail, and the form whirled mockingly before my eyes. As if by a flash of lightning I awoke; and this time also I spent the rest of the night working out the consequences of the hypothesis.

It is a good story. Unfortunately some doubt has been cast on it by S. Rudofsky and J. Wotiz who suggest that Kekulé invented it because he didn't want to acknowledge any credit due to non-German investigators who had worked out cyclical structures for other molecules before Kekulé's discovery of the benzene ring. They also point out that he first publicly claimed to have had the dream ten years after the event.

However, Kekulé's account does ring very true if one assumes, as all the evidence suggests, that he was in a hypnagogic state rather than a true dream state. He does not, after all, actually claim to have been asleep. He says his "thoughts were elsewhere." He "dozed." He made his observations using his "mental eyes." The vision of the twining, twisting atoms he describes sounds typical of the imagery of the hypnagogic state. Although he says, "As if by a flash of lightning I awoke," arousal from a hypnagogic state can feel like an awakening. In any case, his "waking" can be regarded as more metaphorical than actual, the sudden realisation of the significance of what he had seen.

W.H.R. Rivers (1923, pp. 7–8) describes how he too found that ideas often crystallised for him in this special state between sleeping and waking.

. . . as soon as I become aware that I am awake, I find that I am thinking, and have for some time been thinking, over some problem usually in connection with the scientific work upon which I am at the time engaged. Many of the scientific ideas which I value most, as well as the language in which they are expressed, have come to me in this half-sleeping, half-waking state directly continuous with definite sleep. When I began to analyse my dreams I frequently had a similar experience in which as soon as I was awake I found that I was already having, and had for some time been having, thoughts about a dream, the dream itself being still clearly in my mind.

Insights in this state of altered consciousness may seem to appear as if by magic, often in the form of the vivid visual images which are characteristic of hypnagogic experiences. But in reality, there are no free lunches. Einstein's basic insight into the relativity of time, for example, came to him as the culmination of ten years' thinking about the subject. His ideas finally "gelled" early one morning while he was still dozing soon after he awoke, but the insight was only gained because of the previous years of hard work.

The hypnagogic state seems to provide the necessary conditions for a perceptual shift, so that information already acquired is looked at in a new way. The final edifice may seem to materialise spontaneously, but it can only do so if the relevant information—the building blocks necessary for its construction—has already been stored somewhere in memory. It is like a jigsaw puzzle, where the individual pieces have been shifted around, looked at this way and that, until suddenly a key piece of the pattern emerges and the whole falls rapidly into place. But without the preparatory work, the period of incubation, there is no miracle.

Several creative artists have suggested that, for them, the creative process consists of first, a period of hard work, then a time when the ideas are not worked on and allowed to lie fallow (the process the writer Richard Asher described as "leaving the manuscript to simmer in a drawer for a week or two to allow the impurities to rise to the surface"), and finally the dawning of a synthesis or solution, in which the mind seems to make a spontaneous creative leap.

This final creative leap often seems to happen more easily when the logical mind is no longer active. The French mathematician and philosopher Henri Poincaré gives a lovely description of the way this process worked for him.

Then I turned my attention to the study of some arithmetical questions, apparently without success and without

a suspicion of any connection with any preceding research. Disgusted with my failure I went to spend a few
days at the seaside, and thought of something else. One
morning, walking on the bluff, the idea came to me with
just the same characteristics of brevity, suddenness and
immediate certainty . . . It is certain that the combinations
which present themselves to the mind in a sort of sudden
illumination after an unconscious working somewhat prolonged, are generally useful and fertile combinations
which seem the result of a first impression. Does it follow
that the subliminal self having divined by a delicate intuition that these combinations would be useful, has found
only them? Or has it rather freed many others which were
lacking in interest and have remained unconscious?

Poincaré saw the period of conscious thought as one of loos-
ening and shaking up of all the ideas—"atoms"—on which
he was working in an attempt to create new and fruitful combinations. During the time in which his thoughts were lying
fallow, the atoms "freely continued their dance," allowing
new combinations to arise. Dreams, of course, are a state *par
excellence* in which the logical mind is quiet but the "atoms"
may continue to dance.

7

The Creative Power of Dreams

... When an obstacle seems insurmountable, I read the day's work before sleep ... When I wake the obstacle has nearly always been removed: the solution is there and obvious—perhaps it came in a dream which I have forgotten.

Graham Greene

The old idea of "sleeping on a problem," and waking to find we know what we ought to do, is a familiar one. When we have problems in our waking life we tend to dream about them. No one who has studied their dreams can doubt that they reflect the concerns, problems and anxieties of everyday life. But can they help to solve them? A dream may not help us directly to work out our problem or find a solution. But sometimes it may do so indirectly, perhaps by making us, when we wake, look at the problem slightly differently, or think more clearly about it.

However, problem-solving in dreams is seldom a matter of hey presto. Answers don't usually appear out of the blue, from nowhere even if it seems as if they do. The pre-conscious mind can work away at problems even though the conscious mind is unaware of its activity. Then during sleep, the answer may well surface in a dream. Sometimes a dream depicts one of several possible options, most likely (if we've been thinking about the problem for some time) an option that has already occurred to us, even if only peripherally, in waking life.

Several dream researchers have tried to set problems for dreamers to solve in their sleep, and quite often they have been apparently successful. The difficulty is that the problem always has to be given to the dreamer while he is awake, and however much he tries not to think about it before going to sleep, with the best will in the world he will find it hard to stop the wheels of his conscious mind turning and trying to solve it. Even if a dream seems to offer a solution, there is no real way of knowing how much of the problem was worked out while awake. Psychiatrist Dr. Morton Schatzman, in an article in the *Sunday Times* in 1983, set the following problem for people to try to solve in their dreams. "What is curious about the sentence, *Show this bold Prussian that praises slaughter, slaughter brings rout*?"

One person sent the following reply. Two days after the article had appeared, she went to bed, having memorised the problem, but without much expectation of success.

Between three and three thirty a.m., I woke up aware of terrible indigestion and of having had a rather weird dream. In my dream I'm watching Michael Caine in one of his spy roles, possibly *The Ipcress File*. He's in the Centre, or whatever spy headquarters is called.

He walks up to a door marked "Computer Room" and opens it; behind the door is a heavy wire-mesh screen. He passes a folded copy of the *Sunday Times* to someone behind the screen.

From the Computer Room come sounds of whirring tapes, clickings and other computer-type noises. I see that through a slot in the grille is being pushed a coloured comic postcard with a caption at the bottom. Michael Caine takes it, looks at it, chuckles briefly and hands it to me.

The postcard comes to life, and I'm sitting in an audience watching a stage show. On the stage, a comic Elizabethan figure in doublet and hose, wearing a hat with an enormous feather, is kneeling with his head in a guillotine. He looks apprehensively at the audience and rolls his eyes. The audience rocks with laughter, and the comic figure struggles to his feet, comes to the front of the stage and says, "Sh-sh-sh! Laughter is a capital offence!" More riotous laughter from the audience. The comic figure doffs his hat with a flourish and bows extravagantly.

For some reason I feel very grateful to Michael Caine and turn to thank him. He says nothing but points over his shoulder to indicate that he must dash, and with a friendly wave walks off.

At this point the dreamer woke up, turned on the light and from her bedside table picked up the *Sunday Times*, which was open at the article on dreams. At no time during the dream had she been aware that it might relate to the problem, but now she found that she knew the answer: the first letter of each word in the sentence can be lopped off to produce *How his old Russian hat raises laughter, laughter rings out*.

It is interesting that there are complex associations within the dream which point to the solution but are only apparent when you look at the dream in detail. It is clear that the dreamer recognises that the sequence is being triggered by the *Sunday Times* rolled up under Michael Caine's arm. And that the solution is behind a wire-mesh screen. The solution is acted out as a play. The first point of the play is that it is like a charade, with all the actors in costume. The actors say nothing; it is their gestures and setting that give the solution. The first striking feature is the hat. This has two meanings, firstly that it is itself a key word in the answer, and secondly that the removal of the hat from the head of the actor is a symbolic beheading, equivalent to the beheading of each word. The guillotine, in which the actor is discovered when the curtain rises, makes the same point again.

The only words which are spoken are that laughter (another key word in the answer) is a capital offence, again suggesting the relationship between beheading and laughter, or perhaps even more directly between slaughter and laughter. The repetition of the word "laughter" and the riotous laughter from the audience ("ringing out") is almost a direct transcription of the sentence itself. The dream ends with the dreamer's feeling of gratitude to Michael Caine—presumably because she has been given the solution.

Another problem set by Dr. Schatzman was this. How can you make four triangles, all touching, using six matches? One person gave the following account. She remembered the problem before she went to sleep and was determined to dream of it. As she fell asleep she had an image of a triangle in her mind. In her drowsy hypnagogic state she remembers holding on to one corner of the triangle and pulling on it. It behaved as though it was made of India rubber: as she pulled, it extended into the shape of a three-sided pyramid, which of course is the solution to the problem. She immediately awoke fully to draw it out and confirm that she had the answer.

Some years ago, Dr. Morton Schatzman and I were occasional guests on a late-night radio phone-in programme on dreams and their meaning. We decided to see if we could increase our understanding of dream creativity by setting listeners problems to work on in their dreams. One of the first problems they had to solve was to come up with two words in the English language which begin with "he" and end with "he." I asked listeners to hold the problem in their minds as they went to sleep, but not to make a determined effort to solve it. They were then asked to send in whatever dream solutions they found.

The two words I was thinking of were "heartache" and "headache." There were several correct answers but it was apparent from the letter I received that very few of these had come in the form of a dream. Much more often the solution had materialised when the person was falling asleep, in the hypnagogic state. One listener said, "It suddenly came to me as I was falling asleep, thinking about something else." Another wrote:

> I awoke and between sleep and waking was presented clearly with the word: heartache. Normally I do not remember dreams—and sometimes have a vague sensation of having had a pleasant/unpleasant dream. This time I felt that I had a sad-type of dream which I could not recall. The nature of the dream, however, leads me to believe that it did contribute to the word conclusion . . . I am still amazed that the word should have been presented so clearly and think it unlikely that I should have found the word in an awake state.

A few people found the solution suddenly came to them immediately on waking.

I thought about the problem before going to sleep and fell asleep while doing so. In the middle of the night I came round from a dreaming phase because I was feeling cold. I decided to get out of bed and turn the fire on, which I did in an instant. No sooner was I back in bed than the word "heartache" popped into my mind.

Only occasionally did the dream itself give a direct answer. For one listener the word itself actually appeared in the dream, and, even more interesting, the whole notion of the experiment was in the forefront of the dream, almost as if the dreamer was having a lucid dream at that time. The dream gave an answer that was not disguised by any dream imagery or symbolism; the waking mind did not have to decode the dream or work out its significance.

The word "heartache" appeared to me at the start of an unusually vivid dream. I had begun a holiday in the US (a place I've never visited) when the word came to me while I was sitting on a verandah. I mentioned it to someone sitting nearby, who said I must phone LBC [the radio station]. The dialling code was different and I got a wrong number. I was informed that my call had got through to the carrier HMS *Ark Royal* . . .

Dreams tend to incorporate elements of our waking lives. At any one time we may have several things on our mind. Simply by chance a particular dream may seem to take the form of a "solution" to a particular problem—especially as many problems have several solutions. William Dement, for example, gave 500 students a list of letters—H, I, J, K, L, M, N, O— and asked them to dream the one-word solution. One student dreamed of water, but did not even realise that this was the solution (H to O, H_2O). Does this mean that the dream actively solved the problem? Or is it more likely that out of the 500 students given the problem, one, quite coincidentally, dreamed of water? Supposing that a student had, coincidentally, dreamed of water, but that when contemplating the dream in the cold light of day had made a link—Eureka! Water! H_2O! Would we then have given credit to the dream-mind for conjuring up the image of water, or to the conscious mind for making a fortuitous link with the problem? It is at least possible that in many cases of problem-solving it is thinking about the dream after one wakes that provides a solution. Certainly the images and analogies of dreams can be illuminating, but perhaps only the same way that tarot cards can be illuminating. The images are presented to us; the links that we make depend on the circumstances and concerns that surround us. But it is important to remember that if dreams arise from the same cognitive structures that create the waking world for us, then the dream will have within it at some level this waking logic. The dream produces symbols. But these dream symbols should have hidden within them traces of the logic and thus of the interconnections which are part of the problem experienced in our waking life, and also point the way to its solution.

The dream-mind has access to memory, and so it is perhaps easier to see how a dream can provide a solution to a problem that involves memory rather than one that involves logic. A dream may remind us of something we already know, but have forgotten, or draw out attention to obvious clues that we simply failed to pick up when awake. A friend, for example, dreamed that she was looking for the back of an earring that someone (not her) had lost. She found it in a rubbish bin, in a tangle of matted tea bags. When she woke she felt her own ears, realised she had gone to bed without taking her (very precious) earrings off, and that the back of one of them was missing. She searched the bed, and found it. Sometimes the dream can nudge our memory through symbolism, sometimes, as in the following dream, through the remembrance of a bodily sensation.

I went to bed late on Saturday evening, falling asleep dressed in my jeans and a shirt. At about 5.40 a.m. on the Sunday morning I woke up, changed into my pyjamas. As I was getting into bed again I noticed that on the table by my bed was a single die—there should have been a pair of them. I spent about an hour looking for it and then got into bed and went back to bed thinking, oh well, perhaps it's a problem I'll be able to solve in my sleep. I went to sleep and started to dream, and during the dream I felt a pain in my hip as though I was lying on something hard. When I awoke I thought about the feeling I'd experienced in the dream, as if something was pressing into me. I suddenly remembered that I'd put the die in the back pocket of my jeans. I went across, felt in my jeans pocket, and there it was.

Robert van de Castle in his book *Our Dreaming Mind*, has highlighted a fascinating area in which the creative influence of dreams on problem-solving has been little recognised. He points out that much dream activity is concerned with vigorous physical movement—in our dreams we can run and jump (or even fly) over obstacles—and that some professional athletes and sportsmen have found that their dreams reveal ways to improve their waking athletic prowess. He quotes an interview with the acrobat Tito Gaona, published in the 8 April 1974 issue of *Sports Illustrated*:

I have sometimes dreamed my tricks at night . . . and then tried to master them from the dream . . . I also do what I call a double-double . . . It is a double forward somersault with a double full twist at the same time. It has never been done before. No one else does it. It is a trick I dreamed one night.

In an interview with the *San Francisco Chronicle* on 27 June 1964, the golfer Jack Nicklaus described how his game was going through a bad patch. Despite intensive analysis of what was going wrong, he couldn't improve. Then he had a dream in which he was holding his golf club differently and swinging perfectly. He told the reporter, ''When I came to the course yesterday morning, I tried it the way I did it in my dream and it worked . . . I feel kind of foolish admitting it, but it really happened in a dream.'' This bit of dream-coaching rapidly improved his scores.

Finally, van de Castle describes the experience of an acquaintance of his who had acquired an old-fashioned penny-farthing bicycle. He spent about three months repairing it, and during this time had several dreams in which he was happily riding it—which surprised him, as he had never actually been on such a vehicle in his life. However, when the bicycle was finally ready for the road, his friend found that he was able to ride it successfully at his very first attempt. It was as though the "rehearsals" in his dreams had enabled him to develop penny-farthing-riding skills in reality.

A very similar example of dream-coaching was told to us by Donald Turpin, a man who in 1955 lost a leg in a road traffic accident, and was fitted with an artificial limb. Walking, particularly up and down stairs, had always been difficult for him. He had been using his artificial leg for a number of years, and was well accustomed to the difficulties when he had this dream.

I was asleep in bed when suddenly, in the form of a dream, I found myself going up a spiral staircase, whose stairs ascended to the left, with a handrail to the left. I was ascending the way I had been taught, i.e. "put the good leg up, bring the artificial foot level, then put the good leg up again," when somebody came to me from behind, standing about one step behind me to my right and asked why I was going upstairs like that. When I told him I had lost my leg he told me he was aware of that, but instructed me to do it a better way, insisting I follow his instruction, viz. "When bringing the artificial foot up, lean back slightly so the arch of the foot might come against the edge of the upper step, then let the good foot go up to the step immediately above." When I told him I was afraid the knee would bend, thus causing me to fall backwards, he said this could not happen, and to prevent it, took the belt of the artificial leg and held it tight, so I could feel his knuckles digging into my spine, but I could feel too a greater strength, pressure as though the belt were pulling tight against my hips. I tried, following his instruction, and found it quite safe, so ascended quite a number of steps. He then told me to turn round, and for descending, told me to place the arch of the artificial foot on the edge of the step and lean forward, as this would enable my good foot to fall through to the step beneath. Then let the artificial foot come against the next edge. For going both up and down I found this method quite safe and realising it was still in a dream, I wanted to try again. This he permitted me to do, but having gone up a few and then following his instructions to come down again, imagine my surprise when I saw him standing at the bottom of the stairs, not holding my belt as the pressure on my hips and spine indicated. The one thing he insisted on, though, is that I do not try it unless I have a good handrail to my left for ascending, and to my right for descending. He then wished to take me elsewhere, so took me through the large twin doors behind him, and then, and only then, did I realise we were in a church, whose seats were facing to our right, and having gone with him to the other side, I went through metal gates, then up a metal spiral staircase, then along a little passage. To my right was a little dark "room" which was far too dark to see inside. That was it then, the dream was finished, but although feeling quite well otherwise, I could still feel the pressure on my hips as though the artificial leg belt had been put to unexpected pressure that I had not previously experienced.

Details of the dream seemed hard to forget, because the pressure lasted for about nine months, and although I had gone to Roehampton to have other artificial legs serviced, its reason for coming seemed just as mysterious to them as it was to me, but one morning I woke up finding those pressures gone. Try as I might I just could not cast its memory away, so one afternoon I went to try to go up and down stairs as instructed, just to see its effect, and having done so, after about thirty minutes, found it quite easy to do, so that when travelling on the Underground I seemed no obstacle for fellow travellers.

This dream is interesting because, first of all, it shows the dreamer how to solve a problem (going up and down stairs) in a way which hadn't occurred to him in waking life, and secondly, just as it did for Jack Nicklaus and Tito Gaona and Robert van de Castle's bicycling friend, the solution worked— not always the case in dream solutions. How could the dreamer possibly have acquired this information?

We tend to think that we have only to will a movement and it occurs. In fact it is not quite as simple as that. Movement is a whole brain process and for even a simple movement to be carried out correctly a number of different brain structures have to be activated in a precisely timed sequence. Because most of the movements we do are so well learned and practised, we don't realise how difficult it is to modify the normal sequence. The only time we get an inkling of this is when we try to learn some new motor skill—playing tennis, say, or riding a bicycle.

As far as the brain is concerned, dream movement is just the same as waking movement. Work with lucid dreamers has confirmed that the complex reflexes which we use every day are activated in a similar way during a dream (see p. 233). If, for example, we dream of drawing a triangle on a board, then if we were not paralysed, our arms will indeed draw a triangle in the air. If this is so, there is no real reason why "training" in a dream should not be effective. All the mental correlates of the movements could be "practised" in the dream, only the physical movements themselves would be unrehearsed. We can look on the dream as a simulator, and one which can make quite adequate preparation for the actual activity. I suspect that Donald Turpin must have spent a lot of time since his amputation trying to conquer the problem of going up and down stairs before he finally tumbled to the solution which was given to him in the dream. I doubt very much whether anyone could have had a dream like this if they had not actually had the experience of wearing a false limb, or had worked closely with and observed the problems of people who had.

Jack Nicklaus would undoubtedly have had many golf dreams, and when he dreamed a stroke the relevant motor structures in his brain would be activated. Before this particular dream, he had been devoting a lot of thought to his swing, and working hard at alternative strategies, which might well have appeared in his dreams too. On the night in question it seems likely that his motor mechanism was again firing to produce movements of golf swings in his dream, and a particular combination arose which left him well balanced and poised. In so experienced a golfer this might well have triggered a recognition that his motor system was functioning in a more efficient way, and this would then have been clothed in the imagery of movement. It was this imagery that Nicklaus took to the golf course the next day. Similarly, Tito Gaona's dream would have been a rehearsal for the actual trick. It is likely, too, that riding a penny-farthing in a dream, if you really understand what a penny-farthing is (as you would do if you were rebuilding one), would help you develop the postural reflexes which would keep you balanced, and would certainly be some preparation for doing it in real life.

But the creative influence of dreams is not limited to problem-solving. Dreams have long been held to be a source of artistic creativity, and certainly they have played a central role in the work of numerous artists, writers and poets. The story of the conception of "Kubla Khan" as narrated by its author, Samuel Taylor Coleridge, is literary history. In his preface to the poem, Coleridge describes how, in the summer of 1797, he was staying at a lonely Devon farm between Porlock and Linton. In consequence of "a slight indisposition" he had been prescribed an "anodyne" (which is to say, opium). He then fell into an opium-induced slumber just as he was reading the following sentence in Samuel Purchas's *Pilgrimage*: "Here the Khan Kubla commanded a palace to be built, and a stately garden thereunto. And thus ten miles of fertile ground were inclosed with a wall." Coleridge's own account of his subsequent dream continues thus:

> The Author continued for about three hours in a profound sleep, at least of the external senses, during which time he had the most vivid confidence, that he could not have composed less than from two to three hundred lines; if that indeed can be called composition in which all the images rose up before him as things, with a parallel production of the correspondent expressions, without any sensation of consciousness of effort. On awaking he appeared to himself to have a distinct recollection of the whole, and taking his pen, ink, and paper, instantly and eagerly wrote down the lines that are here preserved. At this moment he was unfortunately called out by a person on business from Porlock, and detained by him above an hour, and on his return to his room, found, to his no small surprise and mortification, that though he still retained some vague and dim recollection of the general purport of the vision, yet, with the exception of some eight or ten scattered lines and images, all the rest had passed away like images on the surface of a stream into which a stone has been cast but, alas! without the after restoration of the latter!

The untimely interruption by the person from Porlock has ever since been held responsible for depriving posterity of all but fifty-four of the two to three hundred lines which Coleridge claimed had been dream-given. There are, however, doubts about this famous and particularly stunning example of dream creativity. Nicholas Fruman, in his book *The Damaged Archangel*, has pointed out that Coleridge was in the habit of claiming that a poem which had been well worked over for months or even years was in fact an act of spontaneous creation. The origins of "Kubla Khan" are uncertain. Coleridge, prodigious correspondent that he was, would almost certainly have written to someone, most probably his friend Robert Southey, describing its composition, but there is no record of him having done so. Moreover, in 1934 an autographed manuscript of "Kubla Khan" was discovered which showed that many earlier drafts of the poem had been written before it was finally published in 1816. This seems to prove fairly conclusively that the poem was not entirely the spontaneous product of an inspirational dream.

Nicholas Fruman also points out many other inconsistencies and questionable statements in Coleridge's account, not least the very presence of the person from Porlock. "Why any man on business would be meeting Coleridge in a lonely farmhouse twenty miles from his home is baffling. There would have had to be an appointment, and Coleridge could not have been in the habit of meeting men on business in such places."

But perhaps, as is so often the case, the story of "Kubla Khan" is one of embellishment rather than deception. To dismiss the story as a fabrication, or to belittle the part the dream played in the genesis of the poem, is to misunderstand the creative process. Inspiration alone has never produced a masterpiece. Fundamental to any creative process is the skill of the artist. A painter has to appreciate the rules which govern the application of paint to canvas, the creation of light and shade and perspective. A writer must have a feeling for words and a knowledge of sentence structure. A creative act does not arise *de novo*, but always against a background of an understanding of the subject, hard work in its elaboration, and a desire to push out the boundaries of that subject to find novelty.

Other writers besides Coleridge have claimed to have the

experience of having a work virtually dictated to them in a dream, more or less in its entirety. Katherine Mansfield, for example, once dreamed a short story, even down to its title. John Masefield has described how the poem "The Woman Speaks" appeared to him in a dream engraved on a metal plate. Voltaire and Goethe also claimed that many of their poems had come to them in dreams. It is difficult not to suspect that a certain amount of artistic licence lies behind these claims, and that the works in question were more likely to have been a combination of dream inspiration and hard work.

The value of a dream, any dream, lies in the use to which the dreamer puts it. The dream may provide the germ of an idea, a starting point for something that must subsequently be worked out and polished until finally the dream materialises— more or less.

"The Invention"
by Gerard Benson

At first it was just an idea
(As a matter of fact, a dream).
I woke up not exactly seeing it
But knowing it could be.

Then it was a question of trying things.
Glue, elastic bands, clockwork motors,
A chopstick and a magnet, a needle,
The heel of a boot, a washing-up bowl.

The problem started in the mind
But soon turned itself into *things*,
My clumsiness caused difficulties,
But I kept on. I kept on and on.

Once I had drawn it, it got easier;
And the man at the garage helped
When he gave me some old scrap.
"Scrap" he called it! If only he knew!

And now here it is. I made it and it works
(Not quite the same as the dream)

> And I am going to make another one,
> Only better—and easier to construct.

Every dream is a new experience, and so a potential source of creativity which the artist can use to enrich and stimulate his waking vision and imagination. Bunyan's *Pilgrim's Progress* was inspired by a dream; Mary Shelley based *Frankenstein* on a dream; and a dream, or rather a nightmare, gave Robert Louis Stevenson the plot for *Dr. Jekyll and Mr. Hyde*. At the time he was desperately short of money, and equally desperate for a plot—any plot—that might produce a story to resolve his financial crisis. Then one night he dreamed "the scene at the window, and a scene afterwards split in two, in which Hyde, pursued for some crime, took the powder and underwent the change in the presence of his pursuers." In fact dreams were a constant source of inspiration to Stevenson, who relied on the "Little People" of his dream life when he needed an idea for a story: ". . . What shall I say they are but my Brownies, God bless them! who do one half my work for me while I am fast asleep."

Graham Greene was another author who used an anxiety dream as a fictional and financial lifeline. Greene's financial plight at the time was dire—his last two books had lost money, he had £20 in the bank, and his wife was pregnant. He then had a dream which suggested a plot for his next book, a dream in which he himself had been condemned to death for murder. Unfortunately the novel it inspired, *It's a Battlefield*, is evidence that dream inspiration alone is not enough; it was probably the least successful book Greene ever wrote.

Greene has also described in *Ways of Escape* how his identification with his characters sometimes went so far that he dreamed his character's dreams and not his own. "That happened to me when I was writing *A Burnt-out Case*. The symbols, the memories, the associations of that dream belonged so clearly to my character Querry that next morning I could put the dream without change into the novel, where it bridged a gap in the narrative which for days I had been unable to cross . . ."

The dream world is a continually replenished source of fresh and unexpected images presented to us anew each night. They are our own images, drawn from our own imaginations, and yet when we see them in a dream they may still be a source of wonder and surprise. It is not surprising that so many visual artists have found inspiration in their dreams and used fragments of dream imagery and incident in their work. Salvador Dali was one of many who have tried to re-create their dreams in their paintings. He liked to sleep with a bright light on, to heighten the visual imagery of his dreams, which he referred to as "hand-painted dream photographs." For the visionary artist William Blake, too, dreams were a vital creative source; there even exists a pencil sketch by the artist entitled *The Man Who Taught Blake Painting in His Dreams*.

Many creative artists in the cinema and theatre also acknowledge a debt to their dreams. The Swedish film-maker Ingmar Bergman and the Italian director Federico Fellini both used dreams and dream imagery to give a characteristic surreal, dream-like quality to many of their films. Orson Welles, asked about the dream-like rooms in his film *The Trial*, said he had "tried to make a picture like a dream I have had . . ." William Butler Yeats maintained that his 1902 play *Cathleen ni Houlihan* had come to him in a dream.

Music, too, has often been dream-inspired. The story is told of Richard Wagner, who, having spent the day walking in the hills trying to find a suitable opening for the overture to his opera, *Das Rheingold*, returned home exhausted. He lay down and slowly sank into a dreaming sleep. At this point the medium through which he seemed to be falling took on the nature of a musical sound, the tonic chord of E flat minor, which increased in intensity until he awoke suddenly realising that he had found his opening.

Is the dream state as potentially creative for scientists as for artists? Most of the often-quoted "dream inspirations" of scientists—Kekulé's discovery of the structure of the benzene ring, Einstein's conception of the theory of relativity, Poincaré's establishment of a hitherto unproven class of mathematical functions—occurred in a hypnagogic and not a true dreaming state, perhaps because logic plays a greater part in scientific insights than in artistic ones, and logic is not the forte of the dreaming mind. However, Susan Greenberg has described how the Austrian neuroscientist Otto Loewi had what seemed like a similar intuitive "dream leap." He had been trying to devise an experiment to show whether nerves communicate with their "target" organ by releasing a naturally occurring chemical. Loewi had been working with a heart and its nerve supply suspended in a fluid nutrient medium, and he already knew that stimulating the nerve to the heart made the heart slow down. But how was he to show whether a chemical was involved? The answer he finally came up with occurred to him in a dream, and was simplicity itself. It was to transfer the fluid surrounding the heart he was stimulating to a second heart, which had not been stimulated. When he did this he found that the second heart, bathed in the fluid which had perfused the first heart, also slowed down. The chemical nerve messenger, acetylcholine, which had been released from the nerve terminals when the nerve to the first heart was stimulated, was transferred in the surrounding fluid to the second heart. It was only because Loewi had already done the necessary preparatory work that he was ready to have this final creative hunch—and, when the dream provided the vehicle for it, to recognise the significance of the idea.

Dreams—especially morning dreams—were one of the many springs which fed Dante's creative genius, as were the "waking visions" and hypnagogic phenomena which enriched his imagination and formed some of his most important sources of inspiration. William Anderson, in his biographical analysis of the nature of Dante's creative inspiration, suggests that there is a difference between most dreams and experiences of mental imagery and the inspiration, both artistic and scientific, that is sometimes experienced in dreams.

> First of all, in most dreams the dreamer has no control over the actions he sees or takes part in, or the emotions aroused in him; he is a helpless performer and his deeds in dreams have no practical outcome. By contrast the inspiration, though it may arise in a dream or dreamlike state, brings with it a sense of order and a pure objective emotion which the poet notes and obeys but ultimately controls, and the inspiration does lead to a finished artefact.

It is not the dream, then, but the mastery of the dream, that is the source of true creativity. Kekulé, describing his own revelation of the structure of the benzene ring some years later, acknowledged both the importance and the limitations of the contribution that dreams can bring to the act of creation when he said, "Let us learn to dream, gentlemen, and we may perhaps find the truth, but let us beware of publishing our dreams before they have been tested by a discerning mind that is wide awake."

8

Insights into Illness

Some years ago a friend of ours, Helen, a young woman who is also a doctor, developed a rare kidney disease. While we were talking to her one day after her illness had been diagnosed, she said, "It's strange it should have happened like this, because all my life I've had this dread of having something wrong with my kidneys." She then went on to describe a series of dreams she had had between the ages of about five and twelve years old. This is her story.

I dreamt very vividly, and each one was of a different story in which I played a part. The remarkable thing about the series of dreams was that at the horrific and terrifying end of the dreams the same thing happened. I experienced a sensation of being poked in the back which remained with me in my waking state for several minutes. If I went to sleep too soon the dream started again where I'd left off and the poking would go on even longer.

I didn't record the dreams at the time, but I can still remember vague details of a couple of them.

One was a Hansel-and-Gretel type of dream with me as the Gretel character. At the end of the dream the witch had caught us and she was trying to push me into the oven. She had horrid bony fingers like a skeleton's and she poked me in the back with one of them to get me to move. I was terrified. The thought of going into the oven was almost preferable to the horrid feeling in my back. I woke up.

The second dream had a war-type scenario. My comrades and I were soldiers. We were being attacked. At the end of the dream we had been caught and were to go into a hollow in the ground. Not particularly terrifying, but to make us move on a guard poked me in the back with the barrel of his gun. I was immediately too petrified to move. I woke up.

I don't remember which side of the back experienced the poking, or even if it alternated, but this discomfort was always in the same place in the small of my back and was quite definitely present when I awoke, although I could see nothing that could be poking me and my back itself felt normal.

Many years later—in my late twenties—I became very ill. It was obvious that for some reason my kidneys were failing and I was sent for a renal biopsy. I was apprehensive but was given both valium and pethidine.

At the moment the biopsy needle was inserted I became unreasonably terrified. The sensation was exactly what I had had in my dreams and my body responded to the sensation as if something terrible was going on. It took some time to settle me down though I was not someone prone to hysterics. The biopsy showed I had a rare and serious kidney disease and ultimately my kidneys did fail.

It is also interesting to note that as a medical student in excellent health I became cold with fear when I read of glomerulonephritis (I had a form of this disease). No other disease I read about had this effect on me. It is also interesting that at some time in my early twenties a reflexologist ("dowsing" with a pendulum) had told me to "watch my kidneys."

Helen was convinced that the series of dreams was a premonition of the future kidney trouble and that the other two incidents gave her more detailed information of what that trouble was to be.

One of the difficulties people have in accepting the idea of precognition is that it is apparently incompatible with both free will and with causality. If we can get in touch with future events, this implies that they already exist in space and time, and this in turn suggests that we have no free will to act in the present in a way which would change the future.

"Prodromal" dreams, which seem to be premonitions of illness, don't present quite such a challenge to our accepted way of thinking. Firstly, the problem of free will does not arise. In the case of illness one can nearly always argue that the events to which the dreamer gains access really are pre-determined—there really is nothing the dreamer could do to alter their course. If, for example, someone dreamed that they developed lung cancer, and subsequently gave up smoking and so avoided it, it could still be argued that they would retain the susceptibility to the disease which might have triggered the dream precognition.

Secondly, it is often possible to argue that the dreamer is gaining information which is at some level already accessible in the present, and does not have to be accessed from the future. Aristotle believed that dreams give a magnified con-struction to small stimuli arising during sleep, and that in a patient's dreams the physician might detect the early signs of some bodily change of which they were not consciously aware. Galen, the second-century Greek physician, believed that dreams could foretell impending physical illnesses, and in his book, *Prophecy in Dream*, cites a man who dreamed that his leg was turned to stone: a few days later, the dreamer devel-oped a paralysis of this leg.

The dream of an illness may seem to be precognitive, but it might also be, as Aristotle suggested, an indication of the special insight that the dreaming mind has into the body. In the dream state we are cut off from almost all sensory input from the external world, and may therefore be more sensitive to internal cues. It is very possible that subtle physical changes or sensations of which we are quite unaware when we are awake, or which are drowned out by the far more insistent barrage of sensory information from the outside, are more readily picked up during sleep and incorporated in our dreams. It is difficult to believe that this was so in Helen's case, be-cause her "kidney dreams" occurred so long before her ill-ness. But there are many examples of prodromal dreams for which this may be at least a partial explanation.

In his book, *Awakenings*, Oliver Sacks describes how sur-vivors of the sleeping-sickness pandemic which raged for a decade, between 1916 and 1926, were "awakened" by the drug L-Dopa from the zombie-like state in which their illness had imprisoned them. After the acute phase of the illness had passed, most survivors entered a decades-long metaphorical "sleep," their minds still clear, their being virtually speechless and motionless, melancholic and apathetic. Here Dr. Sacks describes the dreams, remarkable in their prescience, which one of these patients had at the onset of the illness:

> The acute phase announced itself (as sometimes happened . . .) by nightmares of a grotesque and terrifying and premonitory nature. Miss R. had a series of dreams about one central theme: she dreamed she was imprisoned in an inaccessible castle, but the castle had the form and shape of herself; she dreamed of enchantments, bewitchments, entrancements; she dreamed that she had become a living, sentient statue of stone; she dreamed that the world had come to a stop; she dreamed that she had fallen into a sleep so deep that nothing could wake her; she dreamed of a death which was different from death. Her family had difficulty waking her the next morning, and when she awoke there was intense consternation. "Rose," they cried, "wake up! What's the matter? Your expression, your position . . . You're so still and so strange." Miss R. could not answer, but turned her eyes to the wardrobe mirror, and there she saw that her dreams had come true. The local doctor was brisk and unhelpful: "Catatonia," he said, "flexibilitas cerea . . . Keep her quiet and feed her—she'll be fine in a week."

But for the next forty-three years Miss R. remained a prisoner of her illness, as she had dreamed, "a living, sentient statue of stone."

Patricia Garfield, in *The Healing Power of Dreams*, describes the very similar case of a woman who dreamed many times over a period of several months of people who were ominously still—seated corpses or waxwork figures. She was later found in a deep coma, suffering from myxoedema, a condition in which the thyroid gland is underactive, and the body's metabolism slows down.

Medard Boss, the Swiss psychiatrist and author of *Analysis of Dreams*, gives this example of a dream which seems to precognise mental breakdown.

> A woman of hardly thirty years dreamt, at a time when she still felt completely healthy, that she was a fire in the stables. Around her, the fire, an ever-larger crust of lava was forming. Suddenly she was entirely outside this fire and, as if possessed, she beat the fire with a club to break the crust and to let some air in. But the dreamer soon got tired and slowly she (the fire) became extinguished. Four days after this dream she began to suffer from acute schizophrenia. In the details of the dream the dreamer had exactly predicted the special course of her psychosis. She became rigid at first, and, in effect, encysted. Six weeks afterwards she defended herself once more with all her might against the choking of her life's fire, until finally, she became completely extinguished both spiritually and mentally. Now, for some years, she has been like a burnt-out crater.

In another example:

> . . . a girl of twenty-five years dreamt that she had cooked dinner for her family of five. She had just served it and she now called her parents and her sisters to dinner. Nobody replied. Only her voice returned as if it were an echo from a deep cave. She found the sudden emptiness of the house uncanny. She rushed upstairs to look for her family. In the first bedroom, she could see her two sisters sitting on two beds. In spite of her impatient calls they remained in an unnaturally rigid position and did not even answer her. She went up to her sisters and wanted to shake them. Suddenly she noticed that they were stone statues. She escaped in horror and rushed into her mother's room. Her mother too had turned into stone and was sitting inertly in her armchair staring into the air with glazed eyes. The dreamer escaped into the room of her father. He stood in the middle of it. In her despair she rushed up to him and, desiring his protection, she threw her arms round his neck. But he too was made of stone and, to her utter horror, he turned into sand when she

embraced him. She awoke in absolute terror, and was so stunned by the dream experience that she could not move for some minutes. This same horrible dream was dreamt by the patient on four successive occasions within a few days. At that time she was apparently the picture of mental and physical health. Her parents used to call her the sunshine of the whole family. Ten days after the fourth repetition of the dream, the patient was taken ill with an acute form of schizophrenia displaying severe catatonic symptoms. She fell into a state which was remarkably similar to the physical petrification of her family that she had dreamt about. She was now overpowered in waking life by behaviour patterns that in her dreams she had merely observed in other persons.

Dream content does not always reflect mental illness quite as clearly as this. But studies which have tried to relate dream content to mood and mental state have found some fairly predictable dream themes. In people with severe mood swings, shifts to mania are often heralded by dreams of death and bodily injury, and as they become more manic, their dreams become more bizarre and improbable. No consistent dream themes are associated with depression, and when the mood is neutral, dreams tend to be routine or uneventful.

Jung, convinced as he was of the value of dream analysis in psychological problems, believed that it could be used for diagnosing physical illness too. Dr. Robin Royston, a psychiatrist who was intrigued by the fact that Jung took the idea of "prodromal" dreams seriously, has collected several accounts from people who have had dreams which seem to be linked with physical illness. This is one of the most striking, especially interesting as there is a great deal of corroborative evidence for it. The dreamer had been under stress for some time and his GP had recommended that he go for weekly counselling. Usually at these sessions he and his counsellor discussed family history, etc., but on this particular occasion:

I said I wished to describe to her a dream I had the previous night, because of its unusual vividness. In the dream I was riding along on horseback with my wife and three children ahead of me, also on horseback (I have not been on a horse in thirty years). At first we were going slowly, then I spotted lurking in the bushes on my right-hand side two black panthers, crouched and watching us. Seeing the danger I urged my wife and family to gallop away, which they did, on down this dusty road with me bringing up the rear, keeping between them and the panthers. The panthers now began to chase me, and I felt growing terror as they gained on me. At the climactic moment one leapt up behind me, trying to grapple me off the horse with its forepaws. I felt a sharp pain as the claw of its front paw dug into my back, between my shoulder blades just to the left of my spine. I shook it off and galloped on, still pursued. Ahead my family had arrived at the safety of a little town, where several men in white coats saw me coming and waved me to turn to the right, while by waving things at the panthers they diverted them to the left. I felt I was saved, but looking back over my shoulder I saw the last panther turn its head and stare at me menacingly. At this point I woke up.

My counsellor and I could make little of all this in discussion beyond expression of general anxiety, etc. A month or two later, in mid-December, while I was shaving, my wife noticed a new and unusual mole on my back, between my shoulder blades just to the left of my spine [just where the panther had struck]. She persuaded me to go to my GP, who removed the mole and sent it for histology on December 20th. On December 27th I was informed that it was a malignant melanoma. In January I was admitted back to hospital, where they removed a larger section of my back, covering it with a skin graft from my thigh.

Since then I have been in generally good health, though given the highly metastatic nature of melanomas I sometimes think of the panther's parting glance.

Dr. Royston points out that it is highly unlikely that the dreamer could have had any conscious awareness of the melanoma—there was no pain, bleeding or altered sensation. Neither did he realise just how life-threatening a malignant melanoma could be. Despite this, the dream images—the panthers and the "men in white coats" who saw off the first panther—seem very apt. At the onset of the dream the panthers are still, but begin to move, gathering speed until the first panther finally leaps on to the dreamer's horse. Similarly the tumour is first "still" and undetectable, then begins to grow more and more quickly. Both in the dream, and in real life after the tumour was diagnosed, the dreamer's main preoccupation was to protect his family. It is the malevolent glare of the second panther that makes one pause uneasily for thought. Malignant melanomas have a poor prognosis—but remember, the dreamer was quite unaware of this. The second panther might merely represent a potential threat, but it might equally, Dr. Royston suggests, represent residual cancer cells which have spread and might become manifest at a later date.

Certainly the dream imagery in prodromal dreams often seems remarkably appropriate. Russian psychiatrist Vasily Kasatkin, who studied dreams for forty years at the Leningrad Neurosurgical Institute, regarded dreams as "sentries that watch over our health," and believed that the content of dreams can reveal the nature and location of the illness. Kasatkin recorded the dreams of two people who developed tuberculosis of the lungs, both of whom dreamed of having their chests crushed after being buried under landslides. Medard Boss describes a patient, later diagnosed as having acute cystitis, who dreamed three nights running that a demon forced her to sit on a pipe so hot that she had a burning pain between her legs. In this case, it seems likely that the cystitis had already started, and subliminal pain probably triggered the dream imagery. Often, the imagery is more symbolic. In the following dream, the dream "metaphor" of the radioactive milk churns seems particularly well chosen.

I've always written down my dreams—if I can make the effort—and sometimes see telepathic or precognitive trends, not strong enough to convince anyone else, I imagine. This was more definite. I dreamt that there were two milk churns full of radioactive matter, under the control only of a young boy, son of a neighbour. He was inexperienced and this was very dangerous; one would soon explode. I thought when I was awake that this was just connected with everyone's fear of nuclear explosion. However, when I went for a breast check-up at the Royal

Marsden about a year or two later, as I was regularly meant to do, I was found to have cancer in one breast and had to have an operation and chemotherapy. (This was over fifteen years ago, so I survived.)

I wouldn't actually call this precognitive, as I think it showed a current, pre-cancerous state. But I have often wished that I had decoded the easy Freudian symbolism and gone at once for a check-up and perhaps avoided having to have the operation. This is the trouble with autoscopy and any snippets of information psychically gained; one often doesn't recognise or understand them till later. Also wish-fulfilment and fear-fulfilment becloud the whole thing.

There are many other published cases of dreams which have seemed to be forewarnings of the onset of cancer. Robert van de Castle, in *Our Dreaming Mind*, gives several examples. Amongst them are two cases reported by Bernard Siegel, a cancer surgeon at the Yale School of Medicine. The first was a patient with breast cancer who dreamed that her head was shaved and the word "cancer" written on it. She woke with the conviction that the cancer had spread to her brain, a diagnosis which was unhappily confirmed three weeks later. It has to be remembered, however, that this was a patient who was actually suffering from cancer, and presumably well aware of the possibility of its spread. She may also have been suffering from the early effects of a small brain tumour at the time of the dream which were not yet sufficiently marked to be noted by her waking mind. The second case concerned a journalist who dreamed first that torturers were placing hot coals beneath his chin, and in a later dream that hypodermic needles were being stuck into his neck. He became convinced that the dreams were telling him that he might be developing cancer of the throat, and eventually persuaded a doctor to take his fears seriously enough to examine him. This showed that he had cancer, not of the larynx as he had feared, but of the nearby thyroid gland.

If these dreams really were predicting illnesses which were later diagnosed, is there any possible biological mechanism that might explain this? We are only just beginning to understand how strong the links may be between the mind and the body, between physical health and mental states of mind. There is more and more evidence that a human being acts as an integrated whole.

Dr. Royden has suggested that one mechanism by which these links might be made is via the immune system—the system that protects the body from infectious diseases, and probably plays a part in the control of cancer. The new science of psychoneuroimmunology is the study of the relationship between the mind in its most general sense, brain function, and the effects of both of these on the immune system. There are experiments, for example, which have shown that a "mental diet" of miserable thoughts can reduce the efficiency of the immune system and make the body more susceptible to disease.

If we are looking for some way in which information about what is happening in the body can be transferred to the mind without using the usual conscious nervous pathways, then Dr. Royden suggests that the immune system is an obvious candidate. The immune system "knows" about potential physical illness—a developing cancer or a viral infection—long before the mind can have any conscious awareness of it. If a cancer metastasises, the immune system "knows" about this before any secondary tumour is detected or detectable. The immune system has a memory too: acquired immunity to a disease depends on the ability of the immune system to remember that it has encountered a particular micro-organism before and can overcome it.

This hypothesis might also help to explain Helen's story, which opened this chapter. Auto-immune disorders, of which Helen's kidney disease, Goodpasture's syndrome, is one, are cases of mistaken identity. They occur because the immune system mistakes the body's own proteins for invading aliens and attacks them. Perhaps the immune system had detected early invaders in Helen's kidneys. If we can't find a bodily cause for these dreams, and are not prepared to accept coincidence as an explanation, then we are forced to argue that causality and time itself are different from how we normally think of them—an idea that we will come back to in later chapters.

The following pair of dreams, told to us by EL, are in a rather different category, in that although they are clearly linked to the onset of illness, they give no clues about the nature of the illness; they should perhaps be seen as premonitory, rather than prodromal, dreams.

> One night my husband told me of a strange and very vivid dream he had had. He dreamed that his brother, who had died some time earlier, came to see him. He told my husband that he was to hurry up; he was waiting for him and he was late. Very soon after this dream my husband was diagnosed as having cancer, and ten weeks later he died.
> A few years later I had a very similar dream one night. In my dream my husband was waiting for me outside the house in the car. He told me he had been waiting ages for me and it was time I came. The next day I told the dream to a colleague, adding that it was a good job I wasn't superstitious because my husband had a dream just like that just before his cancer was diagnosed. That evening I had a heart attack. I remember on my way to the hospital in the ambulance saying to my husband, I can't come yet, I'm not ready. I want to see Lara's [their daughter] children.

Was the dreaming mind in each case reacting to physical clues which indicated that all was not well, clues which the conscious mind was unaware of or refused to acknowledge? Or were the dreams premonitory, giving the dreamers a glimpse of the future? The following dream, told to us by Rhiannon Davies, seems to contain both elements. Part of the dream appears to reflect the physical symptoms of her illness, but it seems to have a strong precognitive content too.

One night in March 1985, Rhiannon dreamed that she found herself looking up at a mountain. Stretching up it were parallel rows of water pipes, some thick, some narrow, up which she had to climb. Around her were a lot of boy scouts dressed in green with green caps.

> It took me a long time but I struggled up the pipes feeling exhausted and very heavy . . . puffing and panting I eventually reached the top. The view was similar to Cheddar Gorge—a sheer drop and a gap across of about a mile. I

knew that I had to cross that gorge which had a railway line stretched from the side I was on, to the far side. I was petrified beyond measure and almost fainted with fear . . . I started to crawl, the panic was overwhelming. I heard someone say, "She is going to go," and then felt strong arms supporting me, one under each armpit. By this time my level of consciousness, within the dream, was slightly lowered. I was aware that there were two people in light clothes taking me across . . . Then I heard, "She's not going to make it." With that I felt a tremendous thump in my mid-back and then I was lying face down on the grass on the other side of the gorge. I could feel dew on my face and smell the grass. Then I awoke and told my husband word for word about this dream.

This was Monday morning.

Tuesday morning, I got up as usual to prepare breakfast, and was unable to walk even a few steps without fainting and extreme breathlessness. The feeling was distinctly odd. My husband went to work and I tried again to get up, and collapsed . . . My husband came home and summoned the doctor, who sent for an ambulance.

Rhiannon was eventually diagnosed as having blood clots in the lungs and remained in hospital for two months. At one point:

My husband was told that there was a strong possibility that I would not make it, and doctors were surprised when I did . . . During my time in hospital . . . I was taken to the theatre via a series of corridors where there were rows of parallel pipes in different sizes all along the walls. In the theatre there were lots of people rushing around wearing green gowns and green caps. I am, and always have been, petrified of all things medical. During the time spent in hospital I thought I was dying and wrote farewell notes to all the family.

It would appear that during my sleep state I was given a symbolic yet very real preview of the ordeals ahead, but that already two people had ensured that I should live.

Some parts of this dream—the sensations Rhiannon felt, the exhaustion, breathlessness and fainting—are clearly mirroring the real bodily sensations that she felt when she woke. But in the "strong arms supporting me" it also has echoes of a transcendental, mystical dream, and shows Rhiannon glimpses of a future in which she survives her pulmonary embolus.

If there is any truth in Aristotle's suggestion that the dream mind has some insight into the body, then one might expect the dreams of women to reflect these changes. From puberty onwards, women are subject to the cyclical changes and hormonal fluctuations of their bodies. Robert van de Castle is one of the few people who have studied this aspect of dreaming. In 1964 he collected 450 dreams from about fifty first-year nursing students, over a three-month period, and looked at dream content in relation to different parts of the menstrual cycle. Blood, usually on a female dream character's body, tended to figure most often in dreams that occurred just before menstruation. Several women dreamed of red chairs during menstruation—perhaps reflecting their fear of leaving a mark on the furniture. They also dreamed more often of children and babies during this time—but also of death, and of sick or deformed babies, perhaps a reflection of their awareness that a period also means the death of a potential baby. Themes of marriage, engagements and weddings also figured prominently during the women's periods.

Dr. van de Castle found that dream content changed markedly after ovulation, at mid-cycle. In the first half of the cycle, in their fertile period, the women tended to dream more about sex, have more dreams about their boyfriends, and more dream encounters with attractive strangers. In the second half of the menstrual cycle, encounters with men were fewer, and the men in the dreams were less appealing and less friendly—often even threatening or frightening. Relationships with other women became more prominent in their dreams. It is now known that female sexual drive is determined by the level of testosterone in the blood. This is usually measured when it is at its maximum, at mid-cycle. It is thus not surprising that at mid-cycle, the time of ovulation, women dream of sexual encounters with men.

Pregnancy, which is not only a hormonal but also an emotional upheaval, would be expected to influence a woman's dreams. Almost all pregnant women have dreams which are marked by anxiety that their baby might not be normal, for example. But is it possible that long before these major hormonal and emotional upheavals occur, the dreaming mind can know that a baby has been conceived?

I was about forty, all my three children were at school, and I had just decided that I could at last go back to work again. In fact I'd recently been offered a job and had decided to take it. The last thing on my mind was the possibility of another pregnancy—I was using a contraceptive coil and it simply never occurred to me that it might fail.

Then one night I had a dream that I was pregnant. What I recall mostly from the dream are the very ambivalent feelings I had about the pregnancy—what should I do about my job? Did I really want to start all over again now that I felt our family was complete and I was ready to begin a new phase of life? When I woke up in the morning the dream was very much still with me. As I thought about it and started counting I realised that my period was overdue. After three previous pregnancies I reckoned I knew what I felt like when I was pregnant— each time it had been a very definite and characteristic feeling of nausea which had first alerted me. I hadn't had this feeling and didn't have it now—so far as I could tell I just didn't feel pregnant at all. If I'd noticed the dates but hadn't had the dream I am quite sure I would have been convinced there was some other explanation and simply waited. As it was, when my husband came home that evening I told him about the dream and the overdue period and we decided that I had better have a pregnancy test—which proved positive.

I would not class this as a "precognitive" dream, because the event predicted was already under way. But it seems no less remarkable, because certainly it preceded the dreamer's own conscious cognition. The "dreaming mind," in this case at any rate, was noticeably more observant than the waking mind. It seemed at any rate to have noticed, as the dreamer had not, that her period was overdue. Perhaps it was able (as Aristotle suggested) to pick up and magnify small symptoms of pregnancy of which the dreamer was unaware. But the fact that it could take note of this, work out the implications and debate what a pregnancy would mean to her at this time in her life is still an impressive tribute to the power of dreams.

Robert van de Castle quotes another example of the way in which something, perhaps changing hormonal levels, can impinge on a woman's dreams and alert her to the possibility of pregnancy, or indeed the imminence of menstruation. After the birth of her first child, a woman began to dream that she had started her period, a dream that recurred three or four days before she did, in fact, start menstruating each month. So regular was the dream that she began to regard it as confirmation that she was not pregnant. Then one month she did not have the dream, and a few weeks later discovered that she was in fact pregnant. During a subsequent succession of six pregnancies, this same woman had a remarkable series of premonitory dreams, two warning her about impending miscarriages, others indicating what her labour experiences would be like.

Dr. van de Castle quotes several examples of women who had all undergone quite normal pregnancies, associated with no memorable or disturbing dreams, and then experienced terrifying dreams about the death of their baby. In each case the baby was stillborn, or died soon after birth. He describes, too, the case of a woman who dreamed she was carrying twins, a boy and a girl. In the dream the babies' grandmother tried to kill the babies by poisoning her; the girl lived, and the boy died. Eight months later the babies were delivered—a healthy girl and a boy who was born dead.

Perhaps this chapter should carry a health warning. Almost every woman has occasional fears that her baby won't be born normal, and so anxiety dreams in pregnancy are extremely common. Simply by chance, for some women the dream will unfortunately come true. Similarly, for some people health is a major preoccupation, even an obsession. And all of us at some time in our lives (usually as we start to become aware of the first signs of bodily disintegration) worry about our health. Our dreams are faithful mirrors of our anxieties and preoccupations. If you go to bed with toothache, for example, it should not be too surprising if a session with some demon dream dentist that night leaves you entirely toothless. It is very common indeed to dream that you or someone close to you is seriously ill, or dying, or dead; very rarely that we find confirmation of such a dream when we wake. However, don't let this blind you to the fact that the dream mind is sometimes less foolhardy than the conscious mind. The American dream researcher William Dement, for example, had been a heavy smoker all his life, despite knowing the risks perfectly well. He gave up smoking the morning after he awoke from a vivid and distressing dream in which he discovered he had advanced cancer of the lung and experienced all the anguish of knowing that his life was at an end. He awoke, as most of us do when we wake from such a dream, suffused with relief to find it was only a dream. Pay attention to your dreams if, when you analyse them in the cold light of day, you know they make sense. There are times when you have nothing to lose by listening to the messages your body tries to send.

9

Dream Telepathy

Late one night we were driving south along the M1 after a holiday in Scotland. In the car with us was our elder daughter. Our other daughter and her husband, who had been on holiday with us were flying back to America from Glasgow the next day and were spending the night near the airport. It was quite dark, and at this point high banks lined each side of the motorway. Suddenly the car immediately in front of us swerved across from the outside lane and ran up the bank. We watched in horror—in the dark all we could see was his red tail lights drifting upwards almost as though the car was flying. Then, as we passed, it rolled down the bank, over and over, landing finally upside down on its roof on the motorway. We stopped just ahead and ran back.

The next day our younger daughter telephoned us, in great distress, wanting to know if we'd got home safely. She had had a terrible dream and had woken feeling certain that something awful had happened to us. So strong and persistent was this feeling that she finally had to telephone us to find out if we were all right.

Was this a telepathic experience—knowing what is happening to someone else, usually someone close to you, at the time that it is happening? Or was it simply coincidence?

Almost everyone has experienced what may be telepathy, usually involving someone they are close to, and usually only on a trivial scale—knowing who is at the other end of the telephone when it rings, or what someone is going to say before they speak. If you know someone very well, your minds tend to run on parallel tracks and it's easy to explain most of these incidents in this way. Parents and children often have occasional odd experiences which convince them that some kind of telepathic communication occasionally operates between them. We were all upset and distressed by the accident; if telepathic transmission of emotion is a possibility, this would have been a likely occasion for it to happen. The timing seemed about right too, so far as we could tell.

On the other hand, our younger daughter's anxiety dreams are legendary within the family. When she first went to live in the States we were regularly awakened at five a.m. (around *her* first period of dreaming sleep) to reassure her that her latest dream premonition of disaster had, so far at least, no basis in reality. Sooner or later, one might argue, she was almost bound to strike lucky.

This is perhaps the place to define some terms. Telepathy refers to information obtained anomalously by one individual from another, possibly through "mind-to-mind" contact across space. In clairvoyance, information is perceived anomalously across space—the clairvoyant may "see" an object in a sealed envelope, even though no one is trying to beam the information across to them. Precognition is the ability to see future events by gaining information anomalously across time. These "psi" (short for psychic) phenomena are also known as extrasensory perceptions (ESP), or as paranormal, and they present a real challenge to science, because they cannot yet be explained by any known scientific theory.

Dreams have always interested psi researchers, because they seem to be one of the main vehicles in which anecdotal accounts of psi phenomena such as telepathy and precognition are expressed. We should not underestimate the fact that, whatever the doubts of science, many of the people who have worked with dreams and dreamers for many years seem to have few doubts about the existence of telepathy. Sigmund Freud believed that sleep created favourable conditions for telepathy, and collected many accounts from his patients of telepathic dreams. Jung, too, claimed that he had found by experience that telepathy could influence dreams, and that some people were particularly sensitive to its influence and often had such dreams. Wilhelm Stekel regarded the existence of telepathic dreams as "indisputable," and Medard Boss asserted that "such dreams could no longer be honestly dismissed as mere accidents." Boss also made the observation, which, although it may be regarded as throwing down a gauntlet to conventional science, is very important in this context, that "one single *verified* [my italics] prophetic dream could have more importance than a thousand everyday dreams."

Dr. Louisa Rhine, the wife of Dr. J. B. Rhine, founder of the Duke Parapsychology Laboratory, collected several thousand accounts of psi experiences, most of which involved dreams, the majority of which were precognitive dreams. More recently, two large random population samples were asked about telepathic and precognitive dreams. Almost a third reported some kind of psychic dreams.

These dreams are usually said to have a special quality— the dreamer reports that they are particularly vivid and intense, and make such a strong impression that they linger in the mind much longer than an ordinary dream. Women seem to be more predisposed to these ESP dreams than men; in Louisa Rhine's collection women outnumbered men two to one, and Keith Hearne (see next page) also found a much higher proportion of women amongst "psi dreamers."

Why should dreaming apparently facilitate psi experiences? One explanation that has been offered is that we are receiving psi phenomena all the time but are not aware of this because the conscious mind is too active. If there is any truth in this then it makes good sense to try psi experiments when the conscious mind is out of the way, as is thought to happen in dreams. One might expect more experimental "hits" when people are dreaming than when they are awake.

One of the first scientists to investigate parapsychological phenomena in dreams in a laboratory setting was Montague Ullman, an American psychiatrist who had observed that many of his patients reported instances of telepathy and precognition in their dreams. In 1962, together with Stanley Krippner, he established the Maimonides Dream Laboratory in New York, to investigate dream telepathy and precognitive dream experiences under laboratory conditions. The laboratory continues its work to the present day.

The technique of their early experiments was to fasten EEG electrodes to the head of a subject (the recipient), who would then be taken to a soundproof sleep laboratory where he would go to bed and to sleep. A sealed opaque envelope containing an art print would then be randomly selected from a collection of prints, and taken by one of the experimenters to a distant room. The experimenter would open the envelope and fix his attention on the picture. The recipient would be woken when his EEG showed him to be at the end of an REM (dreaming sleep) period, and asked to recount the dream he had just had. The dream reports were recorded and at the end of the study, independent outside judges would study all the dream reports, compare them with the total collection of art prints and try to identify the print used on the night of each experiment.

Ullman and Krippner found that some subjects were able to incorporate the telepathically transmitted material in their dreams. Each study consisted of eight nights of dreaming, and thirteen major studies were carried out. In nine of the thirteen, the results were statistically significant, indicating that the dreamers dreamed of the target object much more often than could have been predicted by chance or coincidence alone. The success of the experiments was at least partly due to the fact that many of them were carried out with one particular subject, Malcolm Bessant, an English ''sensitive'' who had an extraordinarily high telepathy hit rate. In one case, for example, Bessant dreamed about going to Madison Square Gardens to buy tickets for a boxing match. The target picture for that night was a painting of a boxing match. Sometimes the dream/picture match was more symbolic—another recipient dreamed of a dead rat in a cigar box; the randomly selected picture that was being ''transmitted'' to him was of a dead gangster in a coffin. This degree of verification is rare, but as Boss suggested, even a single verified prophetic dream has enormous implications for science.

The suggestion that in the dream state people are more receptive to receiving telepathic information also prompted Dr. Keith Hearne, a British dream researcher, to test this theory by conducting a dream-telepathy experiment with the aid of the readers of a national mass-circulation British daily newspaper. An item published in the paper on 13 February 1986 asked the readers:

Are you a good dreamer? Then join in this scientific mass dream-telepathy experiment. From midnight tonight until

10 a.m. tomorrow, Dr. Hearne will attempt to transmit pictures by telepathy. He will concentrate, in turn, on a set of ten pictures, spending exactly one hour on each. The pictures could be a jar of flowers, say, or a country scene. The idea is you pick up in your dreams what one or more of them is.

Readers were told that if they woke up at any time between midnight and ten a.m. and recalled just having had a dream, they should note the exact time they woke and write a brief description of the most significant part of their dream.

The judges were asked to try to match the dream reports to either of a pair of pictures they were given (one of which was the "target" picture for the time at which the dream occurred, and the other a randomly chosen "control" picture—the judges, of course, did not know which was which). They were asked to note any links they could find between the dream and the pictures, even if it was only, say, the number of people in the dream, and try hard to match the dream to one or other picture. If this was impossible, the report would be put in an "indeterminate" category.

Several hundred people took part in the experiment, but there were no direct hits. Any links that were found between dreams and targets were very tenuous, and most of the dream reports were judged to be indeterminate. The experiment produced no evidence of mass dream telepathy.

Probably most people would not be too surprised at this. Even though many people feel that telepathy is something they have experienced, it is nearly always with someone they are close to. The most convincing stories of dream telepathy that we have been told nearly always involve people between whom there is a close emotional bond—something which has to be lacking in any kind of mass telepathy experiment.

There is some gradually accumulating evidence that thoughts can be transmitted from one person to another, which is to say, from one brain to another, provided there is some empathic contact between the people involved. The same probably holds true for dream telepathy, as several stories told to us seem to confirm. Geoffrey Leytham describes two telepathic dreams he has had, both related to his wife.

My wife, Pat, had been out for the day with a friend, and they had driven into Wales from our home on the Wirral. When I got home from the University, she told me that she had spent a pleasant time, but did not go into any details about her trip. That night I had a dream which I reported to her next morning: it concerned the inside of a café, and I gave a very detailed description of a woman in the café, and the odd black and white dress that she was wearing. Pat recognised the café as the one in which she and her friend had had lunch, and the woman was exactly as I had described her. In fact, her attire was so remarkable that Pat could not take her eyes off it. She said that my account of the café and outstanding woman was as if I had made a video of the situation.

The second dream concerned a book that Pat was reading at the time.

We were in the habit of reading in bed prior to going to sleep but did not discuss the books that we were reading until we had finished them and given our verdict on them. This night I had a long dream about soldiers and houses and various incidents suggesting a war story. I recalled much of it next morning, and told Pat about it. To my surprise, it coincided with the book she was reading, and especially the parts she had read in bed the previous night.

It is interesting to compare the two dreams described below by Betty M., both of which concern people to whom she was close, with the precognitive dream she describes on pp. 174–75, which had a much more tenuous personal connection for her. These two more personal dreams are much less ambiguous, more specific and more convincing. In late January 1971, Betty M. had the following dream.

A "newsflash" interrupted an ongoing dream, the dream environment replaced by a rectangular frame through which I saw a distant image of my cousin B. And I knew, with sudden intuition, that she was pregnant. The significant-feeling quality of the dream persisted—despite the unlikelihood of its ever coming true. B dearly wanted children, but, sadly, after twelve years of marriage it seemed that she was destined to remain childless. I related the dream to Mother on my next visit and we wondered whether B might be thinking of adopting a baby, for that seemed the only way the dream could in some sense come true. Some weeks later Mother learned that B was indeed expecting a baby, and a son was duly born on 12 October 1971, about thirty-seven weeks after the dream. I should add that B lived over 100 miles away and (apart from Christmas cards) I had no direct communication with her for years before and after the dream.

It isn't as though I frequently dream about people having babies! There was only one other notable instance which . . . concerned my cousin S's expecting an illegitimate baby. Now S was forty-seven years old, and I dismissed any idea of the dream coming true in a literal sense. It subsequently transpired that an illegitimate baby was on the way—but to S's son and his partner.

Even though Betty M. dismissed this latter dream as being too unlikely to come true, it had such a special quality for her that she lodged a sealed account of it with Professor John Beloff, then Professor of Psychology at the University of Edinburgh. Professor Beloff was at that time heading researchers interested in the correlation between dream predictions and their subsequent validation (work which is still continuing under the direction of Professor Morris, holder of the Koestler Chair of Parapsychology at Edinburgh University). This was something she had only previously done on one other occasion, when she had a precognitive dream described in the next chapter. It is interesting that this "baby dream," too, occurred very shortly after conception, just over thirty-five weeks before the baby's actual birth.

At the time she had the dream, Betty M. found it hard to believe that it was telepathic, because she thought it so unlikely that B would even have suspected that she might be pregnant. However, what she did not know at the time, and has in fact only recently learned, is that her cousin had started to take fertility drugs a few weeks before the dream; the possibility of pregnancy was therefore very much on her mind. Her cousin estimates her probable date of conception as being around 19

January; Betty M. dreamed about the pregnancy towards the end of January, at a time when her cousin would, she says, have been in a state of high psychological expectancy, even though she would probably not have known for certain that she was pregnant.

One of the earliest and best-documented collections of dream telepathy accounts can be found in *Phantasms of the Living*, published in 1886. The authors were Frederic Myers and Edmund Gurney, joint Honorary Secretaries of the Society for Psychical Research, and Frank Podmore. The three were scrupulous in their approach, and very much aware of the possible sources of error. For each of the cases they documented they sought corroborative evidence by a third party, checking that the experience had been recounted to someone else before the event was known to have occurred, and that the account had not been embellished with hindsight.

There was, for example, the experience of the artist Arthur Severn and his wife, while on holiday by Coniston Water in 1880. One morning Mrs. Severn woke up, with a feeling that she had had a hard blow on the mouth, and a distinct sense that her upper lip was bleeding. So vivid was the feeling that she sat up in bed and held her hankie to her mouth to stem the flow of blood. To her astonishment she saw that there was none, and realised then that nothing could have struck her— she had been lying asleep in bed, and her husband had evidently gone out for an early-morning sail, as he was not in the room. It must all have been a dream. Looking at her watch she saw it was seven o'clock.

When her husband came in for breakfast she noticed that he kept dabbing his lip furtively with his handkerchief, just as she had done. She said, "Arthur, why are you doing that?" and added a little anxiously, "I know you've hurt yourself! But I'll tell you why afterwards." Arthur then told her that his boat had been hit by a sudden squall, which threw the tiller suddenly round so that it struck him on the mouth. It had been bleeding a good deal and wouldn't stop. When his wife asked him what time this had happened, he replied that it must have been about seven o'clock.

Another dream experience was described by the Canon of Winchester, William Warburton. He had arrived in London to find that his brother, with whom he was staying, was at a party.

Sitting up waiting for him to return, the canon fell asleep, and in a dream, saw his brother come out of a drawing room, catch his foot on a stair, and fall. Half an hour later his brother arrived back and explained that he had just nearly broken his neck, when, coming out of the ballroom, he had caught his foot and tumbled full length down the stairs. Recounting this story, Canon Warburton (who told Myers *et al.* that this was the only telepathic experience he had ever had) added: ''My brother was hurrying home from his dance, with some little self-reproach in his mind for not having been at his chambers to receive his guest, so the chances are that he was thinking of me.''

Perhaps the oddest of all this early collection of dream-telepathy stories concerns the Rev. A. B. McDougall, then a scholar of Lincoln College, Oxford. On the night of 10 January 1882, he was staying with friends in Manchester. During the night he was woken ''by feeling an unpleasantly cold something slithering down my right leg. I immediately struck a light, flung off the bedclothes, and saw a rat run out of my bed under the fireplace . . .'' A day or so later the Rev. McDougall wrote to tell his mother of his encounter with the rat. When she replied, her son reported, she told him that

> On the morning of January 11th a cousin of mine who happened to be staying in my own home on the south coast, and to be occupying my room, came down to breakfast, and recounted a marvellous dream, in which a rat appeared to be eating off the extremities of my unfortunate self.

Of his cousin's dream, his mother commented, ''We always said E was a witch. She always knew about everything almost before it took place.''

It is understandable that finding a rat in one's bed might engender strong emotions. Presumably people who witness accidents or disasters are also in some emotional distress or turmoil. TB is a railway inspector who seems to have ''tuned,'' in a dream, to feelings that someone else was experiencing.

> At about 5.30 a.m I had a dream that a train was passing around the curve beside the house where we used to live.

At the same time another train was proceeding along one of the straight fast lines. A moment later I heard the sound of an impact, and upon looking out of the bedroom window saw that a fast train had been derailed and was blocking one of the adjacent slow lines . . .

As I was looking out of the dream window I was awakened by our (real) telephone ringing, which enabled me to easily recall this dream. I work as a railway inspector, and the telephone call came from one of my colleagues, advising me of a mishap which had occurred down the line at 4.20 a.m. and which I was required to attend. At the time I made little of any relationship between this news and my dream, although I did mention to my wife as I got dressed that it was a bit strange as I had been dreaming of a railway accident.

Upon my arrival at the signal box I found that what had happened was that a train had overrun the end of a siding line, become derailed and blocked the adjacent slow line. The layout of lines bore an uncanny resemblance to the dream layout. It became immediately apparent to me that I seemed to have dreamed of an incident that had taken place about an hour beforehand.

In this case there is no way of telling whose were the thoughts picked up by TB in his dream. It would have had to have been a signalman or some other railway worker who was at the scene of the accident. Why should he have "received" such thoughts? TB had, he says, never before experienced any telepathic or clairvoyant communications, but this incident, with its potential for a major human disaster, would clearly have had an emotional impact for him, closely involved as he was with the safe running of the railways.

Timing is clearly crucial when one is deciding whether a dream is telepathic or precognitive. Does it matter? Yes, to anyone who is trying to understand why and how such dreams occur, it does. The painter, Thetis Blacker, in her book *A Pilgrimage of Dreams*, describes a dream she had on the night of the Frejus dam disaster. The emotional intensity of the dream again seems to add weight to Thetis's own conclusion that this was a telepathic dream, that she had somehow "tuned in" to the terror that the victims of the disaster had experienced.

I dreamed I was standing in a modern bungalow type of house with huge glass windows. As I looked out at the nearby hills, I was overcome by a terrible apprehension. At first I thought that the hillside was going to break away in an avalanche of rocks, but then a voice inside me said:
"It is not the rocks; it is the water!"
I turned to the other person in the house, a woman whom I could not exactly see, or whose appearance I could not, on waking, precisely remember, and said in terror:
"For God's sake, we must get out of here before the dam breaks!"
The urgency of my fear was such that, startled and horrified, I awoke; and as I did so, I heard a voice in my dream calling desperately, "*Et toi, Inez, et toi, Inez . . .*"
I knew no one of that name. I was so frightened by this dream that although I awoke to the light of day, my heart was still pounding with fear. I got out of bed and turned on the wireless in order to listen to the seven o'clock news, and so calm myself and take away the horror of this nightmare. But from this news I learned of the actual happening of that dreadful disaster. I was much alarmed by what I had experienced and I hoped that my dream could, despite its vivid atmosphere of reality, be explained as an exceptional coincidence. But later when the photographs of the disaster appeared in the paper, the details of the actual landscape coincided exactly with those of my dream.

Dreams which indicate that a close friend or relative has died, or is about to die, or is in trouble, are very common. Of the 149 "coincident" dreams which Myers *et al.* described in *Phantasms of the Living*, seventy-nine represented or suggested death.

Averil Meallen gave us an unusual example of this type of dream. At the time of the dream her father-in-law, who lived abroad, and to whom she was not particularly close, was in hospital, but was not thought to be seriously ill—certainly no one thought he was going to die. One night she had what she described as a "very strong dream" that a good friend of hers, Maya, had died. In her dream she saw a black "thing"—the nearest description she could give was that it was something like a black, silky scarf—sliding out of her room. This dream was so powerful that she woke her husband to tell him about it; she also checked the time.

The next day she rang her friend and was relieved to discover that she was alive and well. But soon afterwards they received a telephone call saying that her father-in-law had died—at the time she had woken from her dream. What is interesting is that Averil had forgotten that her father-in-law's name was also Maya, although no one ever called him that. Averil's dream was unusual in that she wasn't particularly close to her father-in-law. She herself found the dream puzzling, and could see no reason why she should have had it.

What is always unsatisfactory in these dream connections is that there is usually no way of knowing whether the experience is a two-way one or not—was Averil picking up signals deliberately beamed to her by her father-in-law, for example, or was he quite unconscious of having made any contact with her? The following dream, told to us by Mrs. Pamela Cleary, may give us some clue, because here we get both sides of the story.

Following a miscarriage I lost a lot of blood—I was alone in the house and the bleeding went on so long that I felt I must go to the bathroom to get a towel to try and stem the flow. I remember being too dizzy to walk and crept on all fours. Lying on the bathroom floor I suddenly felt so relaxed and happy, as though any cares I had were lifted. If there is such a thing as being "at peace," this was certainly it. Then I was floating and looking down on myself on the bathroom floor. I can't tell you how long this lasted—but there was a lovely feeling of letting go, not having to worry any more. Help came and I was sent to hospital for a transfusion. However, the really strange thing, in my opinion, was the story told by my daily cleaner, a very pleasant, solid, unimaginative lady with whom I had developed a natural rapport, as two women will, working together daily. As I was in hospital, my husband had driven round to her house the next morning. Before he spoke she said she knew I was ill. She had had a dream in the night and had seen me lying on the floor, dying. She had called to me, "Oh don't go—don't go and leave the children."

What Mrs. Cleary describes—the feelings of peace and happiness, the floating out of her body so that she saw herself lying on the floor—is typical of a near-death experience. But before she reached this state of peace and tranquillity, as she crawled into the bathroom and lay on the floor, she must have been very frightened, and perhaps it was these powerful feelings that her cleaner picked up in her dream. Mrs. Cleary herself, though, had no sense that she had been in communication with her cleaner during the experience. Compare this with the following dream in which Kenneth Gaskell describes his meeting with a friend who was dying, on the night of his death.

I was about thirty-five years old when I had a quite remarkable dream. I was floating gently forward through very black space, when suddenly out of the blackness ahead of me, and floating towards me, was the figure of a friend and colleague who worked for the same organisation as myself, but in an office about thirty miles from my office.

I was surprised to see him and I said, "Hello, Jack, what are you doing here?" He replied in a very sad voice, "Kenneth, I'm dying." I was so overcome that I began to cry, to such an extent that I awakened and my face was wet with tears.

Immediately on arrival at my office that morning I phoned Jack's office and asked if I might speak to him. I was told that he had died during the night.

I was aware that Jack had suffered from leukaemia, but was not aware that he was particularly "ill," so to speak, at that time.

The feeling of floating through a black void is often described by people who have had near-death experiences. It is tempting to assume that in his dream Kenneth was somehow sharing a component of his friend's death. But of course we can't assume this, because we have no knowledge of what the dying friend was actually experiencing. We only know one side of the story. It is as likely that the feelings which Kenneth picked up telepathically from his dying friend were then clothed in dream imagery.

To explain a truly shared dream experience we would have to postulate some common reality which is independent of individual boundaries, and to which, in some states of consciousness, we have access. There are dreams which do seem to offer some evidence of this, and which are impossible to explain unless we are prepared to widen our personal beliefs and scientific assumptions. Although we have come across only a few really convincing accounts of such dreams, this might at least in part be because in our culture we are just not used to looking in detail at dreams or to sharing our dream experiences with other people.

SHARED DREAMS

Jung drew attention to the curious way in which close friends or members of the same family, particularly husband and wife, or parent and child, will dream the same dream. In *The Development of Personality* he gives an example of three sisters who had not only shared dreams, but dreams which, it later transpired, seemed to have been precognitive.

> When they were approaching puberty they confessed shamefacedly to each other that for years they had suffered from horrible dreams about [their mother]. They dreamt of her as a witch or a dangerous animal and they could not understand it at all, since their mother was so lovely and utterly devoted to them. Years later the mother became insane and in her insanity crawled about on all fours and imitated the grunting of pigs, the barking of dogs, and the growling of bears.

This is an interesting story although I rather doubt that it demonstrates true dream precognition. Insanity which takes this form, even in the late nineteenth century, would be extremely unusual; what is described is much more a common stereotype of a mad person than a true picture of mental illness. If I was the psychiatrist treating the sisters I would suspect a degree of family dysfunction and be inclined to question the loveliness and utter devotion of a mother who inspired such dreams in all three of her daughters.

Much more difficult to understand are dreams which seem to be more literally "shared" in that they are dreamed by different people simultaneously. The basic premise which underlies telepathy is that the mind is not bounded by the skull, but that one mind can be responsive to the mind of another. In most of the examples of dream telepathy that have been described so far, one mind is awake and the other asleep. But there is no reason why this should be so, for if telepathy exists at all it is equally logical to assume that it can exist as well between two sleeping minds as two awake minds. Indeed, if there is any truth in the theory that the conscious mind interferes with telepathic experiences, then it could be argued that two dreaming minds have the best chance of all.

Myers *et al.* give several fascinating and very convincing instances of shared dreams in *Phantasms of the Living*, including two examples of couples who shared a simultaneous dream of death. In each case one member of the couple had a vivid dream of their own death, while the other woke in great distress having dreamed that their partner had died. (That in neither case did the partner in fact die is also worth noting, because it is an indication of how often a "premonition" turns out to be false.)

Myers *et al.* quote, too, the experience, in September 1881, of the Rev. J. Page Hopps, of Leicester.

Last week I dreamt of a "dead" friend, and of this friend doing an exceedingly strange thing. It impressed me very much but I said not a word concerning it to anyone. Next morning, at breakfast, my wife hastened to tell me that she had dreamt a singular dream (a very unusual thing for her to say anything about), and then she staggered me by telling me what she had dreamt. It was the very thing that I had dreamed. We slept in different rooms, she having to attend to a sick child, and I not being very well. I do not care to tell you the dream; but the special *action* in *both* dreams was something extremely curious and

monstrously improbable. My wife ended her description
by saying, "Then she tried to say something, but I could
not make it out." I heard and remembered what was said,
and that was the only difference in our dreams. We had
not been in any way talking about our "dead" friend.

I remain consumed with curiosity about the "extremely curious and monstrously improbable" action in which the Hopps's
dead friend was engaged—even when pressed by Mr. Gurney,
the Rev. Hopps refused to divulge any details.

Myers *et al.* are at pains to point out that when people are
living closely together some joint waking experience may be
the common source of both their dreams. But this does not
seem likely to have been the explanation in the Hopps's dream,
or indeed in the following account, told to them by Mr. Edmund Toy of Littlehampton in November 1883.

I dreamed that for some reason or other I had poisoned
a woman, and the same night Mrs. Toy had a very vivid
dream, in which she thought I was going to be tried for
having committed a murder. I do not think I am of a
bloodthirsty disposition, and do not remember to have
been reading anything to have suggested the dream, so
the coincidence was, to say the least, very striking.

There are strong echoes of Mr. and Mrs. Toy's experience in
this next account of a shared dream, by Beryl Statham and her
son, one of the strangest dream accounts we have been given.

When my oldest son, Richard, was about sixteen, in the
fifties, I went to a conference of the Mothers' Union, I
think in Worcester. I woke on the last morning there in
great distress—I think I had woken myself by crying out.
I had dreamt that I had gone into a room and seen a body
on the floor by the fireside. Richard was standing by the
body, a knife in his right hand. I clutched him by the left
hand and dared not let go to get help in case he attacked
me and then there would be no one to explain that he
must have had a brainstorm, because he was a gentle
personality who couldn't hurt anyone. I had no fear of
death myself but a passionate desire to defend him. I

woke in real horror, but dismissed the dream as a nightmare.

When I got home . . . I started to tell the story of my
nightmare to Richard and Enid [a friend who was living
with the family]. While I was talking both were saying,
"What an extraordinary thing!" and when I'd finished
Richard said, "I've already told Enid my dream: I dreamt
I'd gone into a room and seen a body on the floor with
a knife beside it. I wanted to get help but couldn't move
because someone was holding me firmly by the left
wrist."

This is a fascinating account because although it is very clearly
a shared dream experience, there are subtle similarities and
differences between the two dreams. In Richard's dream, although he was in the room and saw the body lying there with
a knife beside it, he clearly saw himself as being uninvolved
and wanting to get help. His mother, on the other hand, saw
him as the attacker, even though this was so out of character,
and even saw the knife in Richard's right hand. They both
agree that it was Richard's left hand that was being held.

The correspondences between these two dreams are too
many and far too close to dismiss the whole thing as coincidence. The most reasonable explanation is that for some moments the two of them did share a common frame of dream
experience, and that the differences between their dreams are
simply due to their own slightly different perceptions of the
common neutral situation.

Some of the most persuasive evidence for shared dream experiences has been collected by Robert van de Castle, professor at the University of Virginia Medical School and President
of the American Association for the Study of Dreams. At the
time Dr. van de Castle was co-editor of the *Dream Network
Bulletin*, and readers of the bulletin were notified that on a
certain specified night he would focus on a target picture. They
were invited to dream that night about the target picture and
to write in describing their dream experiences.

Dr. van de Castle suggested that if telepathy were involved,
three levels of his consciousness might act as a target that
night. The focus might be the target picture itself (a black and
white photograph of an Indian woman standing in front of a

thatched wooden house, a young boy standing on a metal pot behind her, his hands around a wooden pole). Secondly, telepathic dreamers might pick up the associations which the picture had for him, which he had written down. Thirdly, telepathy might target his dreams. He woke up three times that night and recorded several long dreams.

Twenty-seven people responded, and several people wrote in with dreams which included elements both of the picture and of his written associations with the picture. But the most striking correspondences were with the imagery in Dr. van de Castle's dreams. He says:

> My first dream involved a fishing scene: I was sometimes on a boat and sometimes on shore. The man I was with caught two large flounder and a woman insisted that I put them on top of a boat and gut them. I attempted to cut the fish open with a razor blade. Some blood came out; the fish's face turned into a man's face and he was bleeding. I told him to rinse his face with water and said I would need his advice as to how to cut around his ears and nose.

One woman, Claudia B., a complete stranger to van de Castle, not only picked up many elements in the picture and its associations, but described this dream, which is uncanny in its several similarities to his own dream.

> I am outdoors, perhaps on the deck of a ship . . . mounting the fresh, whole wet skin of a small whale or whale's head (fish-sized) on a board, for artistic and maybe ritual purposes. After removing one eye (the only one, it's a side view) with the knife I'm using, I hear a conversation . . . (All of this could be influenced by a recent waking experience of washing flounder for cooking, but not removing their heads.) I feel a kinship, or sympathy, with the whale, which at some point transforms into a person. The wet, stretched, mounted skin is now of a man's face, reddish-brown . . . I don't seem to notice the change from the whale.

It is interesting that the most significant correlations were not with the target picture, but with van de Castle's dreams. This seems to give more weight to the suggestion that two dream minds are more likely to be in touch than a dreaming and a waking mind.

The following account, told to us by Monica Jackson, is an even more intriguing variation on the shared dream theme, involving three people, two of whom did not know each other at all.

Monica Jackson's father was mourning the death of a friend who had been chief overseer on their coffee plantation for many years. One night he dreamed that his friend appeared at his bedside and asked his help in some unfinished business which was causing him distress. The friend had borrowed 500 rupees from Monica's parents shortly before they went away on holiday. He died suddenly while they were away, and this debt must have weighed on his mind. His friend told him that the money was in a box under his bed in his village house where he had died.

Although the experience seemed quite real at the time, my father had convinced himself that it was a vivid dream until he received a letter from a close relative of the deceased, whom he had never met and who lived in another part of the country, describing exactly the same experience. Comparison of dates showed that these identical experiences occurred to two strangers whose only connection was the deceased, on the same night. My father, a coffee planter in India, was not an imaginative man and, incidentally, was a devout Christian, while the friend and his relative were devout Hindus.

My father had no intention of enquiring further about the money or the box until the relative wrote to him repeating the same dream and message. Then he did so, but was told by the dead man's family that while he had indeed kept his money in a box under the bed, his ne'er-do-well son had just absconded with it. So the delay in responding to the request meant that my father failed his friend. Or so I suppose.

If we accept that this dream account is true, then not only do we have to postulate that these two people had the same telepathic experience, but that they both had it with a man who had recently died. We not only have to accept the fact of telepathy, but also that the dead have the capacity to communicate with the living.

The only rational explanation for this is to assume that the dead friend had told both his relative and Monica's father about the location of the money before he died, and that they had both forgotten, and both then remembered this important information in a dream. This is a coincidence theory, and like most coincidence theories it has very long odds. An alternative theory might be that his friend was troubled by the loan as he lay dying, and that these dying thoughts were picked up by the two dreamers some days later in a post-cognitive way. But if this was the case, where was the information stored? Finally, there remains the theory that the dead can somehow communicate with the living. We can accept this as a matter of simple belief, but as yet, science has no evidence of a mechanism to support it.

I have only come across one other account of a shared dream experience comparable to this. It was told to us by a Brazilian in São Paulo. It was a story that was quite beyond our personal boggle threshold, and yet one could not help believing it. I certainly can't offer an explanation and neither could the narrator, but he was clearly describing exactly what he felt had happened, and his story had the ring of truth about it.

The dream was a simple one. He was taking a walk when he met a friend—a close friend with whom he had always had a strong rapport. They chatted for a while, and then he said, "This is a dream, you know." "I know it is," his friend replied. "Do you think we'll remember it in the morning?" "I certainly intend to," he said. "I tell you what, let's meet tomorrow and see if we do." Then they parted and he awoke.

The next day he went into his office, where his friend also worked, remembering the dream quite clearly, and wondering what he should do if he met his friend. In the cold light of day it seemed too fantastic and he felt slightly embarrassed about mentioning it. He'd been sitting at his desk for some time when his friend came into the office, and strode straight over to his desk, smiling broadly. They looked at each other for a moment, then he said tentatively, "Do you remember . . . ?" "YES!" shouted his friend triumphantly. They had, indeed, a shared memory of the dream experience.

Taking all these accounts together, do dreams provide us with any evidence that telepathy exists—that mind can contact mind directly? There is certainly evidence for telepathy, both from formal scientific work using strict scientific procedures to exclude chance effects, cheating or distortions of the evidence, and from numerous well-documented and authenticated anecdotal accounts. The most successful scientific research into telepathy comes from the Ganzfeld experiments. In these experiments, which are described in more detail in chapter 11, the recipient is in a situation in which he is sensorily deprived, but not asleep or dreaming. In this situation there is now unequivocal evidence that telepathy does exist.

Dreaming creates a situation very similar to the Ganzfeld state. The cortex is stimulated and close to an awake state, but its sensory input is very much reduced. The major difference is in memory function which is intact in the Ganzfeld, but reduced in dreaming. So perhaps it is not surprising that dreams, if they can be remembered, are fertile ground for experiences of telepathy. With such evidence science is clearly going to have to reformulate its theories.

Even if we acknowledge that telepathy can sometimes operate in dreams, that mind can contact mind directly, is there any evidence that the dreaming mind can ever tell us anything about the future? This is the field of precognition—and precognitive dreams have been described throughout the dream history of mankind.

10

Dreams Which Predict the Future

In 1902 John William Dunne, a British aeronautical engineer serving with the 6th Mounted Infantry in what was then the Orange Free State, had an "unusually vivid and rather unpleasant dream." This is how he described it in his book, *An Experiment with Time*, published in 1927.

I seemed to be standing on high ground—the upper slopes of some spur of a hill or mountain. The ground was of a curious white formation. Here and there in this were little fissures, and from these, jets of vapour were spouting upward. In my dream I recognised the place as an island of which I had dreamed before—an island which was in imminent peril from a volcano. And, when I saw the vapour spouting from the ground, I gasped: "It's the island! Good Lord, the whole thing is going to blow up!" ... Forthwith I was seized with a frantic desire to save the four thousand (I knew the number) unsuspecting inhabitants. Obviously there was only one way of doing this, and that was to take them off in ships. There followed a most distressing nightmare, in which I was at a neighbouring island, trying to get the incredulous *French* authorities to despatch vessels of every and any description to remove the inhabitants of the threatened island. I was sent from one official to another; and finally woke myself by my own dream exertions, clinging to the heads of a team of horses drawing the carriage of one "Monsieur le Maître," who was going out to dine and wanted me to return when his office would be open next day. All through the dream the *number* of the people in danger obsessed my mind. I repeated it to everyone I met, and at the moment of waking I was shouting to the "Maître," "Listen! Four thousand people will be killed unless—"

When the next batch of newspapers reached them he opened the *Daily Telegraph* to read that there had been a volcano disaster in Martinique. Mont Pelée had exploded, with the loss of over 40,000 lives.

It continued to worry Dunne for some time that his dream figure of 4,000 had been out by a factor of ten. It disconcerted him even more that, when the final figures were published, the true death toll was in fact no possible combination of 4s and Os. Finally he became convinced that what he had had was not a precognitive dream of the eruption itself, but either a precognitive dream of reading the newspaper story, and misreading the number of deaths announced in its headline, or a telepathic communication with the journalist in the *Daily Telegraph* who had written the account.

For Dunne, this was the first of a series of precognitive dreams that convinced him that dreams have access to the "memory" of future events, and that this is as normal as having access to memory of events in the past. His book, *An Experiment with Time*, describes his theory that precognitive dream experiences are simply dreams displaced in time.

These dreams were not percepts [impressions] of distant or future events. They were the usual commonplace dreams composed of distorted images of waking experience, built together in the usual half-senseless fashion peculiar to dreams. That is to say, *if they had happened on the nights after the corresponding events*, they would have exhibited nothing in the smallest degree unusual, and would have yielded just as much true, and just as much false, information regarding the waking experience which had given rise to them as does any ordinary dream—which is very little.

Before we even consider the plausibility of Dunne's idea that dreams can be displaced in time, perhaps we should examine the whole notion of the existence of a "time warp" in more detail. It's an idea that has long been beloved of writers and dramatists (Barrie's play *Mary Rose*, Francis Hodgson Burnett's children's story *The Secret Garden*, H. G. Wells's *The Time Machine* all make use of it). The story I'm now going to quote is notable first of all because it was well documented at the time, and secondly because of the credibility of the person involved, Air Marshall Sir Victor Goddard.

Early in the 1930s, Victor Goddard was a very junior Air Force cadet. One day he was flying a small biplane (the only type of aeroplane the RAF had at that time) over Fife. He was flying over what he knew to be a derelict airfield, abandoned since the First World War, when he happened to look down and saw to his surprise that it had obviously been reactivated. There were aeroplanes on the ground and, even more surprising, they were monoplanes, painted a distinctive orange colour, and with the RAF roundel clearly visible on their wings.

Returning to base, Victor Goddard put in a report about what he had seen. And on the strength of it was court-martialled. The Air Force owned no monoplanes, certainly no orange monoplanes, and the airfield in question was still derelict and abandoned. Victor Goddard could not have seen what he claimed to have seen. Vivid imagination was not an attribute the RAF much cared for in its pilots, and the matter was taken so seriously that had he not been the top cadet of his year he would probably have been discharged from the force.

In 1940, at the beginning of the Second World War, Goddard once more happened to be flying over the same airfield, and again he looked out of the window. To his astonishment he saw exactly what he had seen ten years earlier. He now recognised the small monoplanes he saw on the runway as Miles Manchesters, in current use by the Air Force as training planes and at that time painted orange (a practice that was soon discontinued when the RAF realised it was an unwise choice of colour for trainer aircraft in times of war).

A time warp? There is a final twist to the story which makes it even more interesting—and to my mind more credible. A friend of ours met Victor Goddard towards the end of his life. They were discussing the story and Goddard told him one other odd detail which still puzzled him. At the time he took his first flight over the airfield, the derelict hangars which were actually on the airfield were of a type left over from the First World War, straight-sided with a peaked roof. But the hangars that Goddard had described in his report were of a quite unfamiliar type, with rounded roofs. By the time of the Second World War this curved-roof type of hangar was in common use. One might assume that Goddard's leap forward in time showed the airfield exactly as it was going to be in 1940, complete with 1940-style aircraft and hangars. But it wasn't quite like that. When the airfield was recommissioned at the beginning of the Second World War, the old hangars were not in fact replaced with new ones, but simply dusted off and used again. When Goddard took his second flight over the airfield in 1940, he noticed that the hangars were *not* the ones he'd seen on his first flight—the only detail which was different from his previous "vision."

So one cannot simply say that Goddard had a precognitive glimpse of the airfield as it was going to be ten years into the future. To our knowledge, no modern hangars were ever built there. It seems to have been more a general premonition of what airfields would be like in the future than a specific view of a particular airfield.

Normally we think of time as being a straight line. There is a past, a present and a future. The laws of causality as we understand them fall into this pattern, so, for example, the future can't affect the past. This simple linear flow of time is, however, not the only one available. J. W. Dunne, for example, postulated that the dreamer stood outside the line of time and thus could see future and past equally well and was not tied to the present moment. By the time you come to quantum mechanics, strange things happen to time, and some physicists will deny the structure of time as we understand it, some even going so far as to say there is no such thing as time. In Einstein's theory of relativity, time becomes one dimension of the structure of the universe (space-time). So it is important to keep an open mind concerning the flow of time and to allow that future events may affect past events and that a linear flow of time may not be the only way that the universe answers our questions. With this in mind, let's look further at precognition.

Dream premonitions are common. In October 1980 a questionnaire was published in *The Times*, designed to find out how many people had had what seemed to them to be experiences inexplicable by science. Several questions were asked about dream premonitions. Forty-two per cent of those who answered said they had at some time had a dream that came true, concerning events which they did not know about or expect before the dream. Of these, about two-thirds had had such a dream more than once.

When Keith Hearne, a dream researcher, placed a request for premonitions in a national newspaper he received 450 replies—the overwhelming number from women. He analysed 165 of the most convincing accounts, taken from eighty-eight of these replies, in some detail. Although many of the people who replied had experienced more than one type of premonition at different times, the largest category was of premonitions in the form of dreams (62.4 per cent). By far the most premonitions concerned death or unpleasant happenings (84 per cent). In just under half of the premonitions the "victim" was someone known to the dreamer, as in this dream described to Dr. Hearne by a thirty-one-year-old woman, Marjorie.

In a dream I saw my uncle in a taxi cab. The next thing I knew my uncle had been crushed to death inside the taxi. Two weeks later I did something very unusual for me—I went into the front room and switched on the TV to watch *Calendar*. Within a minute it showed a railway line and gave out the grim news that my uncle had been killed on the line. I went to pieces and dashed into my neighbour's home.

One of the most remarkable things about the accounts Dr. Hearne quotes is how specific many of the premonitions he was given were. One of the problems of verifying precognitive dreams, as we shall see, is that they very seldom make it easy for us to do so. Their meaning is all too often cloaked in vagueness, ambiguity, use of symbolism. For this reason the following dream from Dr. Hearne's survey is very unusual. The dreamer was Doreen, a forty-year-old woman.

In my dream I was standing at my front door, looking towards the school, waiting for my daughter to come home for her dinner (in real life I was working and my daughter stayed for school dinners). I saw this small aeroplane circling the school and then it seemed to dive straight at the school. It pulled round at the last minute and crashed into an alleyway just in front of me. There was nothing anyone could do. I woke up with sweat pouring from me, and crying. I had to wake my husband up— it was still in the middle of the night. About five months later an aircraft did just miss the school at lunchtime and crashed into some houses further to the left than in my dream, and three young children were killed as well as the pilot and co-pilot.

Dr. Hearne found that the age at which the first experience occurred varied from three to sixty-four, but the peak age-range was between ten and fifteen years. It is perhaps not surprising that early adolescence should prove to be the peak age for first dream premonitions. This is a time of massive and turbulent developmental change, mentally, socially and sexually, and at least some of these changes are closely linked with sleep. Release of the hormones which lead to sexual maturation first occurs during slow-wave sleep in puberty. The peak age for sleepwalking is also twelve years of age, and the rate declines during puberty to about 1–2 per cent for adults. Brain excitability also changes during puberty, reaching its peak at around the age of sixteen and then declining. The onset of epilepsy follows this curve as well, again with the peak being at sixteen. Massive neuronal remodelling also takes place at this time. Large numbers of neuronal processes within the brain die out every second as the brain structure changes from that of the child, with large connective redundancy, to that of the adult, which is slimmer, trimmer and more efficient. Socially, the adolescent is taking his first steps away from the family and testing out his new-found sexuality. ESP phenomena are often associated with this age group—poltergeist activity, for example, is often found to be associated with the presence of a disturbed adolescent in the family.

The preponderance of women in this sample led Dr. Hearne to speculate that this apparent female ability to foretell disaster may have been an evolutionary development in the human species, and have some survival advantage. He found that in his sample those women who had their first premonition at an early age (before twenty-one) had significantly more children than those who had their first premonition at a later age. When those fertile young women with a talent for premonition received forewarnings of disasters, they might survive by taking flight or going temporarily missing, a clear advantage for the group in replenishing its numbers after any catastrophe.

Dr. Hearne asked his subjects to fill in the Eysenck Personality Inventory (EPI), which revealed them to be significantly more neurotic than the normal population. The EPI incorporates a "lie-scale," and the mean score of the sample on this scale was also significantly higher than in the normal population. He suggested that this could mean that more emotional people were more receptive to premonitory information, and perhaps that premonitions are mediated through the primitive emotion areas of the brain. Emotional states are sometimes induced deliberately (as in voodoo practices, for example) to facilitate prophecies. On the other hand, Dr. Hearne points out that the increased neuroticism and the higher scores on the liescale in the sample could simply mean that some of the accounts were exaggerated.

THE NATURE OF PRECOGNITION

Precognitive dreams fascinate because not only do they seem to present us with a bridge across time but this bridge does not reflect our current understanding of physical processes. In physics there is an arrow of time which flows from the past to the future. Precognition in dreams raises the question that even this arrow is illusory, and that past, present and future all stand together. Precognitive dreams also throw our ideas about reality into confusion, because we are taught to regard as "real" only information which we gain from the outside world through our senses. If there is truly a non-sensory link between the "reality" of the objective outside world and our inner, subjective world, what form does it take? And how can we "know" things in the dream state that we have no knowledge of in full consciousness?

One of the main intellectual stumbling blocks to an acceptance of the idea of precognition is that foreknowledge of a future event implies that events are predetermined, and this seems to be incompatible both with the physical law of causality and the experiential principle of free will. How can we act in the present to change a future whose course is already predetermined? Parapsychologist Jon Taylor has proposed a way out of this intellectual dilemma. He suggests that people seem only to have precognitions about those events which they are not able, or do not intend, to influence. Certainly in the vast majority of cases this seems to be true. Often the dream is not specific enough to enable the dreamer to take any positive evasive action, even if he wanted to. And even it if were, in our Western culture most people would hesitate to issue, or to heed, any kind of warning on the evidence of a dream alone.

Jon Taylor observes that precognition is more likely to occur when the premonition occurs very shortly before the event it predicts, when the person's attention is focused on a future event and especially when he is emotionally involved with it. Ian Stevenson, a psychiatrist at the University of Virginia, has also suggested that although people seem to dream of impersonal disasters such as aeroplane crashes or earthquakes, nevertheless there may be some connection between the dreamer and the events he dreams, such that the event has some particular significance for him. Stevenson quotes the example of someone who had an extrasensory awareness of a distant plane crash, who had a life-long interest in aeroplanes and had wanted to be a pilot himself. There do seem, however, to be many examples of precognitive dreams of disasters in which it is difficult to make this kind of connection.

Jon Taylor has also suggested that precognitions seem only to contain elements of the future which are already familiar to the percipient. For example, while someone may dream about a person they have not seen for many years, and then meet that person the following day, there is, he claims, no reliable evidence that people dream about someone they will meet *for the first time* on the following day.

There are always difficulties in assessing the accuracy of precognitive dreams. The main stumbling block is that many dreams are so vague or general that it is difficult to link them to specific events. Memory of the dream may be patchy or faulty. When an event has happened, we may, without meaning to do so, reconstruct our memory of a dream so that it fits the facts more closely. Certainly most studies have found that when people are asked to assess their own dreams for precognitions, they find more correlations than an independent observer. In one such study (Besterman), several groups of people (including J. W. Dunne) recorded their dreams each morning and noted any possible precognitions. The subjects themselves felt that about forty-five out of a total of 430 dreams contained some sort of precognition. An independent observer believed that while a *prima facie* case could be made out for eighteen (4.2 per cent) of these dreams, for only two could a really strong case be made. However, this may be because the dreamer has more detailed knowledge of the dream and of the life event than he is able to convey when writing about it.

For a dream to be regarded as precognitive it's essential for it to be reasonably specific. The description in the dream should be of an event which is literally fulfilled, not merely symbolically foreshadowed, and the dream should have been reported to a credible witness *before* the predicted event has occurred. One also needs to know how unusual the dream was for that particular dreamer, and indeed for dreamers in general. If dreams of fire and flood are very common, for example, any apparently precognitive dream of fire or flood immediately becomes less credible.

Then there is the question of setting a time limit. With an open-ended time-frame, almost any dream may eventually be correlated with some future event. Many people dream of the death of a parent; every parent eventually dies. Most researchers specify that to qualify as precognitive, the predicted event must occur within a predefined time of the premonition. One dream researcher, N. Sondow, observed that most of her "hits" were events that occurred within one day of the dream: she noticed a steep decline in precognised events with the passage of time. If a dream predicts an event which does happen, but a long way down the line, then it must be very specific to qualify as a genuine precognition. Dunne's criterion for accepting a dream as precognitive was that two or more unusual events should occur together both in the dream and in the event it foretold. It isn't unreasonable to regard the following dream as precognitive, for example, even though the event in the dream occurred many years later. Jean T. had this dream at a time when she was worried about her father's health.

I was standing in a florist's shop choosing some flowers
for my friend. I looked around at all the flowers and was
unable to find the exact colour that I wanted. It was then
that the assistant, with some meaning, took me over into
a far corner of the shop and showed me a very unusual
display of rosebuds in an unusual vase. She looked at me
knowingly and said, "These will be for your father's
death." I was already worried about my father, and you
can imagine that this made me more uneasy.

For some time after the dream Jean was hesitant about going
into florists' shops in case she saw this flower arrangement,
which was so distinctive and unusual that she would immediately have recognised it. However, her father recovered and
it wasn't until ten years later that he fell seriously ill. One day
she was buying flowers for a friend at a flower shop that she
hadn't been to before as they had driven out into the country
on a visit. The shop seemed familiar, however, and instantly
she recognised it as the one in her dream. In some trepidation
she looked around the shop for the distinctive display, but
couldn't see it. Relieved, she asked the price of a bunch of
flowers, and when she said it was too expensive the florist said
she had a nice arrangement of rosebuds which she went into
the back of the shop to find. She brought out the identical
display to the one seen in the dream. At that moment Jean
recognised that her father's illness was terminal: he did in fact
die one month later.

Dream researchers Montague Ullman and Stanley Krippner,
whose work at the Maimonides Laboratory on dream telepathy
was described in the previous chapter, have also conducted
many experiments on dream precognition. In these experiments, they found that one of their subjects, Malcolm Bessant,
who had been most successful in the dream-telepathy experiments, also proved to have a particular talent for dream precognition.

On the nights before an experiment, Malcolm Bessant tried
to dream precognitively about an experience he would undergo the next day. During the night Malcolm was woken after
each REM period and asked to record what he had just
dreamed. The following day an assistant who had no idea what
Malcolm had dreamed the night before randomly chose a sit-

uation from a large number of possible experiences, which he would then be given. The experience would involve more than one of the senses, e.g. vision and smell, or hearing and touch, etc. He might be given some chocolate to eat while listening to music, or shown sequences of slides with a sound accompaniment. Independent judges were then shown the account of his dream and a set of eight experiences, including the one he had undergone, and were asked which experience they thought matched his dream most closely. Bessant's "hit rate" in these experiments was remarkable, reaching 88.9 percent accuracy, but no other subject achieved anything like that rate of success, and no other studies have been as successful as those carried out at the Maimonides Laboratory. In most cases, when prospective studies are carried out in which subjects are asked to record their dreams each night and then assess them or have them assessed for correlation with future events, the results are seldom very significant.

This was even the case in an experiment Dr. Keith Hearne carried out with Mrs. Barbara Garwell of Hull, who has a reputation for unusually accurate dream predictions. Her two most spectacular "hits" both occurred in 1981. In March of that year she dreamed that two men wearing Nazi SS uniforms shot a person she took to be a well-known actor, although she was uncertain of his identity, as he stepped out of a limousine. Three weeks later Ronald Reagan was shot and wounded as he stepped out of his limousine. In September 1981, Mrs. Garwell dreamed of an assassination taking place somewhere in the Middle East (the men in her dream had "coffee-coloured skins" and there was "sand nearby"). In her dream a row of dark-suited men were sitting in a stadium when two soldiers rushed up and sprayed them with automatic rifle fire. In October, three weeks after Mrs. Garwell's dream, President Anwar Sadat of Egypt was assassinated. The killing of Sadat did bear some uncanny resemblances to the dream. Sadat, wearing a dark uniform, was watching a military parade with other dignitaries from a stand. The assassins (though four in number, not two) leaped from a vehicle in the parade and sprayed the ceremonial party with automatic rifle fire, killing Sadat. In both these instances, there are witnesses who confirm that Mrs. Garwell told them about the dream before the actual events occurred.

Dr. Hearne decided to study Mrs. Garwell's predictions over the period of a year. Because of her reputation, he felt that it was reasonable to expect at least some "hits" over this length of time. Over half the predictions Mrs. Garwell had during this time were in the form of dreams; others came to her as visual images, usually as she got into bed. Independent raters compared each prediction with events reported in the local newspaper (the *Hull Daily Mail*) over the next twenty-eight days, and these events were rated according to how closely they seemed to correspond with the dream. Only three of the fifty-two premonitions were rated as having a good (five or six points of correspondence out of a maximum of eight) or very good (seven or eight points) correspondence with a subsequent event. This dream, which Mrs. Garwell had on 21 January 1982, was given seven points.

> I had a vivid dream. Ron was sat at an old table reading a paper as if he had just picked it up. The headline was "Boat broke in two—sinking." There was a picture. It was coming to England. HMS *Diddy*? I felt that it was an old one—an oil tanker as there were no portholes. It was sinking in the water. It seemed to be a Greek ship. Ron's mother said, "All the people said to me the water was boiling hot."

Just over three weeks later, on 13 February 1982, a story appeared on the front of the *Hull Daily Mail* about a Greek tanker, the *Victory*, which sank in the Atlantic after splitting in two in a severe gale. The crew had described the sea as "boiling." A final persuasive touch was that the ship was sailing from Florida to Liverpool, and "diddy" (as in Ken Dodd and the Diddy Men) is a word specifically associated with Liverpool.

Despite a disappointing hit rate in the study as a whole, there were some interesting correspondences in Mrs. Garwell's dream about HMS *Diddy*, and in two other premonitions, one in which she "saw" an attack on the Pope, another which seemed to predict the outbreak of hostilities in the Falkland Islands.

One argument put forward to account for successful precognition is that there is an emotional relationship between the individual and the events foretold. So why, in this experiment, were correspondences sought only between Mrs. Garwell's dreams and events reported in the *Hull Daily Mail*? It seems unlikely that the *Hull Daily Mail* would be full of events that had much personal significance for Mrs. Garwell. Why not look for correlations between her dreams and future events in her personal life? One reason is that it would then be much more difficult for an independent rater to assess the accuracy of the dream prediction. The rater would have to be Mrs. Garwell herself, and it is acknowledged that when people are asked to rate their own dreams they always score many more "hits" than an independent observer. It is very easy for someone to shape or manipulate events in their lives to "fit" the dream, even if they are not consciously aware that they are doing this, and of course they are bound to have a more intimate knowledge of their own lives than any independent judge.

So perhaps it shouldn't surprise us that Mrs. Garwell's hit rate was low. In fact, it is more surprising that she was successful with HMS *Diddy*, (and indeed with the Pope and the Falkland Islands). We are not told whether Mrs. Garwell was a Catholic, which would mean that an attempt on the Pope's life would have had some personal significance for her, or whether she had a son of fighting age, in which case an outbreak of hostilities in the Falklands might have evoked some emotional response.

Might the *"Diddy"* dream have been simply a fortuitous coincidence? But even supposing Mrs. Garwell had dreamt of a tanker breaking in half every night of her life, how often would such an event have been reported in the *Hull Daily Mail* in the course of a year? I suspect there would have been very few hits. The chances of a random dream occurring with a random disaster with this degree of information must be small enough to make coincidence unlikely.

PRECOGNITIONS OF DOOM AND DISASTER

A natural place to look for dream premonitions is in those dreams which occur before great national disasters, particularly those disasters which move us all emotionally: for example, where children are involved. Ian Stevenson has collected nineteen corroborated reports of people who had premonitions, several of which were in the form of dreams, of the sinking of the *Titanic*. One man, who had a passage booked on the ship, had two dreams in which he saw the ship floating upside down, with people swimming around it in the water. Interestingly, the dream didn't induce him to cancel his passage, though he did eventually do so because his business plans changed.

More than fifty million people in this country dream several dreams each night. So it is not surprising that dream predictions of doom and disaster are common, nor that they are so extraordinarily difficult to verify. Usually, like Nostradamus's prophecies, dream prophecies are so vague or couched in such general terms that it is only with hindsight that they can be linked to specific events. Open any newspaper any day and you are almost bound to find at least one report of a fire, a flood or an air disaster somewhere in the world. It is reasonable to assume that a good many people are frightened of fire, or of drowning, or are phobic about air travel, although we don't know how common it is for them to dream about their fears. However, the chances are high that such fears will sometimes surface in their dreams, and the dreamer may be tempted to make a link between the dream and some quite coincidental event. By sheer chance a few such precognitions may seem to come true, but very many more do not. Kingsley Mitchell, for example, told us about a dream he had the night before the sinking of the ferry *Estonia*.

In September 1994 I had a dream. I saw this black, terribly rough sea where the top of the waves could only be made out by the white boiling froth on the tops. Suddenly an enormous "dragon-like" head broke the water, opened an enormous mouth and let out a roar, while suddenly it swallowed tons of water including a very long black object. The head once more returned, sinking down from whence it had come, leaving only the black storm.

The following day in the fairly early hours of the morning I switched on a little transistor radio only to hear that news was coming in of a ferry in serious trouble.

Mr. Mitchell acknowledges the difficulties that there are in interpreting his dream. It is clearly non-specific; there was nothing to identify the sea monster with the ill-fated *Estonia*. What made it "fit" for him were the feelings of disaster, the swallowing-up of the "long black object" by the stormy seas—and the fact that when he switched on the radio next morning he heard of the ferry disaster. Had he not done this, would it have occurred to him to regard his dream as precognitive? Or would it simply have remained just another nightmarish dream?

He also recounted another dream he had had many years previously, which was again so non-specific that one has to accept that chance is a more probable explanation than precognition. In this dream:

> ... I found myself on a factory floor and in the centre was a large square hole with flames gushing out and various things falling in. "Factory on fire," I deduced, but I was wrong! Next morning I was to hear that a factory ship had a very serious fire in its hold.
>
> Of course the thing is with these events there's no "running commentary": "You are now standing on a ship." You have to be content with the minimum amount of information describing the scene. So that if you think it looks like a factory then when describing the event later it is a factory. Until you learn otherwise.

Even when a dream seems more specific, and even when the feelings it induces are very powerful, the dreamer seldom has the nerve to act upon it. A Canadian academic told us this story, on condition that he remain anonymous, as he has no wish to acquire the reputation of a flake amongst his colleagues.

At the time he was living in New Brunswick, three time zones ahead of the Rocky Mountains. One weekend morning he woke at half past eight, rather later than usual, from a dream which he described as being indescribably frightening, far more terrible than any nightmare he had ever had. He had been looking down on a train, which was travelling through the mountains (a part of the country which he loved and knew well). He could see the faces of the passengers and saw that they were filled with an intense terror. He knew without any shadow of a doubt that the train was going to crash.

The dream made such an impression on him that he wrote it down as soon as he woke—something he had never done before, as he had never been particularly interested in dreams. He even wondered whether he should contact the railway company but realised that he would look ridiculous and no one would be likely to believe him. So he did nothing. The next day, Sunday, he read newspaper reports of a train crash early the previous morning. The crash involved a train which had been travelling through the Rockies; it was due to a points failure, and many lives had been lost. The timing was interesting. At the actual time of the dream (5.30 local time) the train would have been in the same mountainous terrain that he had seen. However, the crash occurred three hours later, when the train had emerged on to the plain. Local time at this point was 8.30 a.m., the same "clock" time that he had had the dream. An explanation for this dream would be that when he awoke, he had precognitive knowledge that the train was going to crash, and this is what he sensed was going to happen. However, his dream had used the actual environment of the train as it passed through the Rockies.

He is certain that the dream was precognitive, and says that he has always felt guilty for not acting on the powerful feelings it induced, even though he knows rationally that it would have been highly unlikely that anyone in authority would have taken him or his dream seriously.

There have been at least two serious studies of precognition related to major disasters. Unavoidably, like all such studies, they are both retrospective; the material was collected *after* the event. But in each study, the researcher checked for corroborative evidence that the dream had been described to someone else before the event occurred, and in each study, there are at least one or two premonitory dreams which seem to offer *prima facie* evidence that precognition may indeed occur.

THE ABERFAN DISASTER

At about 9.15 a.m. on 21 October 1966, half a million tons of coal waste slithered down a hillside above the small Welsh mining village of Aberfan, engulfing the school and obliterating a generation of schoolchildren. It was a disaster so horrific, of such magnitude, that it occurred to a psychiatrist, Dr. John Barker, who visited Aberfan the next day, that it would provide an opportunity to investigate precognition. Through an appeal in the London *Evening Standard* he received seventy-six claims of precognition of the event. Of these, sixty were impressive enough for him to examine them in some detail. He concluded that thirty-five cases, of which twenty-five were in the form of dreams, could be regarded as genuine premonitions. In twenty-four cases the premonition had been related to someone else before the tragedy actually occurred. Most of the dreams occurred in the week before the disaster, and several bore a close resemblance to the actual events. One man actually saw the name "Aberfan" in his dream. One woman dreamed, a week before the tragedy of children buried by an avalanche of coal in a mining village. She woke up screaming. Another, two weeks beforehand, had a dream of a school, screaming children, and a "creeping slimy substance." Mountains, valleys, black pitch and shale, digging, buried houses, schools and children were all themes that cropped up in several of these dreams.

The two following dreams are especially remarkable in their timing (the night before the disaster), their accuracy, and the intense emotional impact the dream had on the dreamer. First, Mrs. M. H. of Barnstaple, who wrote to Dr. Barker as follows:

The night before the Aberfan disaster I dreamt of a lot of children in two rooms. After a while some of the children joined some others in an oblong-shaped room and were in different little groups. At the end of the room there were long pieces of wood or wooden bars. The children were trying somehow to get over the top or through the bars. I tried to warn someone by calling out, but before I could do so one little child just slipped out of sight. I myself was not in either of the rooms, but was watching from the corridor. The next thing in my dream was hundreds of people all running to the same place. The looks on people's faces were terrible. Some were crying and others holding handkerchiefs to their faces. It frightened me so much that it woke me up.

I wanted to get out of bed and telephone my son and his wife and ask them to take special care of my two little granddaughters. When I did get up it was 6.45 a.m. I told my brother-in-law that I had had this terrible dream and that I was going to telephone my son and daughter-in-law, but he said it was too early. I therefore waited until 8.45 a.m. and telephoned, telling them about my dream and that I was very worried as the dream was about children. I told them it wasn't our two little girls in the dream as they looked more like schoolchildren.

The dream upset me very much all the next day. I did not hear about the Aberfan disaster until 5.15 p.m.

Perhaps the saddest story is that of ten-year-old Eryl Mai Jones, one of the children who was to die in the doomed school. Note the intensity of Eryl Mai's dream—she felt she *had* to tell her mother about it, there and then. A local minister compiled this account of Eryl Mai's tragic premonition.

She was an attractive, dependable child, not given to imagination. A fortnight before the disaster she said to her mother, "Mummy, I'm not afraid to die." Her mother replied, "Why do you talk of dying, and you so young; do you want a lollipop?" "No," she said, "but I shall be with Peter and June" (schoolmates). The day before the disaster she said to her mother, "Mummy, let me tell you about my dream last night." Her mother answered gently, "Darling I've no time now. Tell me again later." The child replied, "No, Mummy, you *must* listen. I dreamt I went to school and there was no school there. Something black had come down all over it!"

Any catastrophe on this scale will inevitably generate a number of "false positive" dreams. Most dreams lack specificity and cloak their meaning in symbols. The disaster is on everyone's mind, and anybody who had a disaster dream in the preceding days would believe, after the event, that it must have referred to Aberfan.

As anyone who remembers it will confirm, the Aberfan disaster had an enormous emotional impact on the country as a whole. This was partly because children were involved. But it was also because of the anger it generated. This was a disaster that should never have happened. The public quickly became aware that the Coal Board's inspection procedures for regulating and making safe their slag tips had been totally inadequate. There was a general feeling of guilt that "we" could have allowed this to happen. In that sense almost every person in the country was involved in some way. And yet not everybody in the country in the preceding weeks had had a dream about Aberfan. What is it that singled out those people who did have premonitory dreams in such a countrywide disaster as this? Most of the dreamers had no personal connection with the disaster, no relatives or friends in the area; indeed, many had never even heard of Aberfan. Five times as many women as men reported dreams, and although several said that they had never had a similar dream in their lives, many claimed that they had had premonitions of other calamities and of events in their personal lives.

THE TETON DAM DISASTER

On 5 June 1976 the Teton Dam in eastern Idaho collapsed, causing massive flooding though little loss of life. Dr. Lucille Wood-Trost, who lived not far from the flood area, advertised through the local press, radio and television for reports of precognition of the disaster. Of the eighteen replies she received, nine were accounts of premonition in the form of dreams; one was a hypnagogic vision.

Like all studies of dreams carried out *after* an event, it is impossible to say how reliable all these accounts are. There was wide coverage of the Teton Dam flood in the media, and a wealth of information available. It is always possible that some "precognitions" were dreams which were dreamed after the event, but allocated wrongly in retrospect by the dreamer to the nights before the event. However, Dr. Wood-Trost sought evidence in every case that the dream had been reported before the bursting of the dam had occurred. One interesting point she makes is that the reports she received did not come from people who were directly and severely affected by the flood, who might be expected to be the ones to have such precognitions, certainly if there is any basis for the evolutionary survival theory put forward by Keith Hearne, or for Dr. Ian Stevenson's theory that most people's premonitions are of disasters in which they themselves have some personal involvement. But as Dr. Wood-Trost herself pointed out, even if those most closely involved did have premonitions of disaster, in the aftermath of the flood their lives and homes would have been disrupted and they themselves would have been in the state of disorientation and shock common to disaster survivors. Even if they had been aware that someone was collecting precognitive experiences, responding would be difficult and would certainly not be top of their list of immediate priorities.

Four of the dreams, and the hypnagogic vision, were certainly about floods, but there was nothing to relate them to the Teton Dam in particular. There was, for example, a flash flood in Colorado that same summer, causing many more deaths, and these dreams could equally well be said to predict that flood. However, there were four other dreams which did show more specific correspondence with what actually happened.

Case 1

A fifteen-year-old female, whose dream occurred one week before the disaster. She has had many apparent precognitions, usually trivial things such as phone calls and meeting new people. Her mother confirmed that she told the family about her dream the following day as the vacationing family drove through Sugar City.

The dream: There was a disaster in Sugar City, Idaho, causing everyone to leave. People were running and a bridge with people on it collapsed.

Correlation with actual events: Sugar City was completely evacuated and was devastated by the flood. All bridges in this town collapsed.

Case 2

A twenty-five-year-old woman who had a series of three dreams during the week before the disaster. She was the wife of one of the construction workers on the dam, and her dreams occurred after her husband had told her of a "gut feeling" he

had had that the dam was about to go. It is therefore not particularly odd that she should dream about the flood.

The dream: All her dreams were about a neighbour's goats
being washed downstream and drowned.

Correlation with actual events: The goats were indeed all
drowned. Normally they were nowhere near the water. A day
before the dam break (and *after* the dreams had occurred), the
goats were placed to pasture on an island in the Snake River.
The dreamer had no knowledge of the plan to move the goats.

Case 3

A thirty-five-year-old female whose dream occurred one week
before the event. Although she strongly believed in ESP oc-
currences she had had no personal experiences before. However, she had taken a course intended to develop paranormal
powers. Both her mother and grandmother reported many ESP
experiences.

The dream: There was a big black cloud. Everyone waited.
Water came. The dreamer was not much affected and neither
were her parents. There was a cave full of water. Her parents
went into it "as though it were a natural thing to do." The
grandmother was placed on a high campground with pillows
all around.

Correlation with actual events: The woman lived quite a
way downstream from the dam and waited for almost a day
for the waters to come. When her sister's house was flooded,
the parents went into the cellar (recognised by the woman as
the dream cave) and deeper waters. They did this to save various belongings that were stored in the cellar. The sister and
her family "camped" on the floor with blankets and pillows
at the parents' house. This resembled the high ground in the
dream. The grandmother was also there.

Case 4

A fifty- to fifty-five-year-old woman who lived in Texas but
had many relatives in the Idaho area and occasionally visited
it. Her son planned to attend college in the autumn of 1976 in
one of the flooded towns. Her dream occurred four to six hours

before the flood, and her husband, a psychologist, confirmed her story.

The dream: The dreamer and her family were going to visit her sister in Idaho. As they crossed the Snake River Bridge, huge waves began to come over it. "They were forceful and out of control and finally snapped the bridge in half." The family made it to the other side and the dreamer looked back to see people, cars, houses falling into "the raging water and the panic and confusion as others were trying to rescue those who were being swept away."

Correlation with actual events: The bridge mentioned in the dream was, in fact, destroyed.

The pattern of dream premonitions was very similar to that found in the Aberfan disaster, in that there was a gradual build-up in the number of dreams during the week before the tragedy, reaching a peak on the night before the disaster. All but one of the premonitory dreams occurred during the week before the flood, two only a few hours before. The most reliable dream predictions usually occur very shortly before the event dreamed of.

The fact that a premonition seems especially significant and meaningful is no guarantee of its accuracy. But certainly dreamers of precognitive dreams maintain that it is the dreams which appear to have special significance at the time which do indeed seem to be matched by future events. Dr. Hearne observed when working with Mrs. Garwell that she had a much stronger feeling of conviction about those premonitions that later proved to be accurate. Many other people who have premonitory dreams make a similar distinction between the thousands of ordinary dreams which any individual has in a lifetime—some of which are bound, by chance, to match future events—and the handful of dreams that are "special" and seem to be quite distinct from ordinary, everyday dreams.

In July 1987, Betty M. had a dream which seemed to her to be so significant that she lodged a copy of it with Professor John Beloff.

On 4 July 1987 I experienced one of my "special" dreams, portending an air raid in October. My immediate reaction was that I must lodge an account of the dream with John Beloff—yet the implication of the dream was so unthinkable I sought instead to dismiss it from my mind. However, the sense of significance persisted and I eventually yielded to my initial impulse and prepared the following statement, handing it to John Beloff on 12 September in a sealed envelope.

I dreamt that an air raid siren sounded. A look of dread came over the faces of the people around me. I had some sense that this scene wasn't actually happening, but belonged to another time—a playback from World War II, perhaps. Not, I silently implored, from the future . . . I seized hold of a newspaper and anxiously sought out the date; to my horror it read "October 1987."

I waited apprehensively as October proceeded. Early on the 16th a freak hurricane struck the south-east of England (including the London area where I live), catching even the weather forecasters by surprise. The scenes of devastation were reminiscent of wartime, with repeated references in the media to the Blitz of 1940. Some fifteen million trees were destroyed and thousands of buildings severely damaged. I got off comparatively lightly with a wrecked fence.

The idea of an air-raid warning, if interpreted literally, is highly appropriate—the hurricane being a *raid* by moving *air*! The allusions in the dream to World War II are also relevant. Statisticians are said to have estimated that a storm of such severity would be expected to occur only once in about 500 years in any one place.

Rather, than invoking precognition, one might argue that the weather unfolds in deterministic manner, little affected by human activity—thus allowing a clairvoyant interpretation. Conceivably, the forthcoming hurricane subsisted in the meteorological conditions months ahead of its actualisation and could *in principle* (though not in practice) have been predicted. It may be that my dread of high winds sensitised me, by direct "resonance," to the impending catastrophe.

This is an excellent dream to look at in detail, because not only was it recorded before the event, but there is an unusually accurate predicted date, of October 1987. If only Betty M. had seen the actual date of 16 October on the newspaper she looked at! This would then have been completely persuasive.

Although the hurricane is an impersonal disaster, it did have some personal connection to the dreamer. She mentions that she has a dread of high winds, and also that she lived in the area affected by the hurricane. Does it matter that the dream wasn't literally true—that there was no blitz, and no air disaster in the strict sense of the word? Most dreams do use symbolism, and there is of course a danger that by accepting dream symbolism we abandon any idea of a testable hypothesis that can be falsified, because we can interpret symbols in any way we like, creating a neat win-win situation. But anyone who saw the aftermath of the 1987 hurricane would have no problem in accepting that in this case the "blitz" analogy was close and the symbolism appropriate. In this particular case I think it would be unreasonable to dismiss the dream premonition on the grounds that it was not literally true.

PERSONAL PRECOGNITIONS

Precognitive dreams which are linked to the dreamer's personal life, or the life of someone close to him, often seem more convincing than dreams prophesying some remote or random national disaster, even though they are more difficult for an independent observer to verify. This may be partly because the connection between the dream and the event is more easily recognised and remembered than events which don't concern you personally, and also because the emotional link between dreamer and event might be expected to increase the clarity of the information received.

Most of us will have had nightmares of personal disaster from which we usually awake with a huge feeling of relief and recognition that it was only a dream. Just occasionally the feeling lingers, and even more rarely it is so strong that it colours one's feelings for the next few days. I had such a dream when I was an eight-year-old child in Kenya. With my mother, older brother and sister, I had travelled down from Mombasa to Malindi on the coast—a four-hour journey in an old wooden bus, down a dirt road in the intense heat. Because I had made a fuss about the sun streaming in through the window, I was eventually put on the shady side of the bus, while my brother and sister had to sit in the sun. But it was agreed that on the way back my brother would sit on the shady side while I would endure the sun without complaining. Of course, children always go for immediate gratification, so I accepted this.

Three days before we were due to return home, I awoke from a terrifying dream in which my brother had been in a car crash, badly hurt, perhaps even killed. Until then I had never thought about life and death, and the thought of my brother dying was so real and powerful that I asked my mother and father what life and death meant and what it would be like if my brother died. On the day of the journey I was duly given the sunny side of the bus while my brother took the shady side. I went to sleep, and so apparently did the driver, because the bus veered across the road for no obvious reason and the shady side of the bus struck a large tree close to the edge of the road. My brother received a serious head injury and was unconscious for several weeks, and other people in the bus were killed. I was never in any doubt that my dream was precognitive, the only one I have ever had.

BJ has had several precognitive dreams throughout her life. She says she has dreams, special dreams, and some that are very extra special. "In these extra-special dreams I am accompanied by a woman who always dresses the same and walks the same way with her head slightly bowed. I don't recognise her in the dreams, but when I awake I know that it's my dead sister."

BJ told us of a dream she had the night before she was to have a brain scan due to a pregnancy illness and was worried about the result:

I was in a small office with a filing cabinet in it. The top drawer opened and invisible fingers thumbed through the files. One was lifted out and opened up and my dead brother's voice, sounding very happy, said, "It's all right, Brenda, there's nothing wrong with you." The room was filled with a very bright light. I woke up and knew I was all right, and when I went to the doctor for confirmation he used the same words to me that my brother had.

It's easy to see why, in her state of anxiety about the result of her test, BJ should have had this dream—and why she should have dreamed of a happy outcome. She feels that the dream was precognitive because the words her brother used in her dream were the same as those her doctor used in reality. However, doctors have only a fairly limited vocabulary for breaking either good or bad news, and the similarity here isn't really enough to convince me. What I find most significant about this dream is the sense BJ had that everything would be all right, and the way her room was filled with a bright light. Bright light is often found in mystical dreams (see chapter 15) and is associated with inner truth. It may be that the dream was showing her some truth about herself, something that she recognised and found reassuring.

Dreams were regarded by Jung as warnings of danger. In *The Practice of Psychotherapy*, he quotes the example of a mountain climber who dreamed that he was climbing higher and higher until he finally stepped off into space. Not long afterwards he was killed in the mountains in precisely that way—a friend saw him step off into space. Should he have taken the dream as a warning? The trouble with attaching too much importance to one's dreams is that it seems likely that anyone whose lifestyle involves risk or danger must occasionally have such dreams. They can just as easily be interpreted as very reasonable indications of natural fear or apprehension as precognitive warnings. Equally one could argue that in this case the dream was prompted by suicidal thoughts, and that the climber later chose to kill himself in this particular way, or that even if it was not a deliberate act, he didn't take all the precautions a prudent climber should have done.

The following story, one of the most convincing accounts we have come across of a precognitive dream, is told by Mrs. P. Clare.

My sister, Daphne Carlyon Tweedy, was a well-known horsewoman and trained horses for show at all the big shows. One day she bought a smart green and white check coat that she liked very much. Next day she was going to drive up north to visit a man who bred horses on business, and she wanted to make a good impression. That night she had an awful dream. She was standing looking down into a ditch; in the ditch lay her dead body dressed in her new green and white coat! She woke up very frightened. Next morning the dream had faded somewhat. She really had nothing half as nice as her new coat to wear, so she decided to wear it and drive very carefully.

Some hours later she was driving along a newly tarred country road with high hedges on each side. The road was perfectly straight and free from traffic and she was driving fast. Suddenly she found herself crossing a major road. A motorcycle was coming towards her from each direction! Both bikes hit her car, which turned over on its side (it was a little Austin 7). The door next to her was jammed but it was a little open at the top and she managed to struggle out. Both motorcyclists were lying by their bikes and one of the bikes was on fire. She rushed over and managed to drag the man free from his burning bike and up on to the grass verge of the road. Then she fainted.

When she came to, she was lying in a ditch and a policeman was looking down at her. He said, "It's all right, she's not dead, she's only fainted." Her driving licence was not endorsed, nor was she blamed, as the council workmen had tarred straight across the major road, obliterating all the white road signs.

One might perhaps argue that this was a simple anxiety dream, triggered by the fact that not only was she due to make a long journey next day but was also due to meet someone on whom she wanted to make a good impression. And it is not surprising that her coat figured in the dream because it was new and meant a lot to her. But there is such a close correspondence between dream and reality that it is easier to believe that the dream was precognitive.

There are many anecdotal accounts of pre-death meetings, in which a dying person visits a friend or relative and tells him of his impending death. Philip Healey had one such dream. He was very close to his mother, and knew that she was near death. So it is not surprising that he should dream about her dying. His dream might simply be coincidence, it could be precognitive, or telepathic, or it could equally well fit into the pattern of a near-death visitation.

My mother Alice and best friend contracted dementia. My father, sister and I looked after Mum as she looked after me when I contracted multiple sclerosis, but as the illness got worse and escalated we had to put her in the nursing home. In the end she was a bag of bones, couldn't speak, lost her dignity and it was so distressing for all of us.

On the morning of 26 July I had what I can only call a dream premonition. It was in colour. I have never had a dream like it before. Mum phoned me up on the phone she liked, which was red. We had a new white one but she never liked it. She said, "Hello, Philip." I said, "Mum are you okay?" She said, "Yes, I'm all right. *But I've got to go.*" I woke up and knew it was real. The following morning she passed away. I am not a callous person but I was relieved she was out of that mental torture.

It is very common for people to dream, often with astonishing accuracy, about what is going to happen to them in the future. But do we have to presuppose psi phenomena such as precognition to account for all such dreams? If we know something about the dreamers and about the circumstances in which the dreams occurred, it's often possible to explain them in other ways. I think what we *do* have to presuppose is that the "dreaming mind" can be astonishingly acute, and that often it seems to have knowledge that at a conscious level goes entirely unnoticed. It even manages to make sure that these dreams are brought to our attention, that for the dreamer they are somehow marked out as "special" so that they stand out from the ordinary run of dreams as being more significant.

Martha was nineteen, and at the time she had this dream was helping to run a hotel's trail-riding and carriage business in America. She was working and living with the stable hands and the stable manager at Mohawk Mountain House. The dramatis personae who figured in her dream were Chris, who was the stable manager; Matthew, Tracy, and Don who, with Martha, did most of the work. The work was hard, and she was very tired.

My dream happened exactly the same way on two separate nights, two weeks apart. In the dream we were all playing tarot cards, of sorts, where you pulled a card from the deck, looked at it, and it showed you a small video of the future. We were in a circle and had all drawn the cards and were about to show them to each other. I was the last to show.

My card said, "Stable Manager" and the video was the guest book being flipped quickly so that you saw the first two horses' names on every page and the time that they could be hired out. I was shocked because this was Chris's job and if that became my future, then what of him?

Before I showed anyone I tried to stop my dream. I didn't want Chris to be angry because I was getting his job. Anyway I couldn't stop the dream at that point.

Matthew went next and his was a video of a trail-rider/photographer; then Chris went and said his new occupation was a sort of black hole. He was quite alarmed but figured it to be a mistake. Tracy's had a video of her being a waitress, and then, just as it was my turn to show, I woke up. Phew!

I didn't tell anyone about the dream. Then, two weeks later, I had the very same dream. The next day the senior assistant of the hotel called me into his office and told me that Chris was moving to another place of employment, and I was to be stable manager. He told me that this decision had been made two weeks earlier. This seemed such a coincidence to me that I asked him to check the date, and it did indeed turn out to be exactly the same day as my first dream. The whole thing was very strange, and Chris did move on, and I did become the stable manager, just as the dream predicted.

How much of this can we explain straightforwardly? It may help to know a little bit more about the background to the story. For some time before the dream, Chris had been enjoying the position of stable manager, and drawing the stable manager's (quite generous) salary, but doing very little of the actual work involved. In fact Martha had been doing his job as well as her own, while still being paid the usual stable hand's pittance. This is a situation that might have two predictable consequences. First, Martha could be expected to feel very resentful about the fact that she was doing two people's job, one of them quite a responsible job, for one person's very small salary. And secondly, the stable hands might not have been the only people to notice Chris's tendency to off-load work on to other people; there must have been a distinct possibility that he might lose his job because of it.

Martha confirmed that she had in fact been feeling angry and resentful about the way Chris was behaving. And she also confirmed that Chris didn't simply "move on" but had been fired because the people running the centre realised that he wasn't doing his job properly. She also knew that she was capable of doing the job—had been doing it in fact—and that if he did go, she was the obvious person to take over.

All this explains the actual content of the dream quite convincingly. What it doesn't explain is the timing. There were two dreams, each with a time link to the real events predicted in the dream. There are about three possible explanations for this. The "rational" view is to fall back on that old catchall, coincidence. If it had happened only once I would have found this easy to accept. But it does undoubtedly look less convincing when one has to postulate a second identical coincidence to explain a second dream. A more likely explanation is that on the days she had her dream Martha had picked up subtle cues from the hotel management team without noticing it, that something in their demeanour, or in Chris's, had suggested to her that change was in the air. The final explanation is that telepathy, clairvoyance or precognition were involved— Martha was somehow picking up the intention of the hotel management team to get rid of Chris and to promote her. And as a postscript to the dream, Martha added that Tracy did indeed leave and get a new job—as a waitress.

A TALENT FOR PREDICTION

It does seem as though there are people who have a gift for precognition who are, if you like, premonition-prone. Although a few people report just a single premonition during their lives, much more often the pattern is of multiple precognitions. There is plenty of anecdotal evidence, too, that "psi sensitivity" runs in families, and it is worth noting that in the two most prolific "dream-seers" that we have come across, dream precognition seems to be a family trait.

Fara D., therapist and medical research scientist, says that she has had this kind of dream ever since she can remember—certainly since the age of seven or eight, and that both her mother and grandmother had the same facility. Like so many other people who have experienced this phenomenon, she says that her precognitive dreams have a special recognizable quality and are quite different from ordinary run-of-the-mill dreams. They feel "portentous."

One of the most convincing of Fara's dreams had a curtain-raiser—a weird and inexplicable incident that occurred in 1985. This was not a dream—she was wide awake at the time, and in her university refectory, when she saw her brother (who was not at the university and had no reason to be there) in the queue in front of her. Saying to the friend she was with, "What on earth's my brother doing here? I must just go and talk to him," she went over to him, but he had vanished.

A year later Fara had this dream.

In my dream I saw an intensive care unit. Lying on the bed was my brother. He was wired up to various monitors, and there were holes in his chest, and a mark on his neck. The family were standing around him, though I was not there. I could hear the doctor say to my mother, "I'm sorry. He's dead."

When I woke up I felt I had to tell someone about the dream. The next morning I rang my mother to ask if my brother was all right. She said he was fine—he'd just gone to get some spare parts for his car. I told my mother I had this feeling that something terrible was going to happen and I really needed to get in touch with him. She assured me he was fine, but I was so concerned I rang him anyway, and he too told me he was fine, that there was nothing to worry about.

Three weeks later my father was involved in a terrible car accident in which two other people died. He was taken into intensive care and I went to visit him in hospital. Part of me felt that this must be what my dream was about, but I still had this feeling that it involved my brother. My brother took me to the station after I'd seen my father;

we hugged each other as we said goodbye and again I felt this was the last time I would see him.

About a week after this my brother developed a pain in his stomach. It was Ramadan and he had been fasting; he had also been trying to lift his car in order to mend it and felt that he might have strained a muscle. But to be on the safe side he went into hospital to have some tests. They could find nothing wrong, but kept him in hospital to do some further checks.

The following night I woke up sweating at about half past eleven. I felt I could hear my brother's voice saying, "Will you contact Mother?" and again I had this compelling feeling that I had to ring the hospital to find out how my brother was—even though it was my father who was seriously ill. I stopped myself dialling the hospital's number, and decided to telephone home in the morning, but I couldn't sleep.

When I rang home the next day there was no reply. I had to go to Cambridge that day but soon after my train left the station it stopped for about half an hour for no apparent reason, and again I had this compelling urge to get out and find a telephone. I left my seat and walked to the door of the train and opened the window. It was surprising to see the house my brother owned and in which I was living. This was the first time I viewed it from the train even though I frequently travelled on that route. Still agitated, I tried to relax by listening to my walkman; the tape was of "Yasin," a verse considered the heart of the Koran which refers to the hereafter and is read in ceremonies after death. Eventually, at 3.15 p.m., the train moved off again. When I reached Cambridge I finally managed to get through to my mother. She told me that my brother had died at 3.15 that afternoon.

The next day Fara travelled up to her family, and went to look at the ICU where her brother had died. Fara works in hospitals, she knows what an intensive care unit looks like—but what she saw in her dream was not just an ICU but the particular unit she had seen in her dream. The layout of the room was just as she had seen. The blood gas analysing machine was not one she was familiar with in real life, but looked just like the one in her dream. The holes in her brother's chest, a mark on his neck, were the same as she had seen in her dream. Her mother confirmed that the doctor's words were the same too. She discovered too that at about half past eleven the previous night—the time Fara had woken—her brother had felt ill and had asked if someone could contact his mother.

As a research scientist Fara is both puzzled and sometimes worried by the fact that she so often has dream predictions which prove to be accurate, and makes sure that when she has such a dream she writes it down, and also tells someone else about it. She says that the dreams tend to occur in clusters, but that she hasn't been able to find any common factor that triggers them. They don't seem to be related to diet, menstruation, good or ill health or tiredness. There is usually a time lapse of about four weeks between dream and event predicted.

Fara's mother, too, has had similar dream premonitions, of which at least one was of solid practical value. She dreamed one night that her own mother, Fara's grandmother, came and stood at the foot of her bed and said to her, "Put your dowry on or a burglar will get it." Fara's mother woke and obediently got up and put on the abundance of jewellery which formed her dowry. She returned to bed and to sleep, uncomfortably bedecked with gold necklaces, chains, brooches and bangles. During the night they were indeed burgled, but the dowry, at least, escaped.

Averil Meallen has had several precognitive dreams throughout her life. They started when she was at school. The two she remembers most clearly are, first, a dream of meeting a teacher in the school playground. The next day this meeting was re-enacted in real life—she met the teacher in the same place (apparently not a usual place to encounter a member of staff) and the conversation that followed was exactly the conversation she had in her dream. Averil says that though she might somehow have engineered an encounter with the teacher in that particular place, she doesn't believe she could have directed the conversation so accurately. As both in the dream and in reality, she was being told off for some misdemeanour, a possible rational explanation is first of all that she was feeling guilty, and that was why she had the dream in the first place, and secondly, that conversations of that nature tend to follow a quite predictable course.

Averil had the second dream she remembers from her schooldays after a maths exam. Maths was one of her best subjects—her exam marks seldom fell below eighty per cent, and she says that she felt she had done just as well as usual in this particular exam. In her dream she went into the school staff room and saw her marked paper lying on a table. She had got 59 per cent, which might have been cause for celebration for some of us, but was a disappointing result for her. When she was given the result next day, her mark was exactly that—59 per cent. It is quite easy to guess why she had that particular dream. Simply because she was good at maths, she may well have realised at a subconscious level that she hadn't done as well as usual, but was unwilling to accept this or think about the possibility at a conscious level. Anxiety induced the dream and her "dream mind" forced her to face the possibility that she probably hadn't done as well as usual. But how could she have predicted the actual mark so accurately? That is certainly something that is difficult to explain without dismissing it as coincidence, which is simply a catch-all when used this way.

Averil's daughter, too, has had some uncanny dream predictions. Both Averil and her daughter, for example, had dreams the night before A-level exams, which seem to have involved some accurate "question-spotting." In Averil's dream she saw her exam paper, noticed one question she couldn't answer, woke next morning and mugged it up before the exam. When she saw the paper, there was the question. Her daughter's experience was similar—in her dream she was told by a teacher to study a particular topic; she took the dream advice and the question came up. It isn't necessary to attribute these dream instructions to precognition—only to the ability (just as intriguing as precognition, to my mind) of the dreaming mind to "remember" yawning gaps in our knowledge and draw attention to them. But the ability to spot the question that actually came up might be precognition, or simply lucky guesswork.

However, Averil had several other dreams which are less easy to explain. Every time she was pregnant, at about the seventh month she dreamed what sex the baby would be and what it would look like. So far as sexing a baby goes, of course, in any pregnancy there is a 50 per cent chance of getting it right. But it stretches the chance odds to get it right (as Averil did) for at least three of her pregnancies. It is also interesting that she dreamed so accurately of what her babies would look like—one very dark little girl, one fair-haired blue-eyed boy, and another little girl "covered in dark hair."

Although there are numerous anecdotal accounts of people who might have hit a lottery jackpot if only they had believed the evidence of their own dreams, they usually turn out to be the dream equivalent of fishermen's tales. Gordon Moore is one of the very few people who has given us a convincing account of such a dream, verified by the colleague to whom he described it before events had confirmed its accuracy.

It was a Friday in September 1960, about six a.m. I was deeply asleep, then a dream came. In this dream I saw a football pools coupon, it was stationary for two or three seconds, then as it moved, I saw the coupon was marked with several draws *all* in the groups of numbers 15 to 30. The dream ended. My reception of it was, 80 per cent of me thought it rubbish, 20 per cent of me, perhaps there is something in it. I decided to take no action.

When I arrived at work that morning I told a colleague, Jack Clark, who sent in the office pools syndicate coupon, of the dream. He laughed and said, "What did you eat for your supper last night?"

The following day, Saturday, there were nine draws on the football pools coupon, *all* in the list of numbers 15 to 30.

Kenneth Gaskell recounts a similar experience, which was not strictly a dream, but probably occurred in a hypnagogic state on the borders of sleeping and waking. There was another important difference—Kenneth acted on the information!

It was on a Friday and the day prior to the running of the Grand National at Aintree. I was lying in bed and was just coming into wakefulness when a voice within me said, "Don't back Red Rum—back Legal Eagle." Now, I do not follow the horses, so to speak, but after such an announcement I rushed to check the newspaper to ascertain whether there was indeed such a horse listed in the runners. There was not and I promptly dismissed the matter from my mind.

After breakfast my wife and I set off to drive up to Wigan to visit my daughter and her family. When we were in the vicinity of Birmingham on the M6 we started to listen to Jimmy Young on the car radio. He was accompanied in the studio by a lawyer whom Jimmy referred to as the "Legal Eagle" since he answered listeners' questions on legal matters.

Jimmy announced, apparently rather surprised, that his secretary had entered the room. She explained that she was running a sweep and asked Jimmy and "Legal Eagle" to draw a horse. I don't remember what Jimmy drew, but "Legal Eagle" drew a horse called Lucius.

Immediately I said to my wife, "That's it, Lucius is going to win tomorrow's National."

When we arrived at my daughter's house I asked my son-in-law to place for me a modest stake on Lucius with his local bookmaker. And as history is now able to testify, Lucius did, in fact, win the Grand National at odds of 12 to 1.

I have never understood why I should have been provided with such information since I had no particular interest in the Grand National, nor, in fact, horse-racing in general. It does, however, prove to me that there are many levels of consciousness beyond those which we consider to be the norm.

This is a wonderful example of a precognitive racing tip coming true—something which is about as rare as hens' teeth. But further thought suggests that the dream has another implication. It could equally well be simply a precognitive dream about listening to Jimmy Young and hearing Legal Eagle and the racing tip. The fact that the racing tip was correct could be pure serendipity. Although the dream told Kenneth to back Legal Eagle, it didn't actually tell him which horse would win. It is human nature to regard the win as validation of the premonition, but in fact the real premonition was that he did indeed find himself listening to Legal Eagle on the radio programme. If Lucius had lost, Mr. Gaskell would have dismissed the dream as meaningless, but in fact its precognitive significance would have remained unchanged.

Amongst all the numerous surveys and investigations of dream precognition some truly convincing examples are to be found. But not all are so persuasive. Perhaps we shouldn't expect them to be. As scientists, we may be asking the wrong questions about psi phenomena such as telepathy and precognition. Perhaps the wonder of clairvoyants is, like a woman whistling or a dog standing on its hind legs, not that they do it well, or all the time, but simply that they do it at all.

The great divide between scientists and parapsychologists has always been that scientists believe that anything which is "true" should be capable of replication (and conversely that if it can't be replicated, then it was probably a chance event in the first place). Parapsychologists, on the other hand, know that parapsychological effects in experimental situations begin strongly and then weaken, and that there are both experimenter and subject effects. We can't have the same expectations of a parapsychological experiment as of, say, an experiment in physics or mechanics. The fact that the same effects can't be demonstrated every time, in every experiment, doesn't mean that there *are* no effects. We may get somewhere nearer finding out why this happens by trying to discover the conditions in which it is *most likely* to happen, by studying the experiments which *do* work.

11

Explaining the Inexplicable

There are coincidences which are so serendipitous that it seems churlish to dismiss them as merely due to chance. Jung used the term "synchronicity" to describe such happy coincidences—events that occur together in time but are not causally linked. As an example of synchronicity, here is an experience described by David Hay, Senior Lecturer in the Department of Education at Nottingham University. He had been at an all-day meeting, where he and his colleagues had been discussing a research project and had concluded that they had to find a cognitive psychologist to work with them on the project. The ideal person, somebody said, would be Dr. Margaret X (whom Dr. Hay had never met), if they could manage to persuade her. Driving home, Dr. Hay thought about Dr. X, and about how he could get in touch with her. As he entered his house, the phone was ringing. He picked it up and heard his caller say, "You don't know me, but I'm Margaret X . . ."

Whether we call it synchronicity or chance, whenever explanations are being sought for odd or paranormal events, that old stand-by coincidence must always be the first stop. Can we ever dismiss chance as a possible explanation of any psi phenomena, or are there times when coincidence itself seems as implausible as any paranormal explanation? Coincidence deserves closer scrutiny.

Why is it that some out-of-the-ordinary events are attributed to chance, others to phenomena such as clairvoyance or telepathy or precognition? Is it the nature of the experience which determines the label that is put on it? Do most people dismiss

190

single coincidences as chance, for example, while attributing two or more to some paranormal event? Or is it the nature of the observer? Researchers into the paranormal recognise the existence of "sheep" (people who are successful in paranormal experiments and find no difficulty in accepting the paranormal as an explanation) and "goats" (who block parapsychological results in parapsychological experiments, who tend to be people to whom nothing inexplicable ever happens, and who find a rational explanation for it when it does). While goats probably tend to dismiss all coincidences as due to chance, sheep are more likely to accept an explanation such as clairvoyance, precognition or telepathy. It might be supposed that many human beings have a slight natural inclination towards sheepishness, in that they like to find meaning in their lives rather than to believe they are governed by random chance, and certainly the level of belief in the paranormal which most research studies find seems to confirm this.

Telepathy and precognition are common experiences. One 1985 survey, for example (Harraldsson, 1985), found that a third of the UK population claim to have experienced telepathy. Coincidence, which we can define as the occurrence of two or more odd, inexplicable or personally meaningful events which seem to the person experiencing them to be connected, is pretty well universal. A questionnaire survey devised by Jane Henry, Senior Lecturer at the Open University, health consultant, Ruth West, and the late writer and journalist, Brian Inglis, to explore people's experience of, and attitudes towards, coincidences, and published by the *Observer* newspaper on Christmas Eve 1989, seems to confirm that these odd events play a part in most of our lives, and that in many cases chance alone does not seem a satisfactory explanation for them.

The questionnaire asked about people's coincidence experiences, whether or not these were significant, either because they were so improbable, or because they were useful or had some symbolic significance for the person concerned, and what, if any, explanation they could find for them. There were 1,000 replies, 490 men and 510 women, and the general tone of the replies was, the authors say, one of genuine curiosity about the experiences and open-mindedness about the explanation for them. Nearly all of the sample (84 per cent), but rather more women than men, said that they had had coincidence experiences which were significant, useful or personally meaningful to them.

By far the most common type of experience was the kind of synchronicity described by David Hay. Three-quarters of the sample reported spontaneous association (as when you are singing a particular song and switch on the radio to find it being played). Almost as common was the kind of "small-world" encounter where you meet your bank manager coming up the Grand Canyon as you are on your way down. Two-thirds of the sample had had this kind of experience. About half the sample had had "cluster" experiences—coincidences involving a cluster or sequence of related names, numbers or events, such as going to a race meeting on the third day of March (the third month), and backing the third horse in the third race which comes in, unfortunately, third.

About two-fifths of the sample claimed to have had ESP-type coincidences, knowing about something that is separated from you by either space (telepathy or clairvoyance) or time (precognition). And a similar number had had coincidences where a problem appeared to have been solved by a "hidden hand." This is the type of experience where you are, for example, looking for a particular book in a large crowded book-case and it suddenly falls off the shelf on to the floor in front of you.

What was interesting was the way the people who had these experiences accounted for them. Given a list of possible causes and asked to indicate which of these they believed might explain or have influenced their experiences, the most popular explanation given was "intuition" (71 per cent said intuition was involved, 10 per cent that it was not, 19 per cent did not know). This was closely followed by psi (ESP): 64 per cent believed this was a factor and only 7 per cent were prepared to say that it was not, though 29 per cent said they did not know. Chance came in third place: 60 per cent of the sample felt it played a part. About half the sample cited destiny, fate or karma; rather fewer mentioned divine or diabolical intervention or planetary influences.

THE CASE FOR PARAPSYCHOLOGY

Parapsychology is the study of various unusual phenomena such as telepathy and precognition, which are common in human experience and yet are difficult to explain using current scientific models. Ten years ago a serious scientist would have hesitated even to broach the notion that parapsychology was a concept to be taken seriously. It is a strong statement to say that there is now good scientific evidence that parapsychological phenomena occur. But any reasonable and openminded scientist who is willing to spend a few moments actually looking at the data should at least be convinced that the study of parapsychology has moved from the position of wondering whether or not it exists, to looking for a theory to explain phenomena which have been scientifically shown to happen.

If telepathy and precognition exist at all, then there is no reason why they should not operate in dreams. In fact there are good reasons why they should, because as we shall see, there is some evidence that dreaming is a state in which people are particularly likely to be open to psi phenomena.

A parapsychological experiment will never be repeatable in the way that a simple scientific experiment to show that, say, the frequency of a pendulum varies with its length is repeatable. You won't get the same effect every time. Too many variables are involved, as they are in any experiment which is concerned with people and behaviour. As yet we don't understand all these variables, and we don't know how to control for them. It has to be accepted that parapsychogical effects are both small and unpredictable. Experiments work for some people, not for others, they work sometimes, under some conditions, not at other times or under other conditions. Motivation is important too, and this varies from time to time; people cannot always control their motivation. Even the "best" clairvoyants don't claim a 100 per cent hit rate.

So it isn't appropriate to use repeatability in the old scientific sense as a criterion of success. What we need to know is whether parapsychological phenomena exist at all, and the most reliable way to judge this is by using statistical evidence.

The question that must always be asked is whether the success rate of an experiment is greater than might be expected by chance. It is possible to calculate the statistical probability of an event occurring by chance alone. Clearly if the odds are high that it is occurring by chance, then one must accept that chance is the most likely explanation. If the odds are low that this pattern of results could be found by chance alone, then one is more likely to accept that a psi effect is operating. The level at which you decide whether or not chance is operating is arbitrary, but there are standards which are used throughout science, and these can be applied to psi as well as they can to standard science. If the pattern of results from a parapsychological experiment is such that it could only be found one time in twenty by chance, then it is more likely that a psi effect is occurring than that the results are due to chance alone. This is a significant level of 5 per cent. If the pattern of results is one that might be seen only one time in 100 by chance alone then, clearly, chance is even less likely to be an explanation. In many psi experiments the pattern of significance is very much higher than that, so that the particular pattern found could only occur by chance in one in 1,000 or 1 in 10,000 times. In these circumstances it is very difficult to argue that the results are simply due to chance; much more likely is that they are due to an effect of some kind and, if the experiment is properly designed, that the effect is indeed a psi effect.

Almost all of us underestimate the role of chance in explaining the inexplicable. Mathematician John Allen Paulos has pointed out in his book *Innumeracy: Mathematical Illiteracy and its Consequences* that many apparently precognitive dreams must occur each year on the basis of chance alone. Supposing we define a dream as precognitive if the chances of it "coming true" and matching some future event are as low as one chance in 10,000. We can assume that everyone has one dream a night (in fact we have many more). So although during the course of a year there is only a slim chance that any single person will have such a dream, of the whole population around 3.6 per cent will do so.

This makes mathematical sense. But in reality it isn't quite that simple. For a dream to be convincingly precognitive we need not just a single dream event, but more than one occurring together as a cluster. It is not enough, for example, to dream that you have seen a horse winning a race. You have to know that a particular runner (number 13, for example) has won a particular race (for example, the Grand National). One is dealing with multiple probabilities and not with a single chance, and this racks up the odds against it occurring by chance to many more than one in 10,000.

The statistical method of analysis presents other problems for psi researchers. Any single experiment has a large chance of failure, and most researchers do not have the time or the resources to carry out the huge numbers of experiments needed to produce a clear statistical picture. The solution is to use a method of assessing repeatability called "meta-analysis," which integrates research results of numerous independent experiments. In the last ten years meta-analyses have been carried out on many psi experiments, and have shown that in many cases there have been results which can only be convincingly explained by the existence of psi.

THE GANZFELD EXPERIMENTS

The most persuasive evidence for the existence of psi phenomena comes from a series of experiments, the Ganzfeld ("whole-field") experiments, which are particularly interesting as they relate most closely to telepathy experienced in dreams. Before the experiment starts, the telepathic "receiver" is put into a state designed to reduce all sensory stimulation. He is made to lie on a comfortable bed in a warm, sound-attenuated room. Half ping-pong balls are put over his eyes to remove patterned vision. Often cotton wool is wound round his hands to reduce sensory stimulation to a minimum. It is argued that in this state, called the Ganzfeld state, the brain's inputs from the body sensors are reduced and the mind is allowed to freewheel. In this relatively quiet environment, telepathic information is thought to be received more easily.

In another room, quite isolated from the receiver, the telepathic "sender" is shown a video clip or still picture and asked to send the image to the receiver mentally, usually over a period of about 20–40 minutes. Meanwhile, the receiver is asked to give a continuous commentary on all the visual images, thoughts and feelings that are passing through his mind. At the end of the sending period, the receiver is taken out of the Ganzfeld state and shown four different pictures or videos. He is asked to decide which of these is the true target image, on the basis of the perceptions he experienced during the Ganzfeld state. By chance alone a hit rate of 25 percent—one in four—would be predicted. In fact about 700 such experiments, conducted worldwide by about a dozen investigators have shown that the target is hit on average 34 percent of the time, much higher than the chance hit rate, and statistically highly significant.

But the difficulties for the scientist don't end there. Even if the evidence that mind may directly affect mind and mind may directly affect matter is approaching a point where you would have to be the modern equivalent of a medieval flat-earther to reject it, science still has no theory to explain it.

We know that the brain is continually building models based on information transferred within the neural nets. We know how neurones function and what information they must have to produce a cognitive experience. But we have, as yet, no theoretical basis to explain how such models come into consciousness, and we don't fully understand the relationship between thoughts and feelings and brain function. This lack of knowledge also creates difficulties for us when we come to look at parapsychological phenomena.

Let us assume for the moment that the dream state really is a psychically sensitive one and see whether we can find any explanation for this. One possibility is that psi signals are often present in the brain. But in a normal waking state we are focused on the outside world; the noise of normal sensory input makes it difficult to attend to cues and information from these other sources, even though they may be available for us.

In the dream state, of course, we are very thoroughly detached from any inputs from the outside world and so are perhaps more open to receiving psi information. The evidence of the Ganzfeld experiments seems to support this view—in fact dreaming, a state in which sensory input from the outside world is cut to a minimum, would seem to be an ideal state to receive telepathic transmissions.

Precognition is more difficult to explain because we have to enter the field of causality. In physics, time can run either forwards or backwards, with equal facility. But in the real world time has a definite direction: it goes from the past to the future. It is argued that this is because on a macro scale statistical processes occur and these are not reversible. Consider what happens to an egg when it is struck with a hammer. The change is irreversible. On the other hand, when two billiard balls bounce against each other, the process can be easily reversed. In precognition, information from the future seems in some way to travel into the present. Does this information originate from a sender (i.e., is it a mind-to-mind message) or does it originate from the event itself (a matter-to-mind message)? There is no way we can answer this satisfactorily. Whatever the precognised event, someone at the time would know about it. What about trivial events of which no one knows? In this case, of course, the question is nonsensical, because it is impossible to prove precognition of an event no one is ever going to know about.

CHICKENS DON'T CHEAT

If psi phenomena exist at all it is highly unlikely that they will be found only in man, as they will be a property of nature. It is not possible to set up experiments in animals to see whether or not psi phenomena occur while the animal is dreaming, but it is possible to do this when it is awake. Dr. René Peoch is a parapsychologist working at Foundation ODIER in Nantes who has spent the last fifteen years studying animal psychokinesis and telepathy, using chicks and rabbits. There are advantages in conducting parasychological experiments using animals, because at least the question of cheating by the subjects (always raised to discount parapsychological effects) can be ruled out. Chickens don't cheat. Rabbits can't be accused of colluding with the experimenter.

Dr. Peoch has, for example, demonstrated what appears to be telepathy between rabbits Two young rabbit kittens who were litter mates and had been brought up together for six months were put into separate rooms. A blood pressure transducer was placed on an ear of each rabbit. If one rabbit was frightened so that its blood pressure fell, a correlated fall occurred in its sibling. However, if the two rabbits were not siblings and had not been brought up together, this did not happen. "Telepathy" only occurred if the rabbits had a close "empathic" connection.

One of Dr. Peoch's most intriguing experiments concerned

the ability of chickens to influence a random number genera-tor. It is intriguing because it deals with the question of cau-sality, and shows just how complicated that question is. He programmed a mechanical robot to receive a code from a ran-dom number generator inside it. The code instructed the robot to make random movements. The robot was then put in an experimental area in which chickens were about to hatch. The robot was the first thing the chickens saw when they hatched, and they imprinted on it as if it was their mother, and treated it as their "mother," following it freely around the area in its random walk. After they had lived with the robot for three days the chicks were taken away and in their absence the movements of the robot were recalibrated to make sure that it was still moving randomly. A chick was then reintroduced to the experimental area in a cage so that it was able to see the robot, but not to follow it. It was observed that the movements of the robot became less random; it spent more time close to the chick than it did elsewhere in the area. It seemed as if the chick was influencing the random number generator of the robot so that the sequence of numbers generated was no longer random but one which programmed the robot to move nearer to the chick.

In a second generation of robots, the instructions for the movements of the robot were generated by a computer not inside the robot, but away from the experimental area. This made no difference. The chick still seemed able to influence the robot to spend more time in its vicinity. Chicks which had not imprinted on the robot had no effect on its movement at all. An "empathic" relationship between chick and robot seemed to be necessary for the effect to occur.

However, now we come back to causality. One of the most intriguing aspects of Dr. Peoch's experiment is the implication that time in parapsychological experiments is different from everyday time. In another experiment, the string of random numbers which instructed the robot to move randomly was generated by a computer six months before the experiment took place. This string of numbers was not examined, but stored on disk. When the experiment was carried out six months later, it was decided to use the first half of this code to programme the robot and the second half of the code as a control, to make sure the original number generator was working randomly (until that time no one knew which of the numbers would be used to programme the robot). But when the chick influenced the robot to come towards it, the robot was of course no longer moving randomly. When the string of numbers was examined, its first half, used to programme the robot, was found to be non-random and showed more codes for moving the robot nearer to the chick. But the second half of the stored code, which had not been used in the experiment, still showed a random pattern. It was as if the computer ''knew,'' six months before the experiment, when it was generating the codes, that the first half of the codes were going to be used in a parapyschological experiment and were to be generated in a non-random fashion, whereas the second half of the codes were to be used as a control and were to remain random. Clearly this contradicts the rules of causality and time as we understand them.

If this is really so (and other workers claim to have repeated the experiment), it argues for a very different type of causality and a very different view of time from the one we normally have. It would mean that there is a strong interconnectedness between present and future events, a connection which would make precognition in dreams more credible. But we still have to explain the kind of connection it could be. One explanation is J. W. Dunne's, which suggests that the dreamer stands outside the flow of time and can see both forwards and backwards in time, thus gaining access to information about events that are about to occur. He does not explain whether knowledge of the future allows one to interact with the future and alter its outcome—a crucial point if precognition is to be of any use to us whatsoever. Einstein's theory of relativity presents yet another view of time—that it is one dimension of the structure of the universe (space—time) and not a simple linear function.

Another explanation is that there is an underlying psychic field, the nature of which has yet to be defined, but which links past, present and future. Modern physics suggests that at the quantum level there is a high degree of connection between every particle in the universe, and thus an alteration in matter in one part of the universe affects every other particle to a greater or lesser extent throughout the universe. A modification of this theory could clearly be used to explain both telepathy and other psi effects.

There are some non-mainstream theories in quantum mechanics which could be used to explain a different causality from the one normally accepted by Newtonian physics. Some physicists deny the structure of time as we understand it, a few even going so far as to say there is no such thing as time. Clearly physics is ahead of the game and is already questioning some of our intuitive Newtonian notions about the structure of the universe and its causal principles. But at the moment, although there is good scientific evidence for telepathy, and some scientific support for precognition, science cannot offer any explanation for these phenomena.

HYPERMNESIC DREAMS

Not all dreams which seem to be precognitive demand that we abandon our notions of time, of past and present and future. Dreams are a patchwork of memories, and the ragbag from which we draw them contains not just the memorable and the half-forgotten, but also fragments of perceptions so swift or so trivial that they may not even reach consciousness at all. It is quite possible, therefore, for us to dream dreams which seem to contain information which we believe that we had no previous knowledge of at all. These are called hypermnesic dreams. Alfred Maury, a nineteenth-century French investigator of dreams, describes one such dream.

I passed the first few years of my life at Meaux, and often went to a neighbouring village named Trilport, situated on the Marne, where my father was building a bridge. Some months ago I found myself in a dream transported back to the days of my childhood and playing in the village of Trilport; I saw a man dressed in a kind of uniform, and I addressed him, asking his name. He told me that he was called C, and was the guard of the bridge. He disappeared, to be replaced by other figures. I woke up with the name C in my head. Was it pure imagination or was there really a guard by the name of C at Trilport? I did not know, for I had no memory of such a name. Some time afterward, I questioned an old servant who had once worked for my father and often drove me to Trilport. I asked her if she remembered an individual named C. Immediately she replied that he had been a guard on the bridge over the Marne at the time when my father was constructing the bridge. I must obviously have known this as well as she did, but my memory of it had been forgotten. The dream had brought it into my mind as if it were something I did not know.

Hervey de Saint-Denys (1822–92), a French scholar who made a study of his own dreams, described another hypermnesic dream.

I had a clear, continuous and precise dream in which I imagined myself in Brussels (which I had never visited). I was walking unhurriedly along an animated street with numerous shops on either side and multicoloured signs projecting over the heads of the passers-by. "This is very odd," I said to myself. "It is really impossible to suppose that my imagination is inventing so many details all by itself. Nor can I accept the oriental belief that the mind travels by itself while the body is asleep. I have never been to Brussels, and yet there is the famous church of Saint-Gudule in the distance which is familiar to me from engravings. I have no feeling of ever having been along this street before, wherever it may be. If my memory can retain such detailed impressions without my mind even knowing it, the fact is certainly worth recording, and it would be interesting to try to verify it. The main thing is to have concrete details to work on and therefore to observe closely what I am seeing." Immediately I began to examine one of the shops in minute detail, so that if I was able to recognise it one day there could be no doubt as to its identity. The shop in question was a hosier's and the first thing I noticed was its sign, which consisted of two folded arms, one red and the other white, extending over the street, bearing like a crown an enormous striped nightcap. I read the name of the shop several times to imprint it on my memory. I noted the street number and a small arched doorway decorated at the top with intertwined numerals. Then I shook myself awake with that sudden effort of will that we can always make when we feel we are asleep, and hastened to note and draw details carefully before the vivid impressions faded. I was to visit Brussels some months later, and I intended at all costs to clear up a phenomenon which at first, in spite of myself, created in me these fantastic imaginings. With unbearable impatience, I waited for the time my family was to go to Belgium. When it came, I hurried to the church of Saint-Gudule, which now seemed like an old acquaintance; but when I looked for the street with all the different signs and the shop of my dreams I found nothing remotely resembling it. In vain I walked methodically through all the shopping areas of that attractive town. Finally I was forced to recognise that further investigation was useless, and resignedly I gave up the search . . .

Some years later, when Saint-Denys had almost forgotten this episode, he went to Frankfurt, a city he had visited in his youth.

. . . a whole series of indefinable memories began vaguely to fill my mind. I tried to discover the cause of this curious impression, and all at once I remembered the object of my useless walks through Brussels. Saint-Gudule was no longer to be seen in the distance, but this was indeed the street I had drawn in my dream diary—the same odd street sights, the same people, the same animation that had struck me so forcibly in my dream. As I have said, I examined one particular house in minute detail. Its appearance and street number were engraved on my memory, and with mounting excitement I hurried to look for it . . . Imagine my mingled pleasure and astonishment when I found myself in front of a shop so exactly like the one in my dream that I seemed almost to have travelled back six years in time without waking up . . . Obviously I had already walked down this street on my first visit to Frankfurt three or four years ago before the time of the dream; and without my knowing or being able to explain the conditions on which this depended, all the details I had seen had been photographed by my memory with the utmost precision. Yet, since I had no conscious recollection of the scene at all, my attention, in the sense we normally give this word, had remained untouched by this mysterious and spontaneous process.

Clearly the dreaming mind has access to memories which the waking mind (even when "prompted" in this way by the dream) does not, or, to be more precise, cannot call up voluntarily. A very similar phenomenon in the waking mind is called cryptamnesia. There are astonishing reports of adults who reproduce childhood memories that they have no conscious knowledge of, so that they seem to know things they have no way of knowing. One such case was a woman who had never been taught Latin and claimed she had never seen a Latin text, and yet was able to recite long tracts of Virgil. It was finally discovered that she had seen the text in a book in her father's library which she had looked at as a child, never consciously learned and subsequently forgotten that she had ever seen.

Only a few people have this kind of photographic memory, called eidetic memory, which enables them to look at a page of a book and later recall and read the image of the page from memory. Our current view of memory is not that it acts like a photograph, as it seems to do in Saint-Denys's dream, but that it uses material stored in memory to reconstruct the scene for us. That is why the reconstruction is never exactly the same as the reality. Witnesses to a traffic accident all give different stories because they all reconstruct the scene slightly differently. If their memory simply recorded the information as if it was a photographic process, their descriptions of the scene would be much more likely to tally. Our ability to recall particular memories depends on our current state and the state we were in when we laid down the memory traces. An actor may find that he suffers from stage fright, his mind a total blank, because the lines he learned when relaxed beside the fire at home are just not accessible when he has to reproduce them in a state of anxiety in front of an audience.

PSI PHENOMENA AND GEOMAGNETIC ACTIVITY

Psi activity is notoriously variable. One explanation that has been put forward to account for this is that there is a relationship between the accuracy of psi phenomena such as remote viewing or telepathy, and patterns of geomagnetic activity. It has been suggested that spontaneous telepathic experiences occur most often during days in which global geomagnetic activity is significantly lower than on the days before or after the experience. However, it is never possible to be sure that correlation means causation. Just because two events are related in time does not mean that one causes the other. It is also difficult to assess the significance of any changes in natural background radiation as these are often smaller than, and swamped by, electromagnetic pollution from electrical equipment in cities. Nevertheless there does appear to be a relationship between ESP and geoelectro/magnetic changes.

Stanley Krippner and Michael Persinger, a Canadian neuroscientist, researchers at the Maimonides Dream Laboratory, decided to test this theory by analysing the results of the many experiments in dream telepathy that were carried out at the laboratory during the 1960s. They selected the first night that each subject in a telepathy experiment had visited the laboratory, and matched the results of these nights with geomagnetic data. They discovered that the subjects' most accurate telepathic dreams had occurred during periods of significantly quieter global magnetic activity, rather than on nights marked by electrical storms and high sunspot activity (Persinger and Krippner, 1989; Krippner and Persinger, 1996).

Because records of global geomagnetic activity have been kept since 1868 they were also able to analyse a collection of spontaneous telepathic dreams described in *Phantasms of the Living* (Myers *et al.*, 1886) to see whether they could find a similar correlation. Here too they found the same pattern—the most accurate telepathic dreams had occurred during periods of low geomagnetic activity.

Krippner and Persinger suggested several possible explanations for the observation that quieter geomagnetic activity seems to facilitate telepathy. First, that the environmental conditions at such times promote exchange of information between the sender and the recipient. Secondly, that normal "telepathic factors," factors which are already in the environment, are amplified between the sender and the recipient. Thirdly, that the normal telepathic factors present in the environment don't change, but that there are transient alterations in brain function which can affect the recipient's sensitised temporal lobes.

In the mythology of dreaming, certain places have always had strong associations with significant or prophetic dreams. In the classical world, for example, the sick would sleep at temples dedicated to the god of healing, in the hope that he might visit them in a therapeutic dream. The idea that geomagnetic activity might have some influence on the dreams that were dreamed at these sites prompted an interesting research programme by the Dragon Project, an Anglo-American collaboration set up in 1990 (and still ongoing), to study ancient sites, and especially to look at the natural radiation, magnetism and other environmental factors at such sites, and to see how these might affect people using the site.

Dr. Paul Devereux and his colleagues examined several well-known sites, including the oracle at Delphi, and found either a higher than normal background radiation level of the stones which formed the pillow for the sleeper, or a marked alteration in the magnetic field of the stone pillow. One such stone had a north pole on both sides indicating a complex internal magnetic field structure. They also looked at the background radiation of some of the stone circles in England, and found that some of the standing stones had a much higher than normal level of background radiation. One of Dr. Devereux's colleagues experienced an altered state of consciousness while standing near one particular stone. On checking this stone with a Geiger counter it was found to be the stone with the highest level of radiation in the circle.

The notion that prophetic dreams might be triggered by some natural factor related to the site itself prompted the Dragon Project to include a dreamwork programme. Four ancient sites in the United Kingdom were chosen; one in Wales—a sacred mountain with a strong magnetic anomaly; and three in Cornwall—a Neolithic stone chamber, an Iron Age underground passage, and a Celtic Christian holy well. Volunteers have been asked to sleep at these sites to see if any site-specific content recurs in their dreams. When the sleeper is seen to be in REM sleep, he is woken, and immediately asked to record on audiotape what he was dreaming. The recorded dreams are being transcribed on to a computer database, and the transcribed accounts sent to Dr. Stanley Krippner at the Saybrook Institute in San Francisco for analysis. The site accounts are compared with ordinary dreams, dreamed at home and recorded by the volunteers. An extensive database of dreams will eventually be available for each site, and its analysis should show whether the dreams that are dreamed by different people at each site contain any common recurring characteristics, symbols or images that seem to be specific to that site.

Let us suppose, just for a moment, that they do. What would the implications be? The most rational explanation would be that the place itself induces feelings, thoughts and emotions which conjure up a specific picture. However, this would not explain precognitive or telepathic dreams. To explain these, one needs a wider framework than current science can provide—a theory that could explain the possibility that mind can exist or memory be stored outside brain processes.

Such theories do exist. The first group are the ''field theories,'' which suggest that there is in the universe some ''field force'' which links individual minds. The existence of a ''psi field,'' mediating psi phenomena, has frequently been postulated, though no one has ever managed to produce a theoretical framework to support it, or any real evidence that it exists. Jung's concept of the collective unconscious is another field theory. He suggested that part of the mind exists beyond individual brains and is a reservoir of human experience inherited from ancestors, independent of time and place.

Biochemist and cell biologist Rupert Sheldrake's theory of morphic resonance is a field theory which attempts to explain how memory might exist independently of an individual brain and could be accessed by other brains. He postulates the existence of ''morphogenetic fields,'' which he suggests are part of the structure of the universe, existing everywhere at once. It is thus possible for matter to be influenced by a morphogenetic field at the same time in widely separate areas. He suggests that information relating to a pattern of behaviour can be transmitted from the brain to the morphogenetic field and modify it. The field in turn will modify other similar brains so that they become more likely to reproduce this particular pattern of behaviour. He uses this theory to explain why scientists working in different laboratories and not in contact with each other often tend to make the same discoveries at more or less the same time.

The only field theory for which there is any scientific evidence has been postulated by a Mexican psychologist, Jacobo Grinberg-Zylberbaum. He has suggested that the electromagnetic fields which are produced in the brain by the passage of nerve impulses in some way interact with the fabric of space, allowing the transmission of an effect from one brain to the next. The transmission is strongest when the two people are in similar states, for example, having strong empathic feelings for each other. He has managed to show that the electrical response of one brain to tone pips can be transmitted to another brain, out of earshot.

Another view argues that the brain does not *create* consciousness, but acts as a transmitter for a beam of consciousness which has its origins outside the brain, and that mind and brain are different but linked together in some way. Sense data is transformed by the brain for transmission to an external mind. Mind in its turn can will an action, transmit it to the brain and so initiate brain processes and actions. Although memories are held partly within the brain, a large part of memory is stored external to the brain, and in this personal identity is located.

Transmission theories have always been popular, largely because many people find very appealing the notion that personal identity might exist independently of the body. Transmission theories allow the possibility of soul, personal survival, clairvoyance, telepathy—almost all of the phenomena which so puzzle and intrigue us. Exponents of some version of the transmission theory stretch from Descartes, to William James in the last century, through to Sir John Eccles, one of this century's most distinguished neurophysiologists and a Nobel laureate, who suggested that at the interface between brain and mind, the "dendron" (a hypothetical region of the nerve cell processes of the brain) links with the "psychon" (the hypothetical atom of mind). Despite its illustrious source, the theory has failed to gain ground because no one has yet managed to prove the existence of either dendrons or psychons.

In fact there is no evidence to support any of these transmission theories, any more than there is to confirm the existence of a field which might mediate psi phenomena. All these theories remain, for the moment, entirely speculative. One is, finally, driven to the conclusion that our science is not yet adequate to explain these phenomena. If science does indeed ever find a satisfactory way to encompass them, it would significantly change our understanding of the world in which we live. Perhaps this must be the role of a new non-Galilean science for the twenty-first century.

12

Night Visitors and Visions

British teenager abducted by "Greys"
Headline in the Winter 1994 issue of *Flying Saucer Review*

This incident was not, as you might suppose, the result of a few Guards officers getting out of hand after a regimental dinner, but a reported abduction by "bug-eyed" aliens. The victim, Elaine Marks of Farnham, was woken by a sound like branches knocking against her bedroom window. Because there were no trees or bushes anywhere nearby she became frightened and called out to her mother, who came to sleep in the bed next to hers. She then saw green and red lights shining in from outside and tried to call out to her mother, but found herself unable to speak and becoming gradually paralysed from her legs upwards.

Suddenly everything went black, and I found myself on a type of thick metal table with three or four "people" round me. Their eyes were large, oval and black and filled up a lot of their face. They were quite skinny and had the same type of build as humans, although they were quite a bit shorter, I'd say about five feet tall.
They weren't wearing anything, I think, but they looked as though they had on very tight catsuits, which were plain light turquoise and fitted to them as though it was their skin, so it must have been their own skin. They didn't speak at all—they just looked at each other awkwardly. I screamed, but the scream didn't come from me

209

lying on the table. It came from somewhere in the distance. Everything went black again and I found myself lying in my bed again and I felt myself gradually being able to move again. I called out to my mum and I felt a bit sick.

Since then, Elaine has had other similar visitations by aliens but only, she says, "when I feel paralysed and feel I'm falling, but I always seem to fall asleep straight after it and only remember the next morning that it happened yet again."

Reports of human abductions by small, unpleasant aliens are rare in Europe and most other parts of the world, but over the last two decades they have reached almost epidemic proportions in the United States. The visitation is often at night, when the victim is lying in bed. The abductees always return to tell the tale, and although the details of their stories vary, they have many features in common. The abductors are humanoid, though clearly not human (the "Grey" described by Elaine Marks—a short, huge-eyed, dark-skinned creature—is typical), and their victim is usually transported in some mysterious way to a room in which he is made to lie prone and helpless whilst undergoing some sexual or quasi-surgical intervention such as an operation or implant. Sometimes, before being returned, just as mysteriously, to his starting point, he will be given a warning of some apocalyptic disaster facing the human race.

Although these alien kidnappings are relatively recent they seem to be a modern manifestation of a much older phenomenon. It was, for example, the practice of the ancient Greeks to seek healing by sleeping at the site of a holy shrine associated with healing, in the hope of a visitation by Asclepius, the god of healing. Surviving tablets from the temples of Asclepius at Epidaurus describe dreams in which the god, or various of his attendants, performed operations on the sick sleeping person.

In medieval times night visitors were more likely to be devilish than divine: the medieval parallel to the visitor from outer space was the incubus or succubus—a devil who took human form (the incubus took the form of a man, the succubus of a woman), and consorted with humans whilst they slept.

Fairies, too, have a long folk history as alien abductors.

Iolanthe, of the eponymous Gilbert and Sullivan opera, was by no means the first or the only young woman to be taken away by the fairies as a baby. It used to be believed that infants were sometimes stolen from their cradles before they were christened, and in the highlands of Scotland babies were carefully watched over until the christening was safely over. Parents of an ill-favoured, stupid, weak or sickly child could take comfort in the belief that the infant hadn't simply inherited the least desirable family traits but was a changeling, substituted by fairies or demons for their own normal, beautiful, highly intelligent offspring.

In fact, stories of night visitations by some evil presence that presses on its terrified victims so that they are paralysed and unable to breathe, or escape, or abductions by strange little people, have been part of folk mythology for centuries. Compare this account by Paracelsus, the Swiss alchemist, written during the first half of the sixteenth century, with the story of Elaine's nocturnal visitors.

> ... some people, especially women in child-bed, have been so oppressed in the night in their sleep that they have thought themselves to be as it were strangled. Neither could they possibly cry out, or call any help, but in the Morning have reported that they were Ridden by a Hag: And they are still accounted to be witches or Inchanters that do this; whereas their bodies cannot possibly enter in the chambers, where the doors and Windows are shut; but the Sylphes and Nymphes easily can.

The fact that these tales have been so widespread in folklore for so long suggests that many of these strange beliefs have their origin in actual human experience. David Hufford, an American psychologist working in Newfoundland, decided to test this theory. In Newfoundland the evil night visitor is traditionally known as "Old Hag." Dr. Hufford devised a questionnaire designed to discover whether belief in the Old Hag legend in Newfoundland was reflected in people's experience. He gave the questionnaire to students in his lecture classes, and found that 23 percent reported that they had had the experience of waking up and finding themselves unable to move. When they were asked to write brief accounts of their experience, many insisted that they were awake and aware of their surroundings at the time, and described impressions of a presence, or of hearing footsteps, seeing amorphous figures, or being pressed down on the bed as they lay on their backs. To show that these experiences are not simply the by-product of a superstitious belief, Hufford then went on to collect other very similar accounts when working in the United States, where the Old Hag legend is largely unknown.

What we are looking at is a common experience, which may be interpreted by the victim in many different ways, in the light of some personal belief or superstition. Whether the night visitor is thought to be Old Hag, or angels, or fairies, or that latter-day intruder, the alien from outer space, the elements of the actual experience and the feelings it evokes seem to be remarkably consistent. The sleeper wakes in terror, with the feeling that a heavy weight is crushing his chest. Although he is awake he is paralysed, unable to move or speak. And often he sees strange, frightening images. The visual images tend to be a reflection of personal belief or culture, and so tend to differ between people and cultures. In medieval times, when rats were omnipresent and a perpetual danger because of the plague they carried, the night visitors were often huge rats, intent on devouring the victim. Even today, rats remain an archetypal nightmare image.

As we saw in chapter 2, during dreaming sleep the cortex of the brain is aroused, but the muscles are paralysed. Usually when we awake these two processes stop together; by the time waking consciousness returns, the paralysis of dreaming sleep has gone. Similarly, once we awake, the rich imagery of dreaming sleep vanishes. But sometimes the awakening process does not go through to completion, and either the paralysis or the dream imagery, or both, is experienced as part of waking consciousness. Sleep paralysis can also occasionally occur at sleep onset. Here the sleeper goes straight into dreaming or REM sleep with the accompanying paralysis and REM imagery, but with wakefulness still maintained.

The classic "incubus attack," when the sleeper wakes to feel a crushing weight on his chest, usually occurs during an arousal from REM sleep. This is most commonly seen in a sleep disorder called narcolepsy, of which one of the major symptoms is sleep paralysis.

A young woman in my clinic, Jennifer W., complained of being very sleepy during the day. But she also told me about the terrifying experiences that recurred most nights. She would wake up to realise that she was in her own bed but the room was quite different. Then a giant rat would arise out of the floor and come towards her. Terrified, she would try to scream and run away, but would be unable to move. The rat would start licking her arms or her face or neck, and then she would slowly feel its teeth sinking into her flesh. Desperate to get away, she would struggle, and occasionally at this point she would wake up, be able to move and the rat would vanish.

Jennifer was diagnosed as having narcolepsy, and her description of being eaten by a rat was characteristic of the imagery that she experienced during sleep paralysis. She would partially awake, so that she had some waking consciousness, but the room looked different because she retained part of her dream imagery. The rat was also part of the dream imagery, as were her experiences of being licked or bitten. Her fear, however, was very real, and it may have been the fear that was causing the terrifying dream imagery rather than the other way around, as fear is often associated with sleep paralysis awakenings. In her semi-awake state her muscles were still paralysed, and thus she was truly unable to move. Once she managed to move a limb, the dream imagery would vanish and she would become fully awake. If, on the other hand, she was unable to waken fully then sometimes she would lose the imagery and return to sleep.

Narcolepsy is rare, and has other symptoms as well as sleep paralysis and hallucinations. Like Jennifer, the sufferer continually falls asleep during the day (narcolepsy is one of the commonest causes of excessive daytime sleepiness) but also has insomnia at night, and sometimes cataplexy—a sudden loss of motor tone in response to an emotional stimulus such as laughter or anger or anxiety, so that he may drop something he is carrying, or in severe cases even fall to the ground. Imagine walking down the street with a two-year-old who suddenly dashes into the road. The shock can induce an attack of cataplexy. You become extremely anxious (emotional shock) and are unable either to catch him as you collapse, or call him back, because you are paralysed. Narcolepsy can be disabling, and often dangerous, causing accidents at work or at home or when driving, because you are unable to stop yourself falling asleep. A good question to ask someone you think may be suffering from narcolepsy is whether they fall asleep while eating. If they do, narcolepsy is a real possibility. Treatment for narcolepsy is to try and make the sufferer more alert during the day by giving stimulant drugs such as methyl phenidate (Ritalin) or dexamphetamine (speed). Cataplexy can be helped by the drug clonipramine or setraline (Lustral).

However, sleep paralysis isn't always associated with narcolepsy. Sometimes, it follows a traumatic event, drugs can cause it, and it may also occur spontaneously, for no apparent reason. Sleep paralysis tends to run in families. Mrs. Susan Smith, two of her brothers and her son all suffer (her word) from sleep paralysis.

I was just getting into bed when I felt extreme dizziness. I lay down and found I was completely unable to move anything, not even my eyes. There was a tingling around my mouth. But I was able to see all round the room. It was as if my mind had become separated from my body. I tried desperately to get my daughter's attention. I then hit upon the idea of thought transference. It worked. Slowly she arose out of herself. That is to say there were two of her. I really believe I saw her soul. She knelt over me. I asked her (still by thought transference) to smack me across my face to wake me. She raised her arm slowly and did what I asked. Suddenly I was out of it and everything was back to normal.

My brother, especially, has had his life turned upside down with this problem. From a young child he was troubled with being woken in the night with a complete feeling of paralysis. Then after a time, thinking he's over it, getting out of the bed, looking back only to see himself still lying asleep. As the years went on, the problem became worse. It was usually on waking or going back to sleep. My other brother has had maybe four attacks, but his are accompanied by a rush of wind through the ears.

Many other people have described a sound similar to this "rush of wind through the ears." One young woman, who was so scared by her experiences that she joined a spiritualist church to try to find an explanation, says, "I wake up but I'm asleep. My eyes are open but I can't move a muscle, not even my mouth, but I still have the excruciating loud rushing sound in my ears." Mrs. Margaret Smith describes:

> . . . a noise in the head, more like a noise that is felt rather than heard. The closest I can get to a description of this noise/feeling is to say, imagine holding a cup of water to your lips and quickly suck in the water through your teeth. Imagine this noise with a much higher pitch to it, also the water travelling *much* faster.

Others have described hearing a "humming noise" in their ears or a noise "like a lift coming down."

The fact that sleep paralysis tends to run in families suggests that the malfunctioning of the awakening process is genetically determined. However, many people experience sleep paralysis even when no one else in their family suffers from it. Quite often sleep paralysis develops as part of a post-traumatic syndrome, after some event or experience which has made the person very anxious. The anxiety then seems in some way to disrupt the arousal process.

Often the frightening imagery is a flashback to the original terrifying experience. A patient of mine was unlucky enough to come round during an operation. She was unable to move or cry out because of the muscle-paralysing drugs she had been given before the operation, but she could hear the surgeons discussing their weekend golf while carrying out the operation, and feel the incredible pain as they cauterised her bleeding vessels and cut into her abdomen. For months afterwards she suffered attacks of sleep paralysis, and not surprisingly the recurring imagery in these attacks was of lying on operating tables and being pulled and tortured by vicious surgeons while she was quite unable to move or cry out.

In fact it is characteristic of sleep paralysis that, unlike almost all other sleep phenomena, it is universally described as unpleasant. Mrs. Margaret Smith has had an experience like the one she describes below maybe two dozen times over a period of six or seven years. Sometimes it would happen three or four times in a week, then not for over a year.

I am asleep or just waking when the following takes place; I have a feeling of suffocation, heart beating very slowly, *forcing* myself to breathe to ''wake up'' (although I can see things around me like my arm on the pillow). Scared that I will not be able to wake up . . . I see a dark tunnel that fits closely around the length of my body, the tunnel or tube is spinning very fast. I am not spinning, I am being pulled down through this tunnel. I see no end to the tunnel, just the sides. All very unpleasant. These things happen all at once, the whole event not lasting more than a few seconds. Once I tried letting myself go on through the tunnel to see what would happen, but the longer I left it, the harder it became to pull myself out of it. It seems much more than just a bad dream.

Many people's descriptions make it clear what a terrifying experience sleep paralysis can be. PR:

Just as I am dropping off to sleep I have this horrible sensation of slipping away somehow or somewhere. I know I *must* bring myself back from this. I have always managed to do this but it is very difficult. I just keep saying to myself, wake up, wake up, I *must* come back. I also physically try to move my arms and legs to wake up but I can't move them. I may only be dreaming but I know I *cannot* let myself go to the end, or the bottom, or further, or whatever it is.

PH:

When I first started with these ''feelings'' I was only about seventeen and I thought I was going insane . . . My body feels like it has ''pins and needles'' all over, and although I am aware of what is going on in my mind, I cannot move my arms or legs. It is a very frightening experience and sometimes I've tried to wake my husband up, but as I said I cannot move, and the last time it happened to me the feeling I experienced seemed stronger and I tried to scream but couldn't.

Occasionally an episode of sleep paralysis does not end with a full awakening, but merges into an out-of-body experience (see chapter 14), and PH's account sounds very much as though she was on the verge of such an experience. Certainly people who have spontaneous out-of-body experiences often describe this same feeling of "pins and needles all over" just before they "take off." Mrs. Tracey Ingham has had several such episodes since the age of thirteen. They happen when she is:

> at a stage between asleep and awake, really relaxed. First I hear a humming noise in my ears then I know it's going to happen. Then it is as if I can't move, as if I'm really heavy, and I can't shout although I really try. Then I feel as if I am floating above the bed and going on a journey. It's very dark but I can see a faint light and I am floating towards it. Physically I am trying to wake up but I can't move. I feel as though I am awake not asleep and I feel really frightened. Sometimes I manage to go back to my body quickly, but other times I feel as though I should go to the light but I know if I do I will die, at least I think I will, then I think of my husband and children and realise I mustn't and I return to my body. I can't make this happen to myself, but I half believe it is part of the mind and I half wonder if it is something spiritual, though I am not very religious myself.

Mrs. B. Bartlett had this experience ten days after her mother's funeral.

> I had been to bingo and I don't drink and I've never had any drugs from my doctor so it can't have been that. When I went to bed the same night I hadn't been in bed long when I heard what I can only describe as a lift coming down. I was going to ask my husband if he could hear the strange noise, but all of a sudden I was paralysed and could not move. The next thing I was in black space, my body I can only describe was my shadow as I floated. I passed three eyes, two were further back in the background than the one which was enormous. All three watched me pass by. I went further into blackness. I

shouted, "Where are you, mam?" three times and with
that I was absolutely thrown back on my bed. I washed
my face in cold water and could not believe it had happened to me but I know it did. Who did the eyes belong
to? The experience still haunts me.

It's probable that Mrs. Bartlett was stressed and anxious at this
time, soon after her mother's death, and that her emotional
state induced the sleep paralysis with its terrifying images. The
imagery itself—the blackness, the three watchful eyes—probably has no meaning or significance in itself, but the emotional
tone it carries is significant. It may reflect the feelings of sadness and fear that she had about her mother's death, perhaps
about being left behind, being lonely, or feeling anxious about
what would happen to her dead mother. Her account, like that
of Tracey Ingham above, also has features which are sugges-
tive of the hypnagogic imagery that occurs on the borders of
sleep. In each case the experience seems to have happened as
they were falling asleep; the fact that they were aware of being
paralysed suggests that they had gone from an awake state
straight into dreaming sleep but remained on its borders.

Sleep paralysis is a terrifying experience—everyone who
has suffered from it will confirm this. So perhaps it is not
surprising that the hallucinatory images which often appear in
these experiences—the Old Hags, rats, or alien beings from
outer space which invade our bedrooms and either crush or
kidnap us—are terrifying too. It isn't just the paralysis that
induces these night-time assaults on the sleeper, because we
are paralysed every night during every dream. Even when
someone is given, experimentally, the paralysing drug curare
they don't experience this kind of terrifying imagery. But why
is the imagery so violent? Why should a huge rat gnaw your
arm? Probably the imagery is emotion-led. The awareness that
you are paralysed evokes terror, and the terror triggers stereotyped horrific images from memory. Sometimes the images
are poorly formed, not explicit, shadowy and vague, as when
the feeling of crushing leads to the image of a dreadful nameless black shape. Or there may be a highly structured and very
clear scenario, being taken into a spaceship, for example, or
laid out on an operating table. The difference probably depends on the degree of cortical arousal. High arousal levels in

a state of high anxiety will evoke more vivid dream imagery. Or it could be that it is dropping back into the dream that makes the imagery more detailed and more bizzare.

One of the noteworthy things about alien abduction is that there seem to be a group of unfortunates who, having once been abducted, tend to become natural victims and are repeatedly whisked from their bedrooms for unspeakable experiments or implantation of small metal objects. The explanation UFOlogists usually advance for this is that the abductees have become part of some ongoing alien experiment which requires occasional follow-up. An alternative explanation is that the "Greys" (or the nine-foot giants clad in shiny metallic clothing which have been encountered in Israel, or the Puerto Rican "Chupacabras," creatures with protruding pointed tongues evidently used to extract blood and other body fluids from their victims) have become the stereotypes conjured up from memory each time the terror of the night paralysis arises.

Alien abduction is at any rate a more colourful explanation. Would you rather wake in the morning and say you have suffered a disorder of arousal on alerting from a dream, or claim to have visited a spaceship from the outer reaches of the universe? The second at least makes for a more lively discussion at the breakfast table.

13

Lucid Dreams—A Taste of Virtual Reality

I was out walking in some unfamiliar country place when I realised it was a dream. For a while I scrutinised my surroundings, and then enjoyed a flying and floating session, trying it with and without swimming motions of the arms. I passed a board with a place-name and other wording on it. Presently I remembered that I wished to try passing through a wall in a lucid dream, and looked about for a suitable wall. A short distance away stood a little building like a brick phone box, so I let myself float into it. At first there was no resistance then, to my surprise, I found I couldn't get right through; I felt as though groping in a black bog, and eventually I gave up the attempt. Presently vision returned, and I found that I was lying on the ground inside the little building; through the window I saw again the vivid blue sky and the board with still the same wording on it. I then let myself rise with the idea of passing through the roof—but the same thing happened again, except that this time I woke.

Since early childhood Betty M. has occasionally had lucid dreams—dreams in which the dreamer is aware that they are dreaming. So real do the dream objects appear that it almost seems possible to bring them back into the waking world by holding on to them. But despite the high degree of realism there are fantastic elements in Betty's dreams too—a path may contract as she is walking along it, or she may step directly into the scene on a television screen. Almost every aspect of waking experience is mimicked in these lucid dreams—the visual imagery is always vivid, she can "hear" and "feel" just as she can in waking life. She experiences taste, smell, heat and cold too, but less intensely. She does, however, seem to be virtually immune from pain in her lucid dreams. Often her dreams are of walking or floating through beautiful scenery.

> While walking along a lovely tree-lined avenue I realised I was dreaming, and a sense of peace filled me. It was an autumn scene, and the ground was carpeted with crisp brown and golden leaves. Eventually the avenue opened into a brilliant sunlit glade; a sparrow alighted on my hand and I observed closely its natural appearance and the subtle colouring of the feathers. Surveying the scene I felt a sense of wonder that it was possible to behold— purely in imagination—such vivid detail and beauty.

Lucid dreams are probably the closest human beings can get to a fantasy life that is virtual reality. It is as if you are conscious, even though you are asleep. You can think and reason, make decisions and act on them. And yet the realisation that the world in which you are thinking, reasoning and acting is a dream world brings a wonderful sense of freedom—you can fly, cross the world as if in seven-league boots, fulfil, in fact, your dreams.

One of the first people to write about lucid dreams (and indeed the first person seriously to research the whole topic of dreams) was Hervey de Saint-Denys. Saint-Denys was his own subject. When he was thirteen, he began to keep an illustrated dream diary, each day recording and illustrating the dreams he had had the night before. As his diary progressed, he found his dreams easier and easier to remember. He discovered, too, that he gradually developed an unusual ability. He found that while he was dreaming, he was aware that he was dreaming, and could even "guide" his dreams in whatever direction he chose. The more preoccupied he became with this new ability, the more frequently it occurred.

Since Saint-Denys first wrote about his guided dreams in 1867, many people have become fascinated with the phenomenon. Some have discovered quite spontaneously that they have the ability; others, having heard or read about it, have deliberately set out to teach themselves to dream lucidly. The term "lucid dreaming" was first coined by a Dutch physician, Frederik Van Eeden, who began studying his own dreams in 1896.

For a long time the notion that people could truly know, in a dream, that they were dreaming was dismissed as fantasy—most sceptics maintained that what the dreamers reported were moments of brief awakening, more akin to daydreams than to true dreams. It is only relatively recently that lucid dreaming has been taken seriously enough to inspire research, and has become accepted as a real phenomenon. Now that it has been investigated more thoroughly, researchers have found solid evidence that the lucid dreamer isn't simply *dreaming* that he is aware, but really *is* aware that he is dreaming.

What makes a dreamer "go lucid"? According to most dream researchers, the most common trigger is simply that the dreamer recognises a dream-like quality in what is going on; it just doesn't seem real in the way that real life does. Sometimes realisation is triggered when the dreamer becomes aware of oddities or inconsistencies in the world around him—that he is walking down the road naked, for example, or has met someone whom he knows to be dead. Perhaps he may see an object move of its own accord, or he may feel no physical pain in circumstances which would normally be painful. He may puzzle about these bizarre happenings for a while, and then finally the explanation dawns on him—it is all just a dream. The final major trigger is emotional arousal, especially anxiety—nightmares quite often lead to a period of lucidity. One dreamer described to us the dream event that led to his own lucidity—the appearance of a group of policemen combined with the remembrance that he had a large lump of cannabis in his pocket.

I walked through an arched entrance to a cobbled stable yard that had been elegantly converted into a collection of homes and shop-like premises. The buildings were clad in ivy. Together with the clear blue sky its calm ambience was idyllic. I crossed the yard to what looked like a café, its tables spilling into the yard and its woodwork painted a deep rich blue.

Inside the proprietor and chef told me to take whatever I wanted from the table. Dominating the array of foods was a huge fish pie about a metre across and three centimetres deep. I took a large slice and sat down to eat at a table with a view over the courtyard. Several other people were eating and chatting at adjacent tables. It was the most delicious pie I have ever tasted; its flavour flooded my mouth.

When I had finished I went to the proprietor and asked him how much I owed him. He looked surprised and a little insulted that I should offer him money. He told me that he prepared the food for anyone who might enjoy it and not for money. I thanked him and left.

Outside I met three friends and walked up a long alley running between a number of residential gardens whose branches and shrubbery overhung the path. Hearing a dog barking we turned round to see a group of four or five policemen with a lively German shepherd dog on a lead at the end of the alley. I remembered that I had a large lump of cannabis in my right-hand jacket pocket. As my adrenaline began to flow I realised that I was in a dream. Having realised this I knew that I must do something active and consciously within the dream to earth the experience and to bring that understanding into the dream world. This was most important. I did a little jig, turning my dream body round in a full circle to bring an external action into the flow of my dream. Shortly afterwards the dream ended.

Once the dreamer has recognised that he is, in fact, dreaming, he usually decides to prove it:

I dreamed I was walking along a path through a garden, towards a building with a large arched doorway flanked by stone pillars. My husband was walking beside me, on my right-hand side. On his right-hand side was another friend of ours. As we approached the doorway something, someone, leapt out from the shadows on my left and attacked me. I screamed and awoke terrified and trembling. Soon I dropped off to sleep again and found myself in the same dream, walking again towards the doorway. But suddenly I knew I was dreaming, and I knew what was going to happen. I thought, I know this is only a dream and I know that if this time I walk on my husband's right-hand side, between him and our friend, whatever it is won't attack me and I'll be quite safe. And that's exactly what happened. I skipped round to my husband's other side and walked up to the doorway and through it, feeling no fear at all—in fact feeling very happy and pleased with myself because I had realised it was only a dream and had managed to alter its outcome in this way.

One very common way in which people tend to test their dream world against reality is by attempting to fly—"If this is really a dream then I could jump off this cliff and float down to the bottom." Alan W. describes this experience in the following dream.

I was riding on the back of a small motorbike or moped. It seemed to be driven by Keith, an old school friend. He leaned backwards, thus making me lean backwards. He was heavily built—we used to call him Bomber—and the bike was small, so I was concerned about the weight on the back wheel. As we drove along I leaned over to the right to see how bad the bulge in the tyre at the bottom of the wheel was. I decided it was tolerable so we carried on. I suddenly realised that we weren't wearing crash helmets, which concerned me. I thought we might be stopped by the police . . . Until this point in the dream I'd been acting very much as if I was awake, in my concern for safety and for the law.

At this point Alan realised that he was dreaming and could do whatever he wanted.

Without further reflection I flew up and away from the motorbike. I did this without stopping and dismounting, because I knew it was safe. I began to fly over the area of ground to the left of the road, and had the impression that it dropped away into a valley, but before I had time to observe properly I was distracted by what seemed to be a large insect buzzing about near my face. I tried to get rid of it by catching and squashing it, but it seemed indestructible. One moment it was mangled and in bits, the next it was there again.

Lucid dreams don't always develop from ordinary dreams, though this is much the most common experience—over three-quarters of people who have lucid dreams realise that they are dreaming during an ongoing dream. But "dream consciousness" can also begin in wakefulness rather than in sleep, and this ability to maintain waking consciousness while falling asleep has long been regarded as a gateway to mystical states. As early as the eighth century it was cultivated by Tibetan yogis, who drew from the experience the knowledge that what was perceived by the senses in the waking state and in the dream state was equally unreal. Masters of Tibetan dream yoga are said to be able to pass in and out of sleep without ever losing consciousness (though I have to say that one of the great disappointments of my working life was my failure to persuade a Tibetan master who was visiting London to let me entice him into a sleep laboratory and hitch him up to an EEG machine to monitor his brain waves throughout a night of dream consciousness). Methods using meditative techniques to develop the ability to maintain consciousness through dreaming and even dreamless sleep were also practised in India at about the same time as they were being developed in Tibet.

LEARNING TO DREAM LUCIDLY

As Hervey de Saint-Denys discovered, lucid dreaming seems to be a skill that improves with motivation and practice. Betty M., too, remarked on the ability of the dream mind to respond to the interest of the waking mind in this way. "The dreams," she says, "become richer in quality, it becomes easier to recall dreams on waking and, reciprocally, there begins to arise during dreams some recollection of waking life as a distinct experience."

But why should anyone want to learn to dream lucidly? One reason is that lucid dreams are nearly always more enjoyable than ordinary dreams. A large proportion of ordinary dreams— some estimates are as high as two out of every three—contain unpleasant elements (falling, being attacked or chased, for example) or feelings such as fear or sadness. Lucid dreams rarely incorporate unpleasant events or emotions, or nightmare qualities. They elicit strong emotions, but these are usually very positive emotions—the sensory imagery is vivid, beautiful colours are seen, celestial music may be heard. The dreams are intense and usually highly enjoyable. This may be partly because of the dreamer's awareness that he is dreaming and that there is therefore essentially nothing to worry about. If a dream becomes frightening or threatening, the thought "this is only a dream" means that the dreamer can regard the situation with interest or curiosity, see it as an adventure and be curious about what happens next without feeling any real fear or apprehension. Betty M.:

> While walking with two companions, a woman and a young man, I realised I was dreaming, and I decided to find out what they thought about the situation—did they realise this was just a dream? To my surprise they replied unhesitatingly that they did. I addressed the young man: "But you only realise this through me." "No," he replied, "on the contrary, you realise it through me! For example, there's a river round the corner which is not so in reality, but I have taken this from 1952/53." (I did in fact live near a river at that time.)

In a lucid dream you can make things happen, alter the course of a dream or shape it so that it goes in a particular direction. You are not at the mercy of your dream images, but at least partially in control. You have a sporting chance of being able to decide what you want to do in your dream, and then do it. Often you can decide who you want to meet. But even when people appear in your dream whom you've no desire to meet, or when things happen that are outside your control, you are not entirely at the mercy of dream events—you may be able to decide how you will respond to the person or situation. And you can even choose to waken from it if things are not going your way.

There is plenty of advice for people who want to develop their ability to dream lucidly. Much of it seems to rest on cultivating your state of "dream awareness," and developing "thought sets"—mental habits which it is hoped may eventually begin to appear in the dreaming state. One suggestion is to get into the habit of questioning, during the day, whether you are awake or asleep. Ask yourself as often as you can remember, during the day, "Is this a dream?" Even the simple fact of recalling your ordinary dreams each morning seems to encourage the development of lucid dreams. If you wake from a dream, try to remember as much as you can about it before your mind becomes involved with other thoughts. When you are thinking about it, tell yourself that next time you dream, you want to remember to be aware that you are dreaming. Another important technique is to sit up in bed just before you finally compose yourself for sleep, and concentrate your mind on the fact that you *will* have a lucid dream that night. This is very important, as it gives the mind a "set" just before sleep onset.

Paul Devereux suggests another technique, which is to make a pact with a friend or partner to meet him or her in your dreams at some specific place known to both of you. Make it a place that you see every day in waking consciousness, so that every time you see it or enter it during the day you are reminded of the pact, and keep it in mind as you go to sleep.

Although periods of REM sleep occur about every two hours throughout the night, the longest period is in the couple of hours before your final morning awakening, and it seems to be at this time that lucid dreams are most likely to occur. So you can increase your chances of having a lucid dream by going to sleep at your normal time but setting the alarm so that you only sleep for three or four hours. By doing this you take off the pressure for slow-wave sleep, which occurs mostly in the first half of the night. You then stay awake until it is your normal waking time, when you go back to bed and to sleep—but this time you are more likely to have dreaming sleep. This particular method is very convenient for anyone involved in lucid dream experiments in sleep laboratories, because it means that technicians can come in at their usual time in the morning and wire up the lucid dreamer before he goes back to bed for his final period of sleep at around eight or nine a.m. He can then have his lucid dreams during the working day!

Alternatively, try taking a daytime nap, when you are again

at a higher point on the alertness cycle. You are unlikely to fall too deeply asleep, and lucid dreams are more likely at times when your body would normally expect to be awake rather than asleep. Whenever you go to sleep, though, do so with the determination to become lucid at the forefront of your mind.

Another method is to try to maintain a certain level of mental alertness as you fall asleep. Ouspensky recommended watching one's own mind as one falls asleep. Stephen La-Berge, Director of the Lucidity Institute in California, suggests occupying the mind with some routine, mechanical task (counting sheep or reciting the twelve times table, for example) as one is falling asleep. Think about lucid dreams before you go to sleep at night, reminding yourself that tonight you are determined to notice when you are dreaming.

Dream researchers Celia Green and Charles McCreery took further the idea of asking yourself during the day whether you are awake or asleep, by suggesting that you repeatedly test the physical reality of the world around you to see whether you are awake or in a dream. You might, for example, see if there is anything strange or surreal in your surroundings or behaviour to suggest that it might be an illusion—can you float six inches above the ground instead of walking, for example? Are walls solid, or do they dissolve if you try to pass through them? Can you switch a light on and off successfully, or read a newspaper (both tasks which are straightforward in waking life but difficult for the lucid dreamer)? How much can you remember about the events of the day leading up to the present moment? Dream events occur, self-contained, in a time vacuum; there is seldom any clear notion of what preceded them.

The suggestion is that if someone repeatedly asks himself "Could this be a dream?" or habitually carries out these "normality" checks in the waking state, he may find himself doing much the same thing in his dreams—dreams tend to incorporate events that have happened during the previous day, so it is quite plausible that this might happen. The discovery of some bizarre departure from normality (the ability to jump off a hundred-foot cliff and float safely to the bottom, for example) might jog the dreamer into an awareness that he is dreaming, and thus achieve a state of lucidity.

WHY DO LUCID DREAMS OCCUR?

Our current understanding of the dreaming state is that it is not just one state, but a continuum from what we might call deep dreams, when consciousness is more impaired, to light dreams, when consciousness is fuller. As you rise up the spectrum to the lighter stages of dreaming, the ego functions return into dream awareness. It is the return of these ego functions that changes an ordinary into a lucid dream. We tend to have lucid dreams at particular times of the day because their occurrence is linked to the twenty-four hour alertness sleep cycle that we all experience. We are at our lowest level at two a.m. and our highest level at nine a.m. In the morning, as the sleeping period comes to an end, the alertness level of the cycle starts to rise. If we can dream during a time when the alertness cycle is higher than it is during a normal sleep period, we are more likely to have lucid dreams. This is why going to sleep at the time you would normally wake up is likely to produce a lucid dream.

Can anyone train themselves to enter the magical, adventurous world of lucid dreams at will? Some people clearly find it easy to do, others are seldom successful, no matter what strategies they use. Green and McCreery suggest that your chances of becoming a successful lucid dreamer are higher if your nervous system is relatively easily aroused, and that in the lucid dream the cortex of the brain is more excitable than in the non-lucid dream. Certainly, we know that there seems to be a higher degree of intellectual functioning in the lucid dream than the non-lucid dream. There is evidence, too, that if you have been in a state of high arousal during the day, or if you have had nightmares, lucid dreams are more likely to be triggered. There is also some evidence that lucid dreamers are significantly more likely to suffer from migraine than people who do not seem able to dream lucidly.

LEARNING FROM LUCID DREAMS

Psychoanalysts have always been interested in what dreams can reveal about the dreamer's unconscious feelings, but until the 1970s the idea that dreams might tell us anything useful about how the brain works had never been taken very seriously. Dreaming was considered to be a state apart, and the dream world was believed to have no connection or correlation with the "real" world. But when the special characteristics of lucid dreams were recognised, scientists began to see that these might provide more fertile ground for research. Celia Green was the first person to suggest that if the lucid dreamer was aware of his dreaming state, and had access to his normal waking mind, he might be able to make observations within his dream and possibly communicate them in some way. If this could be done, it might be possible to discover more about the dream world, and see whether many of the preconceptions we had about it were true.

There is the question of time, for example. The general belief has always been that dream time is quite separate from and different to real time, so that events that might take hours or days are telescoped to minutes or even seconds within a dream. There is also the idea that dream bodies are quite different from physical bodies, and that movements in a dream body are like imagined movements and don't make use of the motor mechanisms of the brain.

COMMUNICATING WITH THE LUCID DREAMER

Many people have had an occasional lucid dream, and it seems to be a facility that most people can learn, if they are interested and know how to go about it. Some people deliberately set out to develop the ability, and may become so adept at it that they can "go lucid" almost at will. Obviously for any scientist who wants to investigate lucid dreams seriously, someone with this ability makes the ideal subject. In the early 1980s a psychiatrist colleague, Dr. Morton Schatzman, met just such a person, Alan W. Alan was a psychology graduate who for several years had been exploring his own dream life and developing the ability to dream lucidly. Alan had devised a whole lifestyle that facilitated his ability to have lucid dreams. Lucid dreams occur most commonly at the end of each sleep cycle during REM sleep. Alan's habit was to go to bed at two thirty a.m. and wake himself at eight a.m., just before the dreams of the fourth sleep cycle were due. He would breakfast on wheatgerm and cheese (a diet which he believed encouraged lucidity) and then return to bed and to sleep.

Alan agreed to be the subject in a series of experiments Dr. Schatzman and I wanted to carry out on the nature of lucid dreaming. But we first of all had to discover whether there was any way Alan could communicate with us while he was dreaming. Even if it could be assumed that lucid dreamers could learn to communicate rationally with an experimenter by signalling with some sort of movement that they had "gone lucid," what kind of signal could they make? Lucid dreams arise in the same rapid-eye-movement stage of sleep as ordinary dreams. And as we have already seen, in REM sleep the body is physically paralysed. But there is an obvious exception to this—the eye muscles clearly are *not* paralysed. Lucid dream researchers found that if, in a dream, the subject looked to one side or the other, their real eyes moved in a corresponding way. Electrodes placed around the eyes were able to detect and measure these muscle movements. The subject could therefore signal to the experimenter simply by moving his or her eyes. By establishing a code using these eye movements the subject could give information to the experimenter—he could indicate when he was lucid, and even what he was doing.

When we started our work on lucid dreaming there was little information about the way the dream body was related to the real body, or even if there was any connection between the two at all. There was no information about dream time and about whether the thought processes in dreams were the same as thought processes in the waking state. We devised a series of experiments, and Alan's ability to become lucid almost at will was a great asset to us.

Our first set of experiments concerned the relationship between the dream body and the real body, and we used the eyes as an indicator of what Alan was doing. He was instructed that if he had a lucid dream he was, in the dream, to draw a triangle on a board with his hand and to watch the tip of his hand while he was doing this. When Alan became aware that he was lucid, he was to flick his eyes from side to side a preset number of times, to indicate to us that he was lucid. After waking, Alan narrated this dream into a tape recorder.

I searched for something to draw triangles on. There were several pieces of paper, but most of them looked too small and had things written on them. I shouldn't use them, I thought, in case they were somebody's valuable notes. (In so far as I was supposing that the notes were real and valuable to someone, I was not completely lucid.) I walked through two (I think) rooms and found a blackboard with writing on it and some red chalk. I hesitated to use the blackboard, again in case somebody had left the writing there for further use.

Nevertheless, I started to draw the triangles on the blackboard. The chalk seemed greasy and didn't write very well, which momentarily concerned me. (Had I been more lucid, I might have realised sooner that it wasn't necessary for the chalk to write well.)

I tried to mark each attempt to draw a triangle with eye flicks: one flick for the first attempt, two flicks for the second, and so on. I drew five triangles altogether. Between the second and third triangles, I had to pause briefly—a man was in the way and I took a few seconds to move round him. Each triangle was about a foot high or a bit more, so I needed plenty of room. Between the third and fourth triangles—or maybe the fourth and fifth— I ran out of space on the blackboard, and moved across the corner of the room to another blackboard.

After finishing drawing these five triangles, I wondered what else to do. I wandered round the EEG department, looking at things. I noticed a fair amount of detail, pieces of equipment and so on, but somehow nothing struck me enough for me to remember anything significant about it. People were around too.

I'd say the whole dream took about five minutes.

The dream account corresponded well with the electro-oculogram [EOG] recording. From REM onset to awakening was just over five minutes, so Alan's dream estimate of the time was remarkably accurate. We then analysed the pattern of electric potentials and were able to show that his eyes were indeed following a path of a triangle being drawn. This allowed us to say that dream eyes and real eyes are the same. By this we meant that when the dreamer moves his dream eyes, his real eyes also move. Thus dreams are not like imagination; imaginary movements of the eyes do not lead to movements of the real eyes.

We next wanted to know if the rest of the dream body was the same as the real body. We put electrodes over the muscles which move the fingers, toes, arms and legs, etc., and Alan was given a series of tasks which involved moving the limbs and indicating to us by means of his eye signals which limbs he was moving. We found that when Alan moved a dream limb or part of a limb, there was activity in the muscles which would move the limb in the real body. Actual movement, however, was limited to little movements of the fingers. The muscles that move the central body musculature are more severely paralysed than those that move the fingers and toes, and so there were no large body movements of the real body. This finding is extraordinary, because it means that whatever we do in our dreams we do, as it were, for real. In other words, leaping and skipping and running in our dreams make use of the movement mechanisms in our brain, and we would carry out these movements if we were not paralysed.

We then went on to ask if the concept of numbers in dreams is the same as in waking life. One feels intuitively that it should be, but there was no scientific proof that it was. We put an accelerometer on Alan's finger, so that we could measure the tiny movements that he could make, and asked him to flick his finger during a lucid dream first once, then twice, then three, four and finally five times. Alan was able to do this in a lucid dream, and did it absolutely accurately, showing that his dream concept of numbers was exactly the same as his concept of numbers in the waking state.

We used this same experiment to look at dream speech. We placed electrodes over his larynx to see if we could pick up activity from the muscles which control speech, and then asked him in his lucid dream to say "one" when he moved his finger once, "two" when he moved his finger twice, etc. We weren't able to pick up any evidence of the speech muscles functioning, but we were able to show that when Alan said a number in his dream, it always coincided with the out breath, just as it does in normal speech. This led us to conclude that dream speech probably makes use of the same mechanisms as ordinary speech.

In our final set of experiments we tried to answer questions about the nature of dream reality and whether stimuli from the outside world could be perceived in a lucid dream. We designed an electric-shock machine which Alan could activate when he was lucid. The electrodes surrounding his eyes were monitored by a computer, which could recognise Alan's lucidity signal. When the signal was detected Alan received an electric shock. In his dream he felt this as no more than a pricking sensation in his wrist, but it jolted him into the realisation that he was dreaming, and that he had to signal to us by making five eye movements which showed up as blips on the machine. This showed us that Alan certainly could receive sensory information from the outside world in his lucid dream, and that he felt it in the appropriate part of his body. Dream sensation was similar to waking sensation.

One of the most interesting experiments we conducted with Alan showed us clearly how far dreaming is removed from imagination. We wanted Alan to dream of moving his finger smoothly from side to side, and follow it with his eyes. This sounds very simple, but to see the implications, try to carry out this experiment with a partner.

Sit in front of your partner so that you can observe the movements of his eyes. Ask your partner to hold a finger in front of his eyes and to move it slowly from side to side, all the time tracking the movement with his eyes. You should be able to see his eyes move smoothly in pursuit of the finger. These smoothly coordinated pursuit movements are only possible because of a reflex mechanism in the brain which stabilises an image on the retina. They are very difficult to produce in the absence of a "real" stimulus, and to prove this, ask your partner next to raise an *imaginary* finger and to move it slowly from side to side as he did the real finger, following its movement all the time with his eyes. You should be able to see that the eye movements are no longer smooth, but move in jerks. This is because the mechanism for producing smooth controlled tracking movements is not functioning. Now, the question we hoped Alan could help us answer was, if a lucid dreamer moved a dream finger from side to side and tracked it with his dream eyes, would his real eyes show jerks—i.e. behave as if they were tracking an imaginary finger—or would they behave as if they were tracking a real finger in real life and make smooth pursuit movements?

When Alan succeeded in carrying out this task in a lucid dream, his eyes showed that he was tracking his dream finger quite smoothly, as if it was a real finger, not an imaginary one. We could therefore say that dream fingers and dream eyes are connected together in a similar way to real fingers and real eyes. In other words, the complex reflex pathways used to stabilise the retinal image in waking life are also used to stabilise the dream image in dream life.

Quite often, in his dream accounts, Alan describes "false awakenings," which are dreams of awakenings, in which the dreamer merely "awakens" into yet another dream. False awakenings can be experienced in ordinary dreams, but are much more often associated with lucid dreaming. The lucid dreamer knows he is dreaming, and therefore he expects to wake. Expectations are often incorporated into dreams, and what seems to happen is that as the lucid dream starts to fade, it becomes a dream of awakening. One young woman described how she awoke from a lucid dream, got up, dressed, breakfasted, went off to work—and then woke up realising it had all been a dream. So she got up, dressed, breakfasted, went off to work—and then woke up realising it had all been a dream. This was repeated yet a third time before she had a final—and actual—awakening.

CONTROLLING LUCID DREAMS

Lucid dreaming does not provide *carte blanche* for the dreamer to go anywhere, do anything. Alan W. found that by concentrating on what he wanted to dream about he could often influence the content of his dreams, and it is true that a lucid dreamer can to some extent direct the course of a dream. But by no means does the dreamer have complete control over the dream. The lucid dreamer who, for example, finds himself on a snow-clad mountain is likely to find it very hard to shift the scene of the dream to the tropical beach setting he might prefer. On the whole the dreamer has to accept the basic scenario of the dream, let it evolve but perhaps establish some control over his own actions and reactions within it. Alan found that when it came to sex, he could not establish quite the control he might have enjoyed over his dream scenario. He has found that while he often meets an attractive girl at a dream party, and may even slip away with her, he usually wakes up before anything can happen. In one dream he managed eventually to get the girl in his arms, but further progress was interrupted because the ceiling above them started to crumble and slowly covered them in debris. The closest he got was a dream in which he was on a lonely beach with an attractive girl. "Come on," said Alan, "what about it?" The girl seemed doubtful but said, "Yes, in a minute." Just then they saw some people in the distance walking towards them down the beach. "Hurry and make up your mind," said Alan, and added, "After all, you know this is only a dream." "All right then," said the girl, "if it's only a dream then I can make you wake up!" Which she did.

This probably says less about the erotic possibilities of lucid dreams than about Alan's own psychological make-up, and perhaps the fact that he has a good relationship with a very attractive wife. Other lucid dreamers have reported very intense and erotic dream experiences. Patricia Garfield, in her book about lucid dreaming, *Pathway to Ecstasy*, says that from her own experience, "Orgasm is a natural part of lucid dreaming." But another woman, a subject in one of Charles McCreery's studies of lucid dreaming, declares of her own experiences, ". . . there seems to be an inherent resistance to anything erotic." In fact, dream content very much reflects our own expectations, inhibitions and desires, and this is as true for lucid dreams as for ordinary dreams.

However, there are dream activities which present definite problems to most lucid dreamers. Lucid dreams seem real, but perception in a lucid dream is often deficient. It seems, for example, to be particularly difficult to control the level of illumination in a lucid dream. Although in a lucid dream Alan W. could flick his fingers as though they were a cigarette lighter and produce a flame from them, he found that he could not simply come into a darkened room and switch the light on. However, he could turn a spotlight on, or turn the light on in a room that was already filled with daylight.

Other dream researchers have found the same problem. Dr. Keith Hearne asked eight subjects, all experienced lucid dreamers, to experiment with light switches during their dreams. Only one of them was able to switch the light on, and she was able to do so only by covering her eyes with her hands, so as to abolish her previous dream imagery.

This has nothing to do with an inability to see bright lights, which are often reported in lucid dreams. It is as though the brain cannot cope with a sudden and total change of image. It seems, for example, to be quite possible to switch on a light using a dimmer switch, so that there is a gradual change of illumination rather than a sudden one. Probably for the same reason, Alan found that the brain also has difficulty in producing sudden loud noises. Alan decided one night to dream that he was firing a gun. But although he says he was prepared for a powerful bang, and had a clear idea of what it would be like, when he pulled the trigger there was only a click, and a piece of fluff emerged from the barrel. Still dreaming, he decided the gun was not loaded, and so he put in a bullet and fired again. This time he saw the bullet emerge slowly from the barrel of the gun, but again, there was no bang.

A possible physiological explanation is that a lucid dream is occurring in a cortex that is not as fully activated as it is in the waking state. This may mean that it is difficult for the cortex to produce a sudden change in activity in a specific brain area—the visual cortex, for example, may fail to activate at the flick of a light switch as it would do if the retina was stimulated by light in the waking state. What is interesting is the way in which the brain seems aware of its deficiency and often makes the dream incorporate a perfectly logical reason for this apparent failure such as a defective light switch or a defective bulb to account for a light that won't switch on, or, in the case of the silent gun, the discovery that the gun was not loaded. Most lucid dreamers find that reading is difficult too. The dreamer may only be able to bring a line or two of print into focus, or he can "read" but discovers that what he is reading is nonsense, or the symbols he is reading are meaningless hieroglyphics. This may be because the images in dreams are never still. Alan W. noticed that when he examined the backs of his hands in a dream they changed slowly; the flesh might seem to be melting, or plants might sprout out of the fingers. When he tried to read in a dream the print disintegrated so that he could seldom get beyond the end of a sentence. He found this dissolution of apparent sense into nonsense happened in a very similar way when he tried, in a lucid dream, to switch on a radio and listen to the shipping forecast and news. To begin with it sounded to him just as the shipping forecast usually sounds, but as he listened more carefully he realised that instead of the usual sea areas—Rockall, Biscay, North and South Uitsera, etc.—he was hearing the weather in non-existent places such as Wolf and Sofa.

Psychological barriers are just as important in lucid dreaming as they are in the waking state. A lucid dreamer may know, for example, that if he wants to extend his arm in his dream so that it is twice its length there's no reason why he shouldn't do so. It's a dream; anything is possible. And yet dream extension of an arm is not a simple matter of making it elastic; the brain has to devise some crazy logic that makes the exercise credible—tiptoeing your fingers along the floor, for example, so that your hand is carried down the corridor, and thereby extends your arm.

Again, although it is perfectly possible to go through a wall in a lucid dream without any difficulty, it is hard to convince yourself in a lucid dream that you can. Alan found that the best way to go through a wall was to approach it backwards, so that he was through it before he saw it. We devised a terrible experiment for Alan, asking him to put his hands behind his head and then to draw them through his head until they were in front of him and he could see them. We told him that the point of the experiment was to see whether he could interfere with his visual cortex, which is at the back of the brain. However, we knew that it was really a test of psychological resistance. Alan tried this experiment on several occasions, but each time awoke before he could place his hands in his brain. He persevered and finally succeeded, without, you will be pleased, doing himself any psychological or physical damage.

Pain is said to be very rarely felt in a lucid dream. Alan found that although in a lucid dream he could slice a knife through his wrist, he felt no pain, and his hand did not fall off. One of Green and McCreery's subjects describes how she tried to injure herself in a lucid dream (1994, p. 29):

I realised I was dreaming, and recalled my intention . . . to investigate the possibility of inflicting pain on myself in a lucid dream. Finding . . . a kitchen . . . I entered and selected a knife—then hesitated. For, although knowing I could not harm myself, and accustomed to immunity from pain in lucid dreams—nevertheless, deliberately to court the *sensation* of pain in this way seemed quite another matter and, I imagined, might well induce considerable pain. Gingerly I tried the point of the knife against my arm, producing a disconcertingly real sensation. I therefore experienced great reluctance to carry out my intention . . . However, someone came up and offered to cut a mole off my arm with scissors. I agreed to this but declined to watch, and presently she declared that it was done. I had felt nothing, but when I examined my arm, the flesh, it seemed to me, had not been cut through at all, the mole hidden rather than removed . . .

To some extent the lucid dreamer is capable of logical thought—much more so, at any rate, than in an ordinary dream. He can recall the tests he has been asked to do in his dream, for example, and can devise strategies to carry these out. Green and McCreery describe how B. G. Marcot gave himself the task of memorising (in waking life) the value of *pi* to 16 decimal places, and then tried to test his powers of recall by reciting these during a lucid dream. He describes consciously thinking the numbers in his dream. "However, as I reached the seventh decimal place, and was forced to exert greater effort to recall the numbers, I failed and rounded the number off at the seventh place, and stopped there."

Green and McCreery point out that seven digits is about the maximum number that a normal person can hold in short-term memory in waking life. But they also point out that the first seven digits are likely to be more firmly fixed in memory than the final nine—many people, after all, are familiar with at least the first few figures of the value of *pi*. In other words, these digits in particular are likely to be stored in long-term memory, and there is plenty of evidence that long-term memory can be accessed in lucid dreams. They suggest that what this experience might show is that in the dream state there is some sort of failure of coordination between short-term and long-term memory, that having accessed as many digits from long-term memory as can easily be stored in short-term memory, the dreamer might have been unable to access any more without forgetting the first seven.

They also suggest an alternative explanation, which is that in lucid dreaming the left hemisphere is relatively inactive, and it is in this hemisphere that this kind of sequential processing of numbers takes place. Tasks of this kind, involving sequences of numbers, might therefore be expected to present some difficulty to the lucid dreamer.

DREAM MACHINES

Unless you are a "natural," it may take a long time to learn to dream lucidly. Saint-Denys records that the first dream in which he had the sensation of what he called his "true situation" while asleep occurred during the 207th night after he had been keeping his dream diary. The second occasion was on the 214th night. Six months later the same phenomenon was occurring on average two nights out of five, and after a year three nights out of four. "Finally," he says, "after fifteen months it was present almost every night, and since that distant time I can truthfully say that I have hardly ever been overcome by the illusions of a dream without recovering my sense of reality, at least at intervals."

To satisfy those who are not prepared to wait that long, and who want quick and easy access to lucid dreams, there have been several attempts to develop a "dream machine." The same principle underlies all dream-machine prototypes. Lucid dreams occur in the lightest phase of dreaming sleep. A machine that aims to induce lucid dreams must first of all be able to detect when the sleeper is in dreaming sleep (relatively easy) and then give the dreamer some external stimulus, sufficient to arouse them slightly so that their sleep lightens, but not so powerful that it actually wakens them. Understandably, this has proved more difficult.

Most dream machines identify dreaming sleep either by detecting the rapid eye movements which occur in dreaming sleep, by placing a pressure sensor on the eyelids, or by monitoring the rate of breathing, which increases during this phase of sleep. The arousal mechanism varies. It may be an auditory stimulus such as a buzzer, or a slight electric shock. Keith

Hearne has developed a dream machine which has other facilities as well—a "nightmare alarm" which wakens the sleeper when his breathing exceeds a certain rate, and a dream-interruption alarm which wakens the sleeper during a dream, for those who want to increase their dream recall.

LaBerge's dream machine works by detecting the movement of the eyes through movement sensors which are placed over the eyes. These then cause flashing lights or other stimuli to be activated which lighten the dreamer's sleep.

However, on the whole, the induction of lucid dreams by dream machine has not proved generally successful—you probably have as good a chance of training yourself to dream lucidly by following the suggestions given earlier in this chapter.

TRAVELING IN TIME AND SPACE

There is some evidence from dream experiments that lucid dreamers are more likely than other people to have other kinds of unusual perceptual experience, such as out-of-body experiences or hypnagogic imagery. Some esoteric traditions which teach techniques for carrying on waking consciousness into the dream state maintain that someone in this conscious dream state can carry out extraordinary feats in the real world. There are Hindu mystics, for example, who claim to be able to use dream control to enable them to visit a number of different places at the same time, appearing in each place in a "dream body" which is nevertheless visible and substantial to anyone who sees it.

What is certainly true is that people in lucid dreams often report the feeling of leaving their body, and the experience is, to them, as vivid and as real as if it were happening in reality.

14

Night Travelers

On 3 October 1863, a Mr. Wilmot set sail for America from Liverpool on the ship *The City of Limerick*. He shared a state room with a librarian, Mr. Tait. There were storms in the Atlantic, and for the first ten days Wilmot slept badly. The first time he managed to get a good night's sleep was the night of 13/14 October. That night he dreamt that his wife, then in the USA, came to the door of his state room. She seemed to hesitate a little on entering, then came towards Wilmot, bent down to kiss him, and withdrew. The next morning, to Wilmot's amazement and embarrassment, Mr. Tait accused him of entertaining a woman in the cabin in the middle of the night. Pressed for details, he described exactly what had happened in Wilmot's dream.

The story does not end there. When Wilmot finally arrived home, his wife asked him if he had received a visit from her on the night of the 13th. Knowing about the Atlantic storms, and having heard that another ship which had left Liverpool just before the *Limerick* had been wrecked, she had, she said, lain awake all that night worrying. Just before dawn it seemed to her that she had gone in search of him. She seemed to cross a stormy sea and finally came to a low black steamer. She somehow went up its side and found her husband's state room, where there were two berths, the upper extending further back than the lower one. She was aware that there was a man (the offended Mr. Tait) in the upper berth, looking straight at her, so for a moment she hesitated to enter. Eventually, though, she went over to her husband's berth, bent down to kiss him, and then went away.

The Wilmot case, described by David Lorimer in his book *Survival?*, is one of the best known cases of dream travel, and was widely investigated at the time. Throughout recorded history, spiritualists and others have valued and tried to foster such experiences, regarding them as an indication that the soul (in the form of an "astral body") can leave the physical body and travel in an independent spiritual realm. Unfortunately, astral travellers usually have little success when they try to verify the reality of what they have seen on these night-time excursions. The Wilmot story, if true, is remarkable in that not only was the experience shared by the two main characters in the drama, but it seems to have been verified by a third, quite disinterested party. Even if we accept that it might have been a dream shared between Mr. and Mrs. Wilmot, or an instance of telepathy between them, it is difficult to account for Mr. Tait's involvement. He and Mrs. Wilmot did not know each other—had never even met. The idea of any telepathic communication between them is highly unlikely.

Out-of-body experiences (OBEs) occur under many different conditions and in every state of consciousness—spontaneously, under the influence of drugs or anaesthesia, as a reaction to pain or stress, as part of the near-death experience. So perhaps it is not surprising that they can also occur in the dream state. But even when they occur in dreams they seem to be very similar to out-of-body experiences in clear consciousness. People who have OBEs describe very much the same premonitory feelings that Mr. J. Hayes mentions in this dream experience—a tingling sensation, vibrations, twisting feelings, anxiety that something is about to happen.

> . . . I remember lying flat out on my back when I started to get this feeling of fear and my insides are pulsating and trying to get outside. (Sounds daft but still true, I remember thinking to myself, is this a heart attack or a nightmare?) I now start to get a tingling feeling at the base of my spine which has started to slowly spread up my back to my head and now throughout my whole body. This sensation is very intense but not painful or uncomfortable although I do feel slightly raised off the bed.

Then a face or presence comes into my view/mind (I'm not sure if I think, feel or see it) and a voice/thought says, "Do not worry or be afraid of anything. You are being cared for." From the start I suppose I was frozen with fear, but after the voice knew I must sit up and conquer this fear, so slowly I started to sit up and swing my legs off the edge of the bed and stand up. I must explain the prevailing atmosphere as it was one of a different "dimension"; the light a beautiful blue/white rather like loads of moonbeams. Movement became easier as I seemed to be travelling on friction-free roller skates. I moved towards the end of the room where there was a closed door that had this blue/white light emanating from around the edges. I was no longer frightened but rather exhilarated . . . All of a sudden I took off like bloody Superman, I'm about four feet off the ground I guess, flew into this very large room, up to one end, turned so my back was to the wall and whizzed up to the ceiling with very little control as I nigh on brained myself in the process, but I just managed to "jack-knife" so that my back and backs of my legs were virtually touching the ceiling.

So here I am hovering off the bloody ceiling feeling really happy when I sense it's about time I went back, so I flew back across the ceiling down through the open door into darkness and woke up. It's funny that the thing that aroused me was the fact that I was laughing.

The strange thing about this dream/nightmare/trip is that with a normal experience of this kind one normally wakes up with a start, literally bathed in perspiration. When I woke up it was gently, I was chuckling and when I felt my forehead, etc. I was comfortably cool.

These experiences are usually so vivid that it is hard for the dreamer to entertain real doubts about what happened, and so powerful that their memory lives on for years. Mr. James Dyer is now eighty, but still remembers a "flying dream" he had more than twenty years ago. He adds, "I do assure you that this is not pure fiction, as the experience is still very real to me and happened on more than one occasion over a period of four or five years, but tends to dim with advancing age."

What was that? What wakened me? Such a strange feeling and yet somehow familiar. I know! I've been flying again. All I have to do is stretch out my arms, give just a little jump, and I'm off. Nobody can come near me. It's so easy! I have only to think of what I want to do next, and there I go. What a wonderful feeling of freedom. It has to be experienced to be believed. No need to worry about a single thing. Come to think of it, I've never seen the countryside looking so beautiful as it does now. Marvellous! Gently rolling hills and vales, and a sparkling stream running through it all. Float lightly down and take a closer look at everything, and enjoy the lovely weather. Spring was never so beautiful.

Someone shouting. Disturbs me somewhat. Whoever it is has no right to spoil the peace of this lovely place. Sounds like a crowd, and in not too pleasant a mood. In fact quite angry. Can't be me they're shouting at. Can it? It is, by gum, and they're after me. Can't make out what they're saying, but it's my blood they want, no doubt about it.

Closer now. I'd better run for it. Run? Why run? I can get away easily, all I have to do is spread my arms and take off. I desperately try to get my arms working but they are so very heavy. Help me, somebody! Panic strikes me, and though I try to run my legs are like rubber, no strength at all, yet I still manage to keep ahead of my pursuers.

At last! A slight downhill and I am a trifle more hopeful. Only to have my hopes dashed as the beautiful green turn comes to an abrupt end under my feet, and I fall over the edge. A tremendous fear grips me. If I can't get my arms working I shall be smashed to pieces below. Phew! Just in time! My arms spread, and the lightness of flight saves me. I swear I must just have skimmed the grass by an inch and I am literally dripping with sweat, and feel as weak as water.

Must hurry and get back home before daylight. Before daylight? It is daylight and I'm scared of what's happened to me. Hurry, before it's too late. Too late for what? I wish I knew what bothers me.

I do wish I could understand why I am looking at me

lying in bed. Because I am floating just under my bedroom ceiling. No one knows the predicament I'm in. Syl-
via is shaking me and asking what is wrong and I can't
answer, being stuck up here on the ceiling. My senses
leave me, and blackness engulfs me until, Oh joy! I struggle upwards through a thick mist of tiredness to see my
darling smiling at me and the wonderful light of brilliant
dawn shows through my window.

Out-of-body experiences seem to be closely related to lucid
dreams, and sometimes develop out of them, and like lucid
dreams, they appear to be a constant part of human experience.
But there is a difference. Betty M., who has had lucid dreams,
out-of-body dreams and also waking out-of-body experiences,
makes an interesting comparison of these states. Perhaps the
most obvious is that in the dream OBE there isn't necessarily
any awareness that this is a dream—in fact it is almost indistinguishable from the waking state, so that often it is difficult
for the person to work out whether he is awake or asleep.
Outside noises such as passing traffic may be audible during
the out-of-body dream, for example, and continue after waking. This is quite unlike the lucid dream, in which by definition, the person knows that they are dreaming, however real
the dream seems.

She has also observed that the out-of-body dream seems to
occur at a lighter level of sleep than the lucid dream, although
she stresses that it is quite unlike the hazy half-dream state.
She has found that the out-of-body experience seems to involve at some stage a change of state, such as a false awakening, or a sense of leaving one's body. Memory seems to be
more accessible in the out-of-body state than in a lucid dream,
and indeed may seem to be as clear as waking memory. In
some respects the OBE provides an even greater degree of
control and freedom than the lucid dream—it is easier to pass
through solid objects in an OBE, for example, and easier to
transpose oneself to some distant place. Betty M. also mentions
the awakening from an out-of-body dream, which she describes as ''clicking'' awake, or like the turn of a switch, unlike the more gradual drifting up through consciousness which
occurs in ordinary or lucid dreaming. Many people who have

had OBEs in other states of consciousness also describe this sensation of "clicking" back into one's body.

Here Betty M. describes how it felt the first time she deliberately tried to leave her body. Although on that occasion she was awake, she says she has learned to induce the same state in a lucid dream in the same way, by lying down and relaxing in her dream.

As I lay awake one morning during the Christmas holiday I let myself relax deeply, trying to imagine I was floating on the sea and concentrating my thought on the experiment I wished to try. Gradually a numbness overcame me until I felt as though floating. My breathing and heartbeat quickened, then suddenly my legs started moving (or so it seemed) down through the bed and back again, swinging through an ever-increasing angle. Excitedly I realised that what I had suspected before was indeed happening now, and I tried to stand up—with the effect of nearly terminating the experience. Quickly letting myself go, the swinging process resumed, until at last my feet touched the floor and I stood free. What a strange and wonderful feeling, like a butterfly newly emerged from its chrysalis.

Many people have tried to learn how to leave their body at will. Waldo Vieira is a Brazilian who has made a study of his own out-of-body experiences since he first had a "spontaneous, whirlwind projection" at the age of nine. He believes that separations from the body are experienced every day by men and women during natural sleep, and describes many of these in his book *Projections of the Consciousness*. For those who want to achieve the out-of-body state and indulge in a little astral travel, Vieira recommends lying on your back with the head pointing east.

Little by little, I mentally ceased to feel the soma [body]. The vibrational state [sensation of tingling and pulsations throughout the soma] arrived, followed by a short period of discomfort. Removing all other ideas, I continued concentrating on saturating the mind with a single thought: a strong desire to leave and float over the soma lying on the bed. The takeoff of the psychosoma [astral body] occurred.

Vieira has formed an institute for the study and teaching of "projectiology"—the art (or perhaps the science) of projecting your consciousness outside your body. His students seem to be of mixed ability—some claim to be able to "project" every night at will; others struggle for years, following his recommendations faithfully without ever achieving the shortest astral journey.

Lucid dreams provide one route out of the sleeping body, but there are others. Sometimes an episode of sleep paralysis culminates in an out-of-body experience, as Mr. B. Henry describes here.

At the time of my experience I was twenty-five years old, participated in a wide range of sports and was extremely fit. At the particular time, I had returned home after playing in a football match; on entering the house I switched on the television and lay back on the sofa in order to listen to the results. Some time later I heard the outside doorbell ring and then the strange thing happened. I tried to stand up and could not move any part of my body. I was mentally aware of what I was trying to do, but unable to move. The outside door was now being banged furiously and still I could not move; instead I appeared to be somewhere above my body looking down at myself. I could see myself in detail, I kept telling my body to move but could not. It was as though I was outside yet inside myself, if you can understand what I mean. It is very difficult to put my experience into words . . . It was a peculiar, yet in a strange way, a pleasant experience. It only frightens me now but it did not at the time. I was completely relaxed, almost floating.

OBEs seem to occur most commonly when you are on the borders of sleeping and waking, a state in which hypnagogic imagery almost certainly plays a part. Waldo Vieira, too, lays great store by sleep onset, and suggests that in the time between waking and sleeping the connection between the body and "the real me" is loosened. What this means scientifically is difficult to say, but the following account suggests that it can have dramatic results.

Martin Pryer was employed as a bus driver for London Transport when he read a book which described a technique for inducing out-of-body experiences. It involved lying in bed, relaxed but not falling asleep, and banishing all thoughts from his mind—very much the same kind of procedure Waldo Vieira recommends and that Betty M. and others have found works for them. Mr. Pryer decided to try it. He describes how for three weeks nothing happened. Then:

> One night as I hovered on the hypnagogic threshold I had my first vision. In full colour, sound and in 3D I was driving a Routemaster bus in Whitehall. I could hear the engine throbbing and feel the wheel vibrating. I was exultant. I was getting somewhere.

As Mr. Pryer suggests, his technique seems to have kept him on the hypnagogic threshold, in a state between waking and sleeping, a state he refers to as his "unusual mode." In this altered state of awareness he had several unusual experiences, some of a very violent nature.

> One night I found myself in a dark room. There was a very large whooshing sound and I was in the grip of a man-like creature. It held me from behind, its arms round my chest, pinioning my arms, and its legs wrapped round my waist. Although I was in the unusual mode, and I dimly knew that I was still in my bed, I cannot emphasise the realness of this experience. And this creature was breathing heavily into my left ear, I could feel its breath. I have never known such terror. Somehow I knew that there was a light switch in the corner of the room. I managed to free my left arm and stagger, still with this creature clinging to my back, to the switch in the corner. It was covered with trailing wires but I managed to find it, and as I switched the light on I was free and back in the normal mode in bed. I was beside myself with fear and remember saying to myself, "What the hell was that?"
> Another night I found myself wrestling with an anthropomorphic creature by my bedside. This creature repeat-

edly threw me to the floor until I managed to resist and I found myself properly awake in my bed.

On one occasion, having entered the unusual mode, I found myself in a colonnaded courtyard. There was a man-like creature there, totally featureless, unclad and completely black, like oil. I hid behind a column. This creature was huge, about eight feet tall, and suddenly a white creature who looked like a real male human rushed from the side. They came together with a mighty crash and fought like maniacs. I hastily departed to the usual mode of awareness in my bed.

Another night I found myself in a circular domed room. It was brightly lit and there were pallets on the floor pointed outwards like the blank "numbers" of some watches. Two ordinary men in white coats came to me. They did not speak but took me to a small door to the left. I looked inside and there was a raging inferno. They took me to a small door to the right out of which emerged three small man-like creatures, grey in colour and leering at me in a knowing way. These three then leapt upon me and began to rip me apart. One stuck his finger in my left eye. I fought my way back to normal reality but was horrified to find that my left eye still felt the pressure as though a finger had indeed been pushed into it.

There are several interesting things about Mr. Pryer's experiences. First is the fine borderline between the "dream" and the reality. Mr. Pryer is able to pass from one to the other but is awake and aware in both modalities, the "normal" mode and what he calls his "unusual" state of awareness. Secondly, he comments on the intense realness of the experiences—even though he knows that they are not in fact real. Finally, there are the strong bodily sensations he has—the feeling of being "ripped apart." Notice that the sensation of pressure, of having had a finger stuck in his eyes, remains even after he has come back to normal reality. People who have had the "alien abduction" experience often describe graphically the operations or physical assaults that have been performed on them. Probably most of these extra-terrestrial kidnappings can be explained by sleep paralysis and hallucination, but hypnagogia may play a part in others. When an experience *feels* as real as Martin Pryer's clearly did, it must be all too easy to convince yourself that it *was* real, and to search for any explanation, however unlikely.

Several people discover by accident that in some particular circumstances they may find themselves and their body disconcertingly parting company. Like other sleep phenomena such as sleepwalking, factors such as stress, tiredness and alcohol sometimes trigger the experience. Kenneth Mountford, who has had many spontaneous OBEs, says that with some effort he has learnt how to induce them. In his experience, they never occur when he is dog-tired. He's had most success producing them by first making sure that he has had plenty of sleep, so first thing in the morning or at the end of an afternoon siesta is the best time. Clearly his experiences tend to occur when he is in only a light sleep, and therefore they probably develop out of lucid dreams. He says:

> The sensation of leaving your body is real, but you are aware you are not conscious in the normal sense but not dreaming either, I do not know what it is. You have some degree of control over where you float, but it's a bit like being weightless with nothing to hold on to. I have sometimes found it difficult to stop the experience and that is very distressing. The experience is a little frightening, but over the years I have got used to it. Although interesting, it is not a pleasant experience.

Whether they find it pleasant or unpleasant, frightening or exciting, almost everyone is interested to find themselves out of their body. Christine Matters had her first experience of an out-of-body dream in April 1992.

> I went to bed and found myself floating above the ceiling. I found this extraordinary. Fascinating in fact. And yet I wasn't scared. I was fully conscious and in a remarkable void. I decided to look down at my body. I scanned from the bottom of my bed up towards my face. While doing this, I thought how vivid the colours of my quilt were from up here. Then I saw my hand overlapping the fold of the quilt. Suddenly I was staring straight at my face. With that, I immediately woke up.

"Interesting but not necessarily enjoyable" is a quite common verdict on out-of-body dreams—unlike lucid dreams, which almost everyone enjoys. One woman who has been having OBEs for over fourteen years, since she was sixteen, says that they are fearful, unpleasant experiences. She knows when she is going to have one and tries her hardest to stay awake, but eventually falls asleep. Several people describe the way that the exhilarating freedom of leaving one's body can quickly turn to terror that one might never be able to return. This is an account of a dream OBE that occurred when the dreamer was about sixteen. She was under stress due to exams and had had little sleep.

At around dawn I felt myself lifting out of my body, like a great weight had just been released from tying me to my physical self. The feeling was amazing—I felt like I was on a luxury water bed. As I ascended up, it was almost like it was on a very calm, rippling wave. What was more prominent was that I was glowing beautifully. There were rays of white, golden light radiating from me, and it seemed I was surrounded by an aura that was very comforting and serene. There were two shelves high on the wall directly next to my bed and I distinctly remembered being able to read the titles of the books as I got closer. There's also a slant in the ceiling directly above my bed due to my low roof. It seemed the top part of my body actually penetrated this solid matter.

I turned myself to turn over and look down on myself. However, at that point the shock hit me that it was happening and this is when things changed and I was very scared.

I said to myself about three times, "I've got to get down to my body." I was petrified at this time. I was very confused and I honestly believed I was about to die at that moment. So many thoughts rushed through me at that time. I kept thinking that I was too young to die and that it must be due to a brain tumour. I thought of my parents waking up in the morning to find me dead in bed.

Suddenly everything around me was black—like a horrible, evil presence was around me. There was a great pressure on the back of my head—as if someone very heavy was pressing down on my head so hard that I could not move. I tried to move my limbs and found everything was paralysed. I can't describe this enough—it was like hell. It's too profound to explain fully what I experienced. I was petrified. Then the pressure on my skull got more and more intense and I heard a "crack" and I was so certain my skull had actually cracked. After this the pain moved down my vertebral column where I felt sharp tingling reaching my arms to my hands and to my legs as the pain moved down further. I was still paralysed and felt pinned down.

This account shows very clearly the gradual transition as the dreamer's sleep lightens from the dream state in which she has the OBE, with its comforting, almost mystical aura and feeling of serenity, into a phase of sleep paralysis where she is terrified, and has the horrifying bodily sensations of being crushed and paralysed, as though by some "evil presence."

It is interesting to compare that experience with the following dream, in which the sequence of events is reversed: the dreamer is first in a "semi-awake" state of sleep paralysis, unable to sit up, and it seems to be his efforts to force himself upwards which catapult him out of his body.

In 1947, when I was twenty-seven years old, I woke up one night in a semi-awake condition. I tried to sit up in bed, I tried to force myself upwards and I thought I had succeeded and then I found out I had not succeeded in sitting upright, and I imagined that I was out of my body, that is, my mind or spirit was, and looking down at my earthly body, only of course one cannot really look because a spirit has no eyes and in the night one cannot see, but I thought this. I was very scared and frightened and there was an uncanny hissing noise all the while and stress as though the body resented this detachment.

Then my spirit started to rise and I could not stop it; it went through house walls and ceiling and on up into the sky, and one thinks you can see the house and other houses all falling away beneath you and it all seems very real, although you must be dreaming. And then suddenly with great relief I awoke as normal in bed, although terribly shaken.

For many people, then, the problem is not how to induce OBEs, but how to stop them happening. JC, who had an OBE as a child of eleven, while she was lying in bed trying to sleep, says that she first had "... a dreadful feeling I was about to die. Then instantly I could see my own body lying on the bed." People who have this kind of experience regularly and do not enjoy it often develop strategies to try and avoid it. Nearly always the experience seems to occur when you are relaxed and lying on your back. One man regularly plagued by OBEs told his wife that if she ever noticed him lying on his back she must turn him over on to his side. Another person finds that she can abort the experience by sitting up in bed. Waldo Vieira's advice that you should lie prone if you want to "project" seems to be soundly based.

According to Celia Green and Charles McCreery, while people can fairly easily train themselves to have lucid dreams, the out-of-body experience is harder to achieve. Some people seem to have a natural facility for slipping out of their body almost at will, and some accounts suggest that children have a greater facility for out-of-body experiences than adults, and that the ability is lost, or at any rate attenuated, with age. This may be because children are not attached as firmly to their bodies' boundaries as adults are. The brain is still setting up its spatial coordinates, and hasn't yet acquired such a fixed idea of where it is.

We know that the brain is capable of creating a whole new, entirely synthetic world from memory—it does just this during dreaming. It can even reset the coordinates of "self," rerunning them so that the brain definition of "you" moves from behind your eyes to a totally different viewpoint, for example, the ceiling. There you will be in psychological and not physical space. What you "see" from up there will be a psychological image constructed by the brain entirely from memory. There are therefore likely to be discrepancies between this and what is actually going on at ground level.

The "psychological model" gives a perfectly adequate explanation for most out-of-body experiences, whether they occur during full consciousness or dreaming. Margaret Coles

used to have OBEs when she was a little girl, when she was
just going off to sleep. She lived by a railway line and when
the trains went by the vibrations would shake the house, and
she would find herself up on the ceiling looking down at herself, or out on the roof of the house. She says, "I was not
dreaming because I could draw a plan of how the slates went
on the roof. A little girl wouldn't have the logic to draw it
unless she had seen it." Although she was convinced that she
could only have known how the slates were laid on her roof
by seeing them in her OB dream, she could almost certainly
have got this knowledge from seeing other roofs, or pictures
or drawings of roofs.

But supposing there is evidence that someone has gained
information during an out-of-body experience which could
only have been gained through the senses, as if they were in
physical space, not psychological space? We have been sent
one or two accounts of these dream adventures which certainly
give one pause for thought. Here is Mr. J. Knight's account
of an experience he had almost twenty-two years ago at the
age of forty-nine.

At the time I was a machinist in a factory working a
6 a.m.–2 p.m. shift. After arriving home at 2.30 p.m. I
would have a light meal and then lie on my bed fully
clothed and have a sleep for a couple of hours. My wife
was school-teaching at the time, and she would often
wake me when she arrived home at 4.30 p.m.

On this particular day, a lovely summer's day I remember, I lay down on the bed and very soon drifted off to
sleep. My next conscious thought was of travelling at a
vast speed. I can still vividly remember my thoughts at
that particular time, "Just go along with it." The speed
sensation stopped and I was floating near the light switch
on the wall. I appeared to be seeing it upside down. I
looked over to the bed and saw myself fast asleep; my
body was turned on its side, and I could hear myself
snoring. I remember thinking, "How can I be here and
yet still be asleep on the bed?" It was all very strange.

I floated over to the window and looked down the road.
I saw a man reverse his car down to the end of his drive-
way. While I watched him he got out of his car and pro-

ceeded to wash the vehicle with a large yellow sponge after soaking it in a bucket of water which his wife had brought out to him. I next thought, "I think I'll see if I can go outside the window and go down the road." Almost immediately a voice, either in the room or in my head, said, "That's enough for now."

Without motivating myself, and with no conscious help from me, the *real me* floated over my body and after seeming to adjust itself, gently, ever so gently, as if this was a regular occurrence, lowered itself into my sleeping body.

I was awake in an instant, not believing what I knew to be true. Suddenly I remembered the man down the road washing his car. With one bound I was off the bed and looking through the window. I wasn't really surprised to see him still soaping his car with the sponge. I couldn't wait for my wife to come home to tell her. Although she did look at me sideways while telling her what had happened, she believed me because I was so full of it.

Of course I told a few friends who thought that I was a slice of bread short of a sandwich. It wasn't until a few years later when I read a book on someone else's experiences that I realised that I was not alone. I have often longed for the experience again, but sadly it has eluded me. I think that the one thing it has taught me is that at death my body dies but the *real me* goes on.

We can't be sure which phase of sleep Mr. Knight was in when he had the experience, but from the information he gives it seems likely that he would have been asleep for an hour. So probably this is an experience that occurred during dreaming sleep, and not a hypnagogic phenomenon at sleep onset. He gives a lovely description, very similar to that of people who have out-of-body experiences as part of the near-death experience, of the splitting of consciousness which occurs when the experiencer's body lies on the bed while what he feels is "the real me" watches it from above. Not only can the "real me" see the body on the bed, but it seems to have been able to gather information about what was happening outside the window—information which he was able to verify on awakening.

But can we be sure that he could not have gathered this information through his senses? Might he not have heard the sounds of his neighbour washing the car as he drifted off to sleep and then reconstructed the image later while dreaming? The yellow sponge is a convincing touch, but he could have seen and remembered seeing his neighbour using such a sponge on previous car-washing occasions.

However, does this matter very much? The real significance of this dream OBE is the meaning it had for the dreamer, the clarity and impact which set it apart from an ordinary dream. This was a dream which left Mr. Knight with the conviction, felt by so many people who have had similar experiences, that there is a "real me" which is quite independent of the body, and which even death cannot extinguish.

GH describes an out-of-body dream which is similar in that it too had a mystical, spiritual quality. It did not need "verification" because it gave her what she needed at the time: confirmation of the existence of some separate aspect of consciousness.

This happened years ago when I was near to having my second child. I was in a deep sleep on the sofa and for no reason I climbed out of my body and I was kneeling down looking at myself asleep. I didn't float or see any bright lights, but I remember it was a lovely feeling and very peaceful. Then I just climbed back into my body. I then woke up straight away . . . I said to myself, if that is dying I am not afraid, it was such a lovely and peaceful feeling. My own explanation of this is my cousin died giving birth to her first boy and I had it on my mind all the time, and I was frightened of dying myself. I felt that she was showing me not to be frightened of death.

In August 1979, Alan Pring was undergoing surgery in Manchester Royal Infirmary. One night, two days after his operation, he had a strange experience, an experience which he says is not like a normal memory (and certainly not like a dream), in that it has not faded with the passage of time, but is retained with complete clarity.

In the hospital ward two beds away from mine was a man who was awaiting abdominal surgery. He was a big, heavily built man, about forty years of age, who at some time in the past had suffered the amputation of his left leg, high up on the thigh, leaving only a short stump.

That night I found myself standing at the foot of his bed watching as he attempted to lift himself out of the bed and into his wheelchair. He had demonstrated that he was quite capable of performing this feat since he had tremendous strength in his forearms. But on this occasion it all went badly wrong.

The ward was almost in darkness and the only bright light was above the man's bed. He leaned over to his left and grasped the arms of the wheelchair, one in each hand, raised his body off the bed, but as he swung himself off the bed towards the chair its wheels rotated and it shot from underneath him. His right foot was still on the bed and he fell from a height of some three feet, landing on the stump of his left leg.

I remained motionless at the foot of the bed, but the noise of the crashing wheelchair and the man's yell of agony brought a nurse running from the office at the end of the ward to my right. She totally ignored me standing there as she rushed past me only inches away. The man writhed in agony on the floor between the two beds as the occupant of the other propped himself up to observe the cause of the commotion. The man on the floor was too big and heavy for the nurse to lift on her own, and she ran past me to the office to summon help before quickly returning to attend to the unfortunate patient, who was in considerable distress. And all the while I just stood there observing but not offering to help.

Very shortly a second nurse came running to help and as they were in the process of lifting the man on to his bed they were joined by a male doctor. The man was groaning and swearing but eventually his pain was relieved when the doctor administered an injection. There were many comings and goings but I was totally ignored as the doctor and nurses dashed to and fro within inches of where I was standing.

The next morning I walked, or rather shuffled, to the

washroom at the other end of the ward. I was still attached by catheter to a plastic bag and its metal holder. In the washroom I overheard two of the ward patients talking about the previous night's events. One asked the other had he been woken by the commotion? Then they decided at what time it had occurred. When they concurred that it had happened at about two o'clock in the morning I felt the hair on the back of my neck rise, for I knew that I could not possibly have been standing at the foot of that bed at that time: each night I had been given two sleeping tablets before ten o'clock and I did not awake fully until at least six in the morning.

On my way back to my bed I stopped at the bedside of the man who had propped himself up in bed to look down on the unfortunate amputee. This man's bed was next to mine. We spoke about the night's events, and then I asked him what he obviously thought was a strange question. I asked him where I was during all the commotion. I had to repeat the question before he replied.

He said that I was in my bed, fast asleep the whole time. I believed him. Nevertheless, I know with absolute certainty that I was standing at the foot of that bed as I have described.

Could Alan have gained such detailed knowledge of the night's events if he was, in fact, asleep? He himself is certain that he was actually *there*, standing at the foot of the bed, seeing everything as it happened. Was this a psychological model created by his dreaming brain from the information available to it—the noise of the crashing wheelchair, the man's cries of agony, the nurse's running footsteps? Within this psychological model Alan generates a viewpoint of his own and then "sees" the events as they unfold. That seems the only rational explanation, and yet models created by the brain with such a limited sensory input from the outside world are not usually as accurate as this one appears to have been. Or might Alan have been experiencing a "false awakening" which would have seemed just as real to him as a true awakening from sleep? In this case he would have been in a light stage of REM sleep, and therefore more able to pick up cues from the outside world which might then have been incorporated into his dream. But here again, it is highly unusual for the dream to match reality as closely as this one seems to have done. Any "model" the brain tries to make in either REM or slow-wave sleep is unlikely to be very accurate, as information reaching the brain from the outside world is necessarily so restricted.

But the alternative is equally difficult for modern science to accept. It is that consciousness and brain are to some extent independent of each other, and that during an out-of-body experience it is possible to gain accurate information not through the senses. It is tempting to go for this explanation, but I don't think in this case the evidence really justifies it. The fact that Alan was in such close proximity to the events of that night means that one cannot rule out the possibility that he might have incorporated cues from the outside world in his dream. One point which should be considered is that Alan was able to see the whole event unfold *before* the commotion occurred, when one would have expected there would be few cues to guide him. However, even if that were the case, one has, yet again, to marvel at the brain's capacity to make very service-able bricks even with a minimum of straw.

However, there are accounts which give another dimension to the out-of-body experience. Some of her out-of-body dreams had led Betty M. to think that these strange experiences might possess an extrasensory element. She gives this account of an expedition she took during an out-of-body experience one night.

Finding myself in the out-of-body state, I desired to see a suitable bungalow where we might live (we were anxious to move house at the time). After a travelling sensation I found myself hovering above an old terraced house in a London street. This is nonsense, I thought, for we would never consider moving *there*, and I tried to induce the vision to change, but to no avail. Then I "clicked" awake.

Several months later, something happened, she says, "out of the blue," and they did move to just such a house as she had seen in her dream. Of course, one London terraced house looks very much like another, especially if you are only hovering above it. "Modelling" could provide a plausible explanation. But still, this wasn't a house she felt she could ever have envisaged living in, and she did end up living there. Was there an element of precognition in her dream?

Certainly dreams have a reputation for providing fertile ground for extrasensory experiences. The late Ian Currie was a Canadian professor of sociology, with an interest in parapsychology and psychical research, who spent many years looking for evidence of man's survival after physical death. It was his contention that "Only the fact that the living temporarily possess a physical body prevents them from realising that they are already as 'dead' as they will ever be, because the essential selfhood dwells in the astral form and is only the temporary tenant of the physical."

Ian Currie regarded out-of-body dreams as astral projections in a state of partial unconsciousness. The following story, an unusual account of haunting by a "living ghost," is taken from his book *You Cannot Die!*

Some time ago, my wife dreamed on several occasions of a house whose interior arrangement she was able to describe in all its details, although she had no idea where this house existed ... Later ... I leased from Lady B— for the autumn a house in the mountains of Scotland ... My son, who was then in Scotland, took charge of the matter, without my wife or I ever seeing the house in question.

When I went there alone later, to sign the contract, and take possession of the property, Lady B—was still inhabiting the place. She told me that if I had no objection, she would give me a room which she herself had been occupying, and which had, for some time past, been haunted by a woman who continued to appear there.

Being quite sceptical about such matters, I replied that I should be delighted to make the acquaintance of the ghost. I went to sleep in the room, but did not see any ghost.

Later, when my wife arrived, she was astonished when she recognised the house as the one of her dreams! She went all over it; all details corresponded with those she had so often seen in sleep. But when she went back down into the drawing room again she said: "But still, this cannot be the house I saw in my dreams, because there ought to be a succession of rooms that are missing here." She was told that the rooms actually existed and that one could reach them through the drawing room. When they were shown to her, she remembered each of them clearly.

She said, however, that it seemed to her that one of the bedrooms was not used for this purpose when she visited it in sleep. It was again explained to her that this room had not formerly been a bedroom but had been changed into one.

Two or three days later my wife and I visited Lady B—. Since they were unknown to each other, I introduced them. Lady B— cried out in amazement, "Why—you are the lady who has been haunting my bedroom."

If we accept the facts as they are presented here, the only rational explanation for them is that this is a case of cryptoamnesia—that the woman in question had at some time in her life been to the house but had totally forgotten the experience. But we are given no evidence that this was the case. Or was she simply experiencing *déjà vu*—the feeling that you recognise a place, have been there before? The fact that she noticed differences between the house as it was and as she had seen it, and that these could be accounted for, makes this less likely. Could she, then, have acquired her knowledge of the house not through the normal sensory channels but by, for example, remote viewing?

Many remote-viewing experiments have been carried out with the appropriate controls and have shown statistically significant results. Stanley Krippner and Montague Ullman, for example, in a pilot study on ESP and dreams, conducted a clairvoyance experiment with a student who claimed to have occasional out-of-body experiences in his sleep. A "target" picture was placed in a box attached to the ceiling of the sleep room. The student was asked to try to "see" the picture if he had an OBE and to try to dream about it even if he did not have an OBE. A second print was chosen as a telepathy target, but the student was not told about this. EEG electrodes were put on the student's head before he went to bed, and he was woken ten minutes after the EEG activity showed him to have entered a REM phase and asked to report his dream. Independent judges found few correlations between the dream reports and the clairvoyance targets. On the final morning of the study the student reported that he had had an OBE the previous night. Inspection of his EEG record showed that just before he was woken from one period of REM sleep the REM sleep was interrupted by an unusual pattern of slow brain waves in the theta and delta frequencies (Krippner, 1996). It is interesting that this was the night his dream (of a sunset) showed the most impressive correlation with the target clairvoyance picture—Berman's *View in Perspective of a Perfect Sunset.*

The student described his dream thus: "It was dark outside and light inside . . . It was dusk . . . It was just getting dark. Sunset. Very hazy . . . It wasn't a clear day. It wasn't either foggy or cloudy. It was sort of muffled. It wasn't a clear sunset . . ." Unfortunately Krippner and Ullman do not give us the student's account of what happened during his OBE, although the relationship of the dream to the target picture is convincing. The most interesting result of this study is that specific EEG changes seemed to be correlated with the out-of-body experience. If this is really so, then it would suggest that the brain functions differently during an OBE than in normal dreaming. We know that changes in body image and projection of the body image outside the body (autoscopy) occur as part of the onset of temporal lobe epileptic seizures, and that in this type of seizure the EEG shows a similarity to the abnormal pattern Krippner and Ullman found. But it is highly unlikely that Krippner and Ullman's student had epilepsy— they are both experienced scientific research workers, and would have mentioned the fact in their paper. They would also have noted if his EEG had been abnormal at any other time. It is more logical to assume that OBEs may be associated with different brain functioning.

If remote viewing is possible at all, there is no reason why it should not also be possible in sleep. But accepting that the mind can somehow pick up information at a distance is the easy bit—or at least, relatively easy. What makes Ian Currie's story even more intriguing, and even more difficult to account for, is the fact that there is independent corroboration of the woman's night travels—Lady B— recognised her as the woman she had seen in her room. The "ghost" was not an internal hallucination specific to Lady B—, but part of a sensory experience held in common between the two women. It was, like the Wilmot case which opened this chapter, an out-of-body experience with a witness.

One of the richest sources of dreams with an extrasensory component is *Phantasms of the Living*, case histories of apparitions and strange experiences collected and examined by Gurney, Myers and Podmore. Amongst them is this dream, experienced by the wife of T. W. Smith, a headmaster. In some ways it is very comparable to the story quoted above.

About six months after their marriage Mrs. Smith dreamed that she had been back at her former place of work, in a room she remembered well. Four women were there, talking and laughing, two of whom she knew, two who were strangers to her. She saw one of them turn off the gas, then the four went upstairs to bed and she followed them. She went into a bedroom with her two friends, and watched her friend Bessie put some things in a box, undress and get into bed. Mrs. Smith then went over and sat on her bed, taking her hand and saying, "Bessie, let's be friends." At that point the dream ended.

Some weeks later she went to visit her mother, and there found a letter from one of these friends, begging her to write and let them know she was still alive. Mr. Smith himself went to see the pair, but said nothing to them of his wife's dream. The two women described how they had gone to bed one Sunday night when Bessie suddenly cried out that she had just seen his wife, who had touched her and said, "Let's be friends." They confirmed other details of the dream, too, for example that the two women she had seen did indeed share a room, and that two new employees had arrived since the wife left.

In this case there is no need to try to explain the fact that Mrs. Smith "saw" the place where she had previously worked—she knew it well and her brain would have had no problem in making a perfectly adequate model of it. The intriguing part of this story is again the shared sensory experience of the two women. It's interesting that only Bessie saw Mrs. Smith, and that Mrs. Smith spoke only to Bessie. Was this, then, a telepathic experience between two close friends, comparable to the shared dreams of two people described in the chapter on telepathic dreams (see p. 145)?

Can we begin to comprehend how, even if consciousness can become separate from the body and able to pick up information at a distance, it can be accompanied by a physical image of that body? The Red Queen was able to believe as many as six impossible things before breakfast, but, sadly, most of us are more limited. It may simply be that we do not yet fully understand the nature of consciousness. There are certainly plenty of anecdotal accounts of masters such as Si Baba appearing to their disciples at a distance. Scientifically, we have to dismiss these accounts simply because there is no theory that will explain how consciousness can extend beyond the skull. And yet these are experiences reported independently and in good faith by sane, intelligent people who have no reason to invent or deceive. All this would become much simpler if the universe was connected at the everyday level of experience, as quantum mechanics currently shows it to be. If, for example, every conscious thought was capable of resonating with another brain under certain conditions, then we would have no difficulty in explaining telepathy, precognition, and other parapyschological phenomena. They will continue to intrigue and puzzle us even if we can so far offer no explanation for them.

15

The Mystical World of Dreams

For most of us, dreams are a product of our memories and experiences, providing us with fleeting moments of drama, entertainment and, occasionally, insight. But can they, as some dream accounts seem to suggest, give us more than this, allow us occasional glimpses of a transcendent reality underlying our normal selves?

When, three years ago, we were collecting accounts of near-death experiences (NDEs) for a book, we found that many people sent us experiences that had occurred when they were asleep. We deliberately excluded all these, on the grounds that they were probably "only dreams." Looking back at many of these, we felt that this was not a logical distinction to make. What became very clear in our researches was that what we call "near-death experiences" are by no means specific to a near-death situation. They are mystical experiences which can occur in any state of consciousness. They occur spontaneously, during illness, during childbirth, under the influence of drugs or anaesthesia, unhappiness or stress, even in the deepest stages of unconsciousness during which it is theoretically impossible for any experiences to occur. When we compared these experiences with the "real" near-death experience (for example, in someone who had been resuscitated after a heart attack) we found that they were indistinguishable.

But if these experiences can occur in deep unconsciousness, why shouldn't they also occur during sleep? Sleep, after all, is simply, another state of consciousness. There is no reason why it, too, shouldn't support similar mystical experiences.

Whether we regard these as a very special sort of dream, or as something of a quite different nature—say, a vision—seems unimportant. Whatever label we attach to it, the quality of the experience is the same. These transcendent dreams, like NDEs, have profound and lasting effects on those who have them.

What exactly do we mean by a mystical experience? The American psychologist Abraham Maslow called these "peak experiences," and R. Bucke, a nineteenth-century Canadian psychiatrist, was one of the first Western scientists to try to define and categorise them. He listed nine features which he believed were the main elements. These were:

1. Feelings of unity
2. Feelings of objectivity and reality
3. Transcendence of space and time
4. Sense of sacredness
5. Deeply felt positive mood—joy, blessedness, peace and bliss
6. Paradoxicality—mystical consciousness which is often felt to be true in spite of violating Aristotelian logic
7. Ineffability—language is inadequate to express the experience
8. Transiency
9. Positive change in attitude or behaviour following the experience

None of these features is unique to the mystical experience. A lucid dream can feel intensely real, so can a drug-induced experience. Transcendence of space and time, feelings of unity and peace and bliss are common in drug-induced states too. Even the quality of ineffability is not limited to mystical experiences. Many people who have temporal lobe epilepsy experience unusual feelings, the "aura," at the start of the attack, but they often cannot describe these exactly, because they are beyond their normal experience; there are no words which will adequately describe them.

Mystical experiences are no rarity, neither are they confined to saints and mystics. In fact they are well within the range of normal human experience, and surprisingly widespread. Profound experiences such as Bucke described probably happen to about one person in ten. "Weaker" experiences are very much more common. Many surveys have asked about people's mystical experiences and tried to discover how common they are, usually by posing questions such as these:

Have you ever felt you are in touch with the universal or at one with the universe? Have you ever been aware of or felt an influence from a presence or power different from your everyday self?
Have you ever felt close to a powerful force that seems to lift you out of yourself?

Most surveys suggest that about a third of the general population have had a "weak" mystical experience at some time in their lives, perhaps the occasional feeling that they are in the presence of some power greater than themselves. Andrew McGreely and William C. McCready found that 35 percent of a representative sample of forty-five million had had such an experience. Another study found an even higher figure—50 per cent of a sample of 1,000 (Wuthnow, 1976).

Even higher estimates have been found. David Hay and A. Morisy, in a survey of postgraduate students at Nottingham University in 1976, found that 65 per cent of those questioned had had this kind of experience. And a social survey by the National Opinion Research Center at the University of Chicago in 1988 found that more than two-thirds of Americans said they had had at least one mystical experience. Five per cent said they had such experiences "often."

This survey also found that, not surprisingly, mystical experiences were more common in people whose lives already had some spiritual dimension, for example, people who regularly prayed or meditated. This may be because some specific esoteric practices such as meditation are thought in some way to modify brain activity, perhaps making spiritual experiences more likely. It is also probable that someone for whom the spiritual life is a reality may more readily accept an experience as mystical, while someone whose view of life is entirely materialist would be less open to these experiences and, if they did occur, more likely to interpret them in some other way and try to fit them into our current limited rational framework.

What is perhaps more surprising is that people who are active members of a church or synagogue were *less* likely to report such experiences. It may be because churchgoing has little to do with true spirituality, and certainly "experience" isn't always highly regarded in some churches. Some years ago I was searching for a control group for a research project which involved studying a group of mediums, and hit upon the idea of finding a group of churchgoers who had had some spiritual experience. When I approached the vicar of one local church and told him what I was looking for, I was soon disabused of the idea. "You won't find anyone in *this* church," I was told frostily, "who experiences anything like *that*."

However, what seems beyond dispute is that these experiences are so common that we have to regard them as part of the normal repertoire of human experience. They must therefore be mediated by brain structures common to everyone. But whether they have their origin within the brain (the only answer permitted by reductionist science) or outside it is a question that we still cannot answer.

What is it that convinces me that some dreams are in the same category of experience as the NDE? First, many of the same phenomena are described. Often the NDE starts with an out-of-body experience. This is followed by the feeling that one is travelling through a tunnel towards a white or golden light which can be seen glimmering at the end, and becomes brighter and brighter, but not dazzling to the eyes, as it gets closer. The light has a very special quality, variously described as love, peacefulness, even bliss. Sometimes there is a sense of some presence or being in the light. Sometimes other people are seen, often dead friends or relatives. Often, there seems to be some sort of barrier which indicates that the person can go no further, or that it is not yet time for them to go beyond a certain point. Occasionally the person may experience a "life review," a sort of Day of Judgement in which they see their own past actions flash by them and themselves feel the hurts they may have inflicted on others. Finally, and perhaps most significantly, the NDE is an experience which leaves a mark. For many people it is one of the most profound experiences they will ever have. It is remembered with extraordinary clarity long afterwards, and it may act as a catalyst to spiritual and individual development.

How do these dream experiences match up to this model?

Here is an account which the dreamer felt was a dream, though not an ordinary dream.

This happened in early 1977 when I was thirty-two years old and in good health. My husband was away on a business trip, my children were three and four years of age. I suppose I was under a slight amount of strain as we had just moved house from Lancaster to near Bristol, away from family and friends, although I am a very optimistic person, easily able to make friends. I also have a very happy life, a good husband and parents and a strong faith in God as a committed Christian—I am fortunate indeed!

It was the middle of the night. I seemed to awake with a sensation that my whole body was tingling and floating. I was very happy and comfortable. I was floating down a tunnel, or passage, towards a very bright golden and white light, surrounded by clear blue. I saw a crowd of people all waving their arms as if beckoning me towards them and I really wanted to go. I then saw my grandmother, who had died a few years earlier, and she was shouting loudly, "No—not yet, not yet."

Somehow, I did go back.

I lay awake for the rest of the night, wondering why this had happened, and if it was a dream, why was it different from anything else I had experienced? It somehow made me feel that my life had a purpose, but also frightened me as I could not understand it.

Years later, when I heard of people having near-death experiences, I wondered if that was what had happened to me—but why, when I had good health?

I lead a very ordinary life as a wife and mother of now teenage children, but somehow feel I always have to try my best to be kind to people and help them and *try* to live up to my Christian principles. I don't always succeed but I keep on trying.

This has all the hallmarks of a "real" NDE—the experience starts with peace and calm, there is then the journey down the tunnel to the light, and finally the decision, made for her by her grandmother, to return. The experience is followed by a spiritual unfolding and has a marked influence on her life.

There is nothing to distinguish this dream from most accounts of near-death experiences occurring in other circumstances.

Religious belief is not central to mystical experience—many people who have no religious belief have these experiences. In the following dream the light is manifested in a vision of the Virgin Mary, a symbol of the transcendent. It is interesting that the dreamer, Mrs. Phyllis Hayes, chose (or was given) that particular symbol, as she is not a churchgoer or a Catholic. But both cultural and religious beliefs do seem to influence the imagery of the NDE experience, and in our culture the Virgin Mary is a strong image of the divine.

> I went to bed and to sleep as usual. Sometime at about dawn, I suppose, while asleep, I was rushing through a long, long tunnel. It wasn't dark nor yet very light. As I rushed upwards along the wall I saw colours as though portraits of every member of my close family, my mother, father, grandmother, grandfather, all spaced apart at various levels. They all gave me a very welcoming smile, they all looked very happy. I went rushing on forever upward. I looked up: at the end of this tunnel was a very bright light, a pure light. In the centre was the head and shoulders of the Virgin Mary, in beautiful colours; over her head was a cover of the most beautiful blue I've ever seen. She looked at me and smiled. I stretched out my arm, calling, ''Mother Mary, Mother Mary.'' I couldn't reach her however hard I tried. Then I felt firm, gentle yet strong hands on my ankles. They firmly tugged me down, ever downwards so fast! Until with a tremendous thump I re-entered my earthly body. I had to stay quiet for several moments.

People who have these experiences are clear that they are in some way different from ordinary dreams. Sometimes they make this distinction by describing them as ''visions'' which occur during sleep. Ninety-year-old Miss E. Lloyd sent us this account. In this dream it is clear that the imagery fits the dreamer's belief system.

> My vision was during the night and was in the form of a dream—but oh so clear to me to this day, eighty-one

years after. I was running down a narrow path in a little wood—not a forest, only what we would now describe as a coppice—and I saw the figure of a youngish man with a most wonderful face dressed in a long robe with some sort of belt at his waist and sandals on his feet. I knew on the instant that it was Jesus Christ and put out my arms and ran towards him. But he shook his head, smiling at me all the time, and put both his hands up signing me to stop. Then again without words he signed me to go back and held out both hands giving me the certainty that I was not to approach him any nearer. He was about twenty feet away from me when I stopped and sadly realised he did not want me to come any closer but to go home. Being a fairly obedient child I knew I must obey him, so turned round and ran back the way I had come. That is all of the vision, but it changed, or rather affected my life from that night up to today. I may be the only person alive in the world who has actually come face to face with Jesus Christ. I little guessed that I should live to be ninety and have always wanted to die and be with Him in Heaven.

Mr. D. Chisholm sent us an account of a dream which is the quintessential essence of the transcendental state. There is the feeling of a journey upwards and towards the light, and eventually towards union with the Divine. The light is manifested as the love of God—an experience which the dreamer says is "indescribable."

Ten years ago I had a "dream" which I still remember vividly. In it, I "floated" up a shaft of light, sloped up like a moving staircase, which came from a window or aperture high up in otherwise dim surroundings.

Nearing the top I experienced what I can only describe as union with God's being, and being engulfed in God's love. Quite indescribable. Then I was outside the light, reluctantly accepting that some day I would be able to return and go right in.

It's interesting how the image of a shaft of light or a ladder or a moving staircase to Heaven is found in our culture. One of the earliest recorded dreamers of this type of dream is Jacob. It's also worth noting that Jacob was so significantly marked by this mystical dream that it determined his actions for many years to come.

> And he lighted upon a certain place and tarried there all night because the sun was set; and he took of the stones of that place and put them for his pillows and laid down in that place to sleep. And he dreamed, and behold a ladder set up on the earth, and the top of it reached the heaven: and behold the angels of God ascending and descending on it. And, behold, the Lord stood above it, and said, I am the Lord God of Abraham thy father, and the God of Isaac: the land whereon thou liest, to thee will I give it, and to thy seed . . . And Jacob awakened out of his sleep and he said, Surely the Lord was in this place and I knew it not. And he was afraid and said how dreadful is this place! This is none other but the House of God and this is the gate of Heaven. Jacob woke up early in the morning and took the stone which he had took for his pillows and set it up for a pillar and poured oil on the top of it.

One of the characteristics of mystical experiences is that they are ineffable—they are so far removed from normal everyday experiences that we don't have the words to describe them. Roger Payne mentions this same feeling:

> I . . . once dreamed—though here words quite fail—that I was somehow myself, or my Self. It was a feeling of the most indescribable bliss, of all I was ever meant to be, or could be, whole, complete, and it is just not possible to put into words what it was. It faded with the light of day, but the memory that I had it remains.

Mrs. Marion S. also refers to the difficulty of describing this kind of dream experience to other people. They are, she says, inexpressible, because nothing in physical experience can provide words to describe what happens. Neither, she says, do ordinary dreams alter one's life or remain in the memory for even a few seconds, let alone thirty-five years, as what she calls her "Real Dreams" have done:

> I call them "Real Dreams" because usually I am asleep or in the half-trance state when waking up, but they are not dreams. Dreams are confused and mine are usually very dull in colour, and they are concerned with things one can easily identify. "Real dreams" are totally different.

Marion S. has had three of these "Real Dreams" during her life (she is now sixty-five), and each, for her, has been a milestone on the path of her own spiritual development. The first occurred when she was only seven years old.

> Previously I had been walking up the garden, asking myself, "Who am I?" I decided that I was not my eyes, nor my ears, nor my brain, nor my body at all. I was *me*. End of cogitation of a seven-year-old, except that I went on later to decide that since this whole world including the *me* that occupied my body definitely existed, then someone must have made it, and in England we call that someone "God." I must have been a Cartesian child.
>
> Then I had a glorious dream, in which a very beautiful person, which I decided was male, came and we had a happy encounter. Definitely nothing to do with awakening sex or any of that. It was an innocent and happy childish "dream." I thought no more about it, except that the person was so beautiful that I wanted more, and turned it into a general daydream. I called him Peter, and he became my imaginary friend, such as many children have. Sometimes the daydreams were fluent and frequent, other times they were totally absent and I could not recall them at will. I just waited and knew they would return, even if I had to wait six months.
>
> The second Real Dream was when I was in my early twenties, about 1955. I was asleep, and knew that I was asleep. I was enveloped in a glorious, inexpressibly beautiful, warm, safe, peaceful golden light, but the light was a person, and I knew without words that it was God. I could not say he or she. Just a person. It was not dazzling

to the sight, but I was prostrated in humble adoration of this wonderful being, and never actually dared to look at the light. It was overwhelming *bliss*. I think that is what St. Paul calls "being caught up to the Seventh Heaven" and the words have passed into our vocabulary. It may also be what people mean when they say they have "seen the light." That was forty years ago, and is indelibly on my memory. I doubt if it will ever be repeated until I die and pass into this presence. I could not turn that into a daydream, just remember it with gratitude for ever.

My third Real Dream—so real that it left me in trembling shock—was . . . what I now call Revelation Day. It was thirty-five years ago and I was twenty-nine years old.

I seemed to be trying to get through those rocks at the entrance to Lulworth Cove. The wind and the sea were rushing and roaring, and all was tumult. Suddenly the Lord was talking to me, and I was stupefied. He knew my name! He seemed amused, and then asked if I knew who He was. I said, "Well, you are God, of course." "Yes, but *who am I*?" I did not understand the question. Then the whole of my life passed by at tremendous speed, and then the same images from my life history were repeated again and again and again. Eventually, I understood. "Oooh! *You're Peter!*" I said. "Oh, yes, yes, *yes, yes, yes*!" He said, and somehow picked me up and whirled me into this state of *bliss* again. I was through the rocks and into Lulworth Cove, which was probably all my subconscious could do to describe the extraordinary things it was dealing with. The wind and the sea were still.

All was huge joy and peace and wonderment, like two lovers who have lost and found each other. My "best friend," who I had always thought was my imaginary friend, turned out to be my Maker, and indeed who better to be an imaginary friend. We had been through thirty years together, with all our secret daydreams, and he knew all about me and more about me than I knew myself. It was breathtaking and indescribable, and left me in a state of shock and trembling.

Since then, I have become a Roman Catholic, which He seemed to want me to do. At first I thought this meant it was the True Church, and perhaps it is, but basically I think He thought I needed it, just as parents choose the right schools for their children depending on the needs of the child. I needed a strong church to teach me right from wrong, which Rome certainly did, although it did not teach me how to obey its instructions, and I am still a very poor example of a Christian—but then, the RC Church is noted throughout its history as being a church of sinners.

The outstanding feature of this dream is its mystical quality and the intense feelings of bliss. The life review in which "Peter" knew all about her is also a feature of some near-death experiences. Again it is worth noting the profound effect that these three dreams had on Marion S.'s life, even to the extent of leading her to the Roman Catholic Church.

Mystical experiences seem very real. But a feeling that a dream is "real" does not in itself mean that it is a mystical experience. Lucid dreams are real, and they may also involve out-of-body sensations and the vivid colours experienced in the next dream, sent to us by Mrs. J. Kelly. What makes this dream seem more than a lucid dream is the experience of golden light and the feelings of intense peace and love emanating from the figure of Jesus. People who have an NDE also often say, as does Mrs. Kelly, that when they meet the Being of Light they "talk" but with their mind, not their mouths.

It happened one night as I lay in bed to sleep. I remember the feeling of being in the sky. I felt very light. I did feel a weight, but it was as if I were as small as a tennis ball. I felt as if I was not in my body at all. Suddenly I started drifting along in a grey sky, for a few seconds. As I came out of the grey sky, I floated along into a beautiful bright blue sky. I could see all around me for miles, although I could not see myself. I saw lovely colours, a blue sky, blue sea, palm trees, sandy hills. I went over a lovely blue lake, with floats. I looked down to see a man standing next to a tree, he was looking upwards at me, it was as if he was expecting me. I recognised the man to be Jesus. I felt myself coming down until I was about four feet away from him. My eyes seemed to focus in on him and

I saw everything in detail. His hair was a golden brown with blond streaks in it. The sun seemed to be shining on him, giving him a golden glow. There must have been a breeze because his hair was blowing softly in the wind. He was wearing a grey/off-white tunic with a white rope tied around his waist. His hands were held in front of him just below his belt. I looked down to his shoes and saw he was wearing brown and gold sandals. I looked up at his face again and thought how lovely this man was. He was smiling at me softly and I felt so much peace and love coming from this man that I did not mind at all how long I stayed, I just felt so happy in this lovely land with Jesus. Suddenly I found myself talking to him! But I was not using my mouth and I could not hear words coming out of my mouth. I could hear the words coming out of my mind. What I said to him was, "Is there really a heaven?" and "Will it be all right?"

And then he answered back, but he did not use his mouth either. I could hear the words in his mind very clearly, and he answered, "Yes, yes there is," "yes." Suddenly I felt myself going backwards and going up into the sky again and saw his eyes looking up at me and watching me go. I went back the same way as I came. Then I woke up. But I knew it was not a dream. I knew it had been real. It was not like a dream at all, it was so different and real.

Like near-death experiences, some mystical dreams carry with them a message specifically for the experiencer. It is as if at some deep level the dreamer needs guidance and help with regard to the path he is following through life. In this dream the culmination of the experience is the answer given to the dreamer's uncertainties about what happens after death. However, it is very seldom that any mystical experience will offer specific advice or instructions about what should be done. The dreamer is much more likely to be given some general comment on his spiritual development, and reassurance that he will be all right.

Roger Payne told us of a dream which he believed to be a "kind of NDE," dreamed by a close friend of his, Brian, who was ill with cardiomyopathy. Roger says that his friend was not conventionally religious and not preconditioned to have such a dream, though he did have a deep sense of God and some transcendent meaning to life. "We knew," he says "that recovery was impossible, but neither of us was consciously aware that it would in fact occur so soon afterwards—about six weeks later. I write the dream as he wrote it in his note-book."

Another bed appeared in my bedroom, ninety degrees to my own, on the left and against the window. A figure in the bed, neat in a white garment. The whole bed floated down the room and stopped at the end of my own bed, with the figure facing me. The figure pointed to some-where on my right and said, "Look at the pictures." "The pictures" consisted of an open-page photo album, the right-hand page consisted of faded grey photos, neatly displayed. But in the top right-hand corner was a brilliant colour scene—the more I looked at it, the bigger it be-came, plus movement of everything (it became a real scene that I was in). It seemed to me to be taking place in southern India or similar environment (all the most wonderful colours, flowers, exotic and beautiful). I en-tered the scene and the whole thing became "real life."

On the left was the most beautiful Pullman train [my friend was a train buff; he loved them, and his father and grandfather worked on the railways]. The colours were Great Western brown with lots of gold linings and pol-ished brass fittings—it was all *new* and waiting for pas-sengers to board [a train going west!]. I stood enthralled at the end of the train, and a small figure to my right resembling ET or similar spoke to me and said, *"Don't miss it!"* The horizon was radiant blue, to which the train was headed.

Roger Payne adds:

I feel the dream hardly needs comment. My friend said he was unsure whether it meant actual death or figurative death, the end of a phase. He had, a year or so before, gone through all his old photos and destroyed many of them (the faded grey photos of his life memories). ET is particularly significant—the extra-terrestrial, the being from another world. His message is enigmatic and seems to imply "be aware," see what is going to happen, don't miss your train to another world. Note too that, as with all such death dreams and NDEs, it is a journey, but not an *end*.

The symbol of a journey recurs often in NDEs—a train, a moving staircase, or (most frequently) a tunnel. It is interesting too that the feeling accompanying this always seems to be of a journey forwards; towards someone or somewhere. There never seems to be any feeling of regret or of looking over one's shoulder at what is being left behind. The future is nearly always positive.

In April 1992 Christine Matters had a dream in which she left her body and floated up to the ceiling, watching herself asleep on the bed below. About a month later she had another dream. This time, she says:

I immediately sensed I had gone further than my ceiling. I was moving at great speed through an air force base about eighteen kilometres away from my home, which I recognised . . . because I had been there before. Once again I felt an incredible feeling of being in control, so powerful it was almost unbelievable. I was conscious and aware and decided to continue my journey. Below me, in a hangar on the base, were men asleep in blue overalls. I was hovering over the ceiling just looking at them. Suddenly one man sat up and looked at me right to my face and yelled out, "What are you doing here?" I didn't know this man but he gave me a hell of a shock. I went through the wall and out into a field. Below me was dark with misty haze just above the grass, but above me were lights. Many lights.

Suddenly I focused on a jeep moving on the road below me. I followed it and yet I felt I was being pulled by it. There were six men dressed in a tan uniform inside the moving jeep. They all spontaneously turned around and looked at me for a second and immediately turned around again to face the road. Next thing, the jeep stopped and the six men got out and climbed a massive staircase, one behind the other. Everything was white and bright lights were now everywhere. I was amazed because I could see a silvery cord attached from behind each of their necks, leading forever with no end. With that, I turned once again and could see the men were all watching me as they climbed the stairs. Now I could see a square white roughly three-inch-square object across each man's mouth . . . I looked up the staircase and the men had disappeared. Now I found myself in the void which I believed the men had entered. I looked at my hand and I had a square object like the men had had across their mouths. I looked down and could see the "me" and my husband lying in our bed below. I floated down slowly to him and stopped just a few inches above him. I took the square object out of my hand and placed it on his mouth. I wanted him to come with me wherever I was going. But my hand was going right through his face. I wasn't surprised and thought to myself, "Oh well, I'm still going."

Back up I went. Whilst in this void I could see a door slightly ajar. I knew that wherever I was going this door had to be closed. I firmly took a grip of the door handle and tried to close it. While doing this I could see, through the slight opening, hundreds and hundreds of lights moving. Suddenly I could feel this void moving. I looked down to where the "me" and my husband were lying, but nothing was moving. I looked around where I was and nothing was moving and yet when I looked out through the gap everything was moving and the sensation of rotating was now quite vivid. I decided I was going to put all my strength in closing this bloody door and took hold of it, when I could sense someone standing next to me. I turned around to see a beautiful woman dressed in white. She had long wavy hair which seemed to be floating round her magnificent face. I looked at her and she spoke with the sweetest voice. "You are not ready. You cannot go yet." The goodness she had was something I had never felt before in my life. I looked into her beautiful eyes without understanding, and suddenly, I woke up in my bed. I gasped for air and tried to open my eyes, but I couldn't. And yet I knew I was back in my body.

Everything was dark, but these lights I had seen before were still high above me. Slowly I concentrated and opened my eyes. Doing so the lights gradually disappeared.

I felt my pulse and just lay for a few seconds to regain control. But I knew something extraordinary had happened. My hand hurt. Hurt badly. I woke my husband up and told him of the pain in my hand. It was closed in a tight clenched fist. I just couldn't open it. When I finally did, I had horrible red bruises round my fingers and palm. I panicked. I began telling my husband what had just happened. Within twenty-four hours all the bruises had disappeared. I showed three people the marks, to verify a) that I had them and b) twenty-four hours later, that they had disappeared.

She adds that the experience changed her. "Not that I was a bad person previously, but just that my priorities differ immensely."

The vivid imagery suggests that this is a REM dream, with the awakening marked by mild sleep paralysis—she was unable to move and felt that she could not breathe—which quickly terminated. But what is very unusual is the state of her hand when she awoke. The obvious reason for the marks on her hand is that her fist was tightly clenched. There were marks on both fingers and palm, as if she had been holding something tightly, and in her dream she was, she says, holding the door handle tightly while trying to push against the door to close it. It must be remembered that in an REM dream, which this clearly was because of the sleep paralysis on awakening, the body is paralysed specifically to stop the acting out of dream imagery. However, on this occasion she seems to have been able to overcome the paralysis and clenched her hand so tightly in the dream that not only were marks left on it, but it was painful.

An alternative explanation is that the marks on her hand were stigmata. Stigmata are marks on the skin surface which have a psychological significance and cause, and yet are mediated by natural body processes. They are seen occasionally in very specific situations, such as when an overwhelming belief in Christ results in the appearance of the stigmata of the

Passion. They often consist of a breakdown of the skin of the hands and feet at the point where Christ is commonly thought to have been nailed to the cross. Certainly this was a dream which had great emotional significance for Christine. She commented that it was no ordinary dream, that it was of such importance that it changed her. The action of closing the door was clearly of great psychological significance to her, something to which she was directing a lot of psychic energy in her dream, and it is possible that her skin responded with bruises. The relationship between skin and psyche is a close one. The commonest example of this is blushing, the dilation of blood vessels in the skin following an emotional stimulus in a sensitive person. Anybody who has suffered from eczema will know the relationship between a worsening of the eczema and psychological stress.

Although stigmata have usually been described in the waking state, we know that emotions can be felt strongly in dreams, and so there is no theoretical reason why stigmata should not be induced by dreams, although I have never come across such a case. However, stigmata are usually painless, so although this would be an interesting explanation, I don't think, in this case, that it is the most likely one. This dream is an excellent example of an "ordinary" dream with vivid imagery overlaid by a transcendental experience.

There are numerous accounts of people who have dreamed that someone close to them has died. Often (but not always) this presentiment turns out to be true. Even more intriguing are two dreams we have been told which are very similar to accounts in the literature of the near-death experience, in which experiences seem to be "shared," as though someone close to the dying person accompanies them on this first stage of their journey from their earthly life.

Mrs. Michelle Rootsey describes this dream she had about her grandmother's death. She was very close to her grandmother, who brought her up and was like a mother to her.

At 3.15 a.m. on 25 March 1991 I woke from the most disturbing and at the same time the happiest of dreams, but so real. I was crying. In my dream I was in a meadow, knee high in wild flowers. It was a warm, sunny day with a gentle breeze blowing into my face. I felt like a little child; I was with my nanny. I felt so young, so happy, so free of all worries. We were both wearing the most beautiful white dresses all smocked and flowing so intricately made with embroidered panels but all white and beaded. We were holding hands, walking and walking, there was peace all around, birds and flowers, trees in the distance and it was so quiet. Nanny was telling me she was all right and not to worry and that she was going to show me around.

She took me to a Georgian house, a mansion with a huge rolling lawn in front. Steps led down on to the grass and the veranda was edged with a beautiful stone balustrade. The building itself was three or four storeys high. Very grand, almost like a country palace. I have never seen anything like it yet. Inside she took me into a very wide and long corridor-type room which was separated into rooms not with walls but draped fabric like muslin, all blowing gently as the warm breezes made their way through the house. In each room was a bed like very old iron hospital beds with ladies again dressed in white. Some were being comforted and all who looked at me were smiling, welcoming me here. All the time there were others walking around this place as though it was a working house. If I remember right, Nanny was saying that she would be going to see her other relatives later on, naming them.

After this she said she had to go and see Grandad and took me to what I can only describe as an underground tunnel, well lit, glowing white. People were coming and going, some sitting on benches, but all dressed in the beautiful white clothes. It was like one of our tube stations in London, but peaceful. There was a wind blowing down here like a train passing but I'm not sure if it was a train.

Abruptly I woke up, laughing and happy, crying and very hurt and sad. It was dead on 3.15 a.m. I looked at the clock and I had to talk to my husband. I woke him and explained what had happened. He promised that we would go and see Nanny in the morning to tell her she was going to be OK and to see her and give her a hug. I could hardly sleep a wink and rang my mother at six a.m., excited to tell her my news and my dream, which I blurted out and said I'll be round soon to pick her up and we'll go and see Nanny early today. I was on such a high. The conversation turned then to my mother. She said at 3.30 a.m. she had received a phone call from the hospital saying that Nanny had died in the night. The nurses had gone in to change her position, then left her for one minute while they got some equipment. When they got back she had died. It was 3.15 a.m.

The imagery in this dream bears some remarkable similarities to the imagery of many NDEs. The idyllic pastoral setting, the flowing robes and peace and quietness, the feeling of being welcomed by the people one sees are all typical of the near-death experience. The scene shifts to a room in a grand house, and the imagery includes hospital beds on which people are lying and being comforted. This vision of healing, of being made whole again, is another theme which quite often recurs in NDEs. People in the NDE often see dead relatives as their younger selves, in the prime of life, even though they may have been ill and elderly when they died. In one instance in an NDE experience reported to us, the person was walking beside a Jesus-like figure. Walking with them were a multitude of crippled, bandaged people, who were taking off their bandages, throwing away their crutches as they went, as if they were symbolically becoming whole again after they had died.

The NDE leaves the experiencer feeling positive and without any fear of death, and this comes through very strongly in this dream. Even though the dream had made her so sad, Michelle was happy for her grandmother and could hardly wait to tell her that she was "going to be OK." Of course, one can argue that Michelle knew that her grandmother was close to death and the dream was entirely in response to this. But is it stretching coincidence too far to say that the fact that she woke from her dream just as her grandmother died was purely coincidental? Michelle was very close to her grandmother, and if telepathy is an element in these experiences it is in just this sort of relationship that one would expect it to occur.

This next dream is in some respects similar, in that the dreamer, June Clark, also seemed to be taking part in the death of a friend. Some of the same imagery appears—including the hospital bed and white gown (I note that she describes this as paper or cotton, and fervently hope it was cotton. Paper gowns were introduced into the health service in a major way as an economy measure in the 1980s. It would be a sad comment on the health service if its cuts were extending even into the transcendental state of the near-death experience).

It was 1979 and I had gone to bed in the usual way, nothing different about the day. I woke up to find myself on a hospital table or trolley. I was covered over with a white sheet. I sat up—everything was pitch dark but I could faintly make out other trolleys covered with white sheets around me. I turned to put my feet to the floor but I realised the legs and feet were not mine, they were a man's legs and feet. I stood up and realised how tall I was. I had a man's body. I was wearing a hospital gown of some kind, it could have been paper or cotton, it was just over the knees. I felt like myself inside and I tried to see around me. It seemed a very large place and so dark except in the distance I could see a pinpoint of light and I knew I had to get to it. I started towards it but my legs were giving way. I started to stagger from side to side. I was so weak, and over and over I kept thinking "If only I could see." I tried to gather the strength from inside to keep going and after a great struggle I reached the light. As I reached it a lift with a bright light stopped at my level and a black iron gate opened and I stepped in. The gate shut and the lift went upwards. There was a little group of people in the lift dressed in black and I felt awkward because I only had the gown on—but then I realised they didn't see me. They went on talking to each other. The lift stopped and I got out. The people had gone, I found myself standing at the bottom of moving stairs seeming to go up through a square in the ceiling. I stepped on the stairs and started going upwards, the light got brighter and brighter the more I went up, suddenly I was me again in my own body, and standing on the step with me going up was a friend's husband I hadn't seen for several years. I had my arm around his waist and he had his arm around my neck, his hand on my shoulder. I was supporting him. I noticed he was smartly dressed.

Side by side we continued upwards. We then stepped off the stairs into a room so large and brilliant with light; as we stepped off the stairs my friend's husband was gone. There were many people there all seeming very busy. Again I felt awkward at only having a gown on, and the light was so bright it was indescribable. All at once I knew I had to find a door to get away . . . I stepped out into the street. It was dull and raining. I stood there waiting, then I saw a funeral cortège coming towards me. I didn't see any people but it stopped in front of me, a door opened and I got in where the coffin goes. Then I woke up.

I hadn't seen my friends for nearly three years but they had known me since I was sixteen. We had spent many happy hours together and I loved my friend's husband like a brother. We lost touch after we moved house, but on that last visit my friend's husband was coming up to retirement—he was a bus driver. One week after the experience I awoke in the middle of the night to find my friend's husband standing by my bed. He smiled at me, he looked like he did when I first knew him, but I did notice he was wearing a butcher's apron and cap. He smiled again and was gone and I fell asleep again.

Six weeks after my experiences I had a letter to say my friend's husband had died six weeks before. I was deeply sad having not seen him for some time. In 1986 my husband died, and I later received a letter from my friend . . . After some visits I told her of my experiences. She was very taken aback. Then I told her of the later visit from her husband. She told me her husband hadn't been well for some time, with heart trouble, plus he was losing his sight and was very tired. She also told me he had a part-time job in a butcher's shop near where they lived and he had collapsed and died there. She said she knew her husband had always cared for me in the same way I cared for him.

Did I help him to the higher realms? Did I take his weakness and do it for him? I shall never know, but one thing I am certain of, I know I went with him, I went through the darkness into the light, but I knew I had to get back.

One can look at this dream in several ways. It is difficult to get an accurate picture of the timing of events, but if the second experience—the apparition of her friend's husband beside her bed—coincided with his death, the first dream, a week before this, would have to have been precognitive. Alternatively, the dream might have been telepathic. Her friend knew he was ill, possibly that he was dying, and his thoughts might well have turned to old times and old friends. A third interpretation is that the dream offered the dreamer a glimpse of her own personal journey towards the light, the revelation that she was not her body. However, a dream belongs to the dreamer, and one has to accept the feelings it evokes in them. In this case she had no doubts. Her dream was a mission in which she took over the weakness of a friend and helped and supported him as he moved after death towards the light.

Miss Jackie White has muscular dystrophy and is confined to a wheelchair. Several years ago she was ill with a really bad cold and felt so weak that she decided to have an early night and go to bed.

While I was asleep I can remember I was in a round room and it was brightly white. If you can think of being in a large can of paint, that is what the room was like. Just round, no corners, just brightly white. I was not alone, there were five or six other people and we were all in a queue about twelve inches off the floor and we were all gliding slowly towards a door that was opening really slowly. We all had white gowns on like hospital gowns. We were still moving slowly towards the door, while it was opening. The light that was shining through the door was really bright, but I didn't cover my eyes. I just wanted to get through that door.

I got so close to the door, suddenly I heard a deep voice that filled the room. It was a man's; he said, "No, Jacqueline, not yet." He said it so slowly. When he said it I can remember I tutted, and I was being pulled back slowly from the door. As I was moving back the door started closing. I felt really annoyed. I wanted to go through that door.

In this dream the bright light, the longing to go through the
door, and the realisation that it wasn't yet time are all typical
of the near-death mystical experience. Jackie also adds, "This
all felt so real it could not have been a dream," a feeling which
is also characteristic of the mystical experience.

BJ told us of a dream she had had before the death of her
mother, whom she loved very much. BJ began to dread the
thought that she might die in pain, and to pray that her ending
might be painless and peaceful.

One night I dreamed that I was in a cobbled street in a
district of Manchester called Ancoats, where my family
came from. I noticed that there was a woman near me
(my sister). I walked along the cobbles and they began to
get wet and I realised they were the beginning of a canal.
The water got deeper and dirtier, really messy, and then
it began to get cleaner and cleaner. I was astounded when
suddenly it was so clear and sparkling that I could see
blue patterned tiles at the bottom and children, some with
armbands, playing and laughing. I felt so proud. The sun
was shining. I turned to the woman and said, "I used to
come from here. Isn't it lovely?" I also felt a little confused, because I felt it shouldn't be me standing there.

Then I noticed that there was a small white fence in
front of me, and a little to the side, and the woman was
on the other side. The sun was just as bright without being
too warm. I heard a man's voice. He said: "Come to me
refreshed." I turned and looked and saw Jesus. He had
shortish curly hair and no beard. I felt His hair was brown
and His eyes were blue, and He was standing looking at
me with His arms outstretched. The light of the sun was
shining on His head and it seemed to radiate everywhere.
I can't put into words how it affected me. Even now it
takes my breath away. Have you ever tried to imagine
what pure love must feel like? That's what I felt when
my eyes met His. I felt I was wrapped up in it like a
cocoon. I woke up and wept with happiness and other
feelings I can't put into words. Even now [two years later]
I weep every day when I remember. For about ten days
after my dream the love and warmth stayed with me. I
was walking on air. It gradually faded, but I feel so hum-

ble, so "blessed" and again so many things I can't put into words.

BJ's mother died a few weeks after she had this dream. "When she died I found it very difficult to cry because I knew there was no need. I knew where she was." Since that time she has had a recurrence of the feelings she experienced in her dream, associated with the need to find some spiritual path, and has started on the road to Roman Catholicism.

BJ's dream is a wonderful example of transcendence. It starts with the journey (this world) where the cobbles are wet and dirty and the water deeper and dirtier. As the journey progresses towards transcendence, the water becomes clean and feelings of universal love start to penetrate through all aspects of the scene. There is, as in many NDEs, a barrier, the small white fence. Although it is not explicit, the implication is that she was prevented from reaching the divine, although she was wrapped in "pure love." As in many NDEs there is the realisation that she should not be there; it was not her time. And as is usually the case in the NDE, there is no sensation of a return journey; just an instantaneous finding oneself back in the body, or in this case, awakening.

One of the hallmarks of a mystical experience is that it changes you. Being "in the light" leaves its mark. It left BJ with the knowledge that she need not grieve for her mother because she "knew where she was." It left her with a memory of the feeling of pure love so strong that for days afterwards she was "walking on air," and even two years later recalling the feeling could make her weep with happiness. And finally, it proved to be a spiritual awakening that set her on a religious path.

Those who have had mystical experiences of the intensity related in this chapter are in no doubt about their meaning. They point inwards and upwards to a universal spiritual dimension of which they themselves are a part. They leave our current science far behind, as Western science is Galilean. Galileo split off the subjective from the objective, ignoring the subjective. Descartes, too, cut off mind from body—body was the domain of science, mind, with spirit or soul, of the Church. The Church has never known quite what to do with Descartes' gift. It has never shown much interest in collecting and examining these experiences, or understood that it is through the mystical experience of the ordinary individual that the transcendent is manifest.

It is now time for the mystics and the scientists together to create a new science which will integrate both the subjective and the objective. The underlying precept of this new science will be that (as is already shown by physics) the world is highly interconnected, and not finally determined by random chance, although there are clearly random processes within it. The transcendental vision is a manifestation of a universe which is highly moral and of an underlying order, one aspect of which is universal love.

In his autobiography *Rain upon Godshill*, J. B. Priestley describes a dream which, he says, left a greater impression on his mind than any experience he had ever known before, awake or in dreams, and which "said more to me about this life than any book I have ever read."

I dreamt I was standing at the top of a very high tower, alone, looking down upon myriads of birds all flying in one direction; every kind of bird was there, all the birds in the world. It was a noble sight, this vast aerial river of birds. But now in some mysterious fashion the gear was changed, and time speeded up, so that I saw generations of birds, watched them break their shells, flutter into life, mate, weaken, falter and die. Wings grew only to crumble; bodies were sleek, and then, in a flash, bled and shrivelled; and death struck everywhere at every second. What was the use of all this blind struggle towards life, this eager trying of wings, this hurried mating, this flight and surge, all this gigantic meaningless effort? As I stared down, seeming to see every creature's ignoble little history almost at a glance, I felt sick at heart. It would be better if not one of them, if not one of us, had been born, if the struggle ceased for ever. I stood on my tower, still alone, desperately unhappy. But now the gear was changed again, and the time went faster still, and it was rushing by at such a rate, that the birds could not show any movement, but were like an enormous plain sown with feathers. But along this plain, flickering through the bodies themselves, there now passed a sort of white flame, trembling, dancing, then hurrying on; and as soon as I saw it I knew that this white flame was life itself, the very quintessence of being; and then it came to me, in a rocket burst of ecstasy, that nothing mattered, nothing could ever matter, because nothing else was real but this quivering and hurrying lambency of being. Birds, men and creatures not yet shaped and coloured, all were of no account except so far as this flame of life travelled through them. It left nothing to mourn over behind it; what I had thought was tragedy was mere emptiness or a shadow show; for now all real feeling was caught and purified and danced on ecstatically with the white flame of life. I had never before felt such deep happiness as I knew at the end of my dream of the tower and the birds, and if I have not kept that happiness with me, as an inner atmosphere and sanctuary for the heart, that is because I am a weak and foolish man who allows this mad world to come in destroying every green shoot of wisdom. Nevertheless, I have not been quite the same man since. A dream had come through the multitude of business.

So even a dream can open us to the mystical or transcendental experience. The dream, in fact, is neither more nor less privileged than the waking state, or even the state of consciousness near death. In a dream, consciousness is clothed in the metaphor of the dreamer, but the transcendent dream appears to show us some aspects of our true selves which seem to point to a spiritual underpinning of the universe. The dreaming mind can touch the very bedrock of creation and see through to the universal love which appears in the transcendental state to be the ground state of the universe. Priestley was one of the lucky few for whom a dream proves to be a revelation, a peak experience that seems to draw together the threads of life and give it meaning.

The real hallmark of these visionary dreams—the dreams that Jung called ''great dreams''—is that they are of an order of meaning which seems to go beyond the personal; touching a chord and having significance for others besides the dreamer.

Through the experience of these few fortunate visionary dreamers, we may all be offered a glimpse of what lies behind the hidden door, and a promissory note that it may indeed prove to be a gateway to the soul.

Bibliography

Anderson, W., *Dante the Maker*, Routledge and Kegan Paul, 1980.

Barker, J. C., "Premonitions of the Aberfan Disaster," *Journal of the Society for Psychical Research*, December 1967, Vol. 44 No. 734.

Benson, Gerard, "The Invention," *Evidence of Elephants: Poems*, Viking, 1995.

Besterman, T., "Report of Enquiry into Precognitive Dreams," *Proceedings of the Society for Psychical Research*, 1933, 41, pp. 186–204.

Blacker, Thetis, *A Pilgrimage of Dreams*, Turnstone Books Ltd., 1973.

Blagrove, M., "Dreams as the Reflection of our Waking Concerns and Abilities. A Critique of the Problem-Solving Paradigm in Dream Research," *Dreaming*, 2, 1992, pp. 205–20.

Boss, M., *Analysis of Dreams*, New York Philosophical Library, 1958.

Broughton, R., *et al.*, "Homicidal Somnambulism: A Case Report," *Sleep*, 1994, 17 (3) pp. 253–64.

Buchanan, A., "Sleepwalking and Indecent Exposure," *Medicine, Science and the Law*, 1991, Vol. 31 No. 1.

Bucke, R., *Cosmic Consciousness: A study in the evolution of the human mind*, Concord, Mass., Ye Old Dept Press, 1961.

Crick, F., and Mitchison, G., "The Function of Dream Sleep," *Nature*, 1983, 304.

Currie, I., *You Cannot Die!*, Element Books, 1995.

Dement, William, *Some Must Watch While Some Must Sleep*, W. H. Freeman, 1972.

Devereux, P., *Re-Visioning the Earth*, Simon and Schuster, 1996.

Dunne, J. W., *An Experiment with Time*, Faber and Faber, 1927.

Fenwick, P., "Somnambulism and the Law: A Review," *Behavioural Sciences and the Law*, 1987, Vol. 5 No. 3.

Fontana, D., *The Secret Language of Dreams*, Pavilion, 1994.

Fordham, F., *An Introduction to Jung's Psychology*, Pelican, 1953.

Freud, S., *On Dreams*, tr. James Strachey, W. W. Norton & Co., 1952.

Freud, S., *The Interpretation of Dreams*, Basic Books, 1953.

Fruman, Nicholas, *The Damaged Archangel*, Allen and Unwin, 1972.

Gackenbach, J. and LaBerge, S., (eds), *Conscious Mind, Sleeping Brain: Perspectives on Lucid Dreaming*, Plenum, 1988.

Garfield, P., *Creative Dreaming*, Simon and Schuster, 1974.

Garfield, P., *Pathway to Ecstasy*, Prentice Hall, 1989 (rev. ed.).

Garfield, P., *The Healing Power of Dreams*, Simon and Schuster, 1991.

Green, C., and McCreery, C., *Lucid Dreaming*, Routledge, 1994.

Harraldsson, E., "Representative National Surveys of Psychic Phenomena," *Journal of the Society for Psychical Research*, 1985, Vol. 53 No. 201.

Hay, D., and Morisy, A., "Reports of Ecstatic, Paranormal or Religious Experience in Great Britain and the United States—A Comparison of Trends," *Journal for the Scientific Study of Religion*, 1978, 17, 255–68.

Hearne, K., "A Survey of Reported Premonitions and of Those Who Have Them," *Journal of the Society for Psychical Research*, February 1984, Vol. 52 No. 796.

Hearne, K., "An Analysis of Premonitions Deposited over One Year, from an Apparently Gifted Subject," *Journal of the Society for Psychical Research*, 1986, Vol. 53 No. 804.

Hearne, K., "A Nationwide Mass-Dream-Telepathy Experiment," *Journal of the Society for Psychical Research*, January 1989, Vol. 55 No. 814.

Hobson, J. A., *The Dreaming Brain*, Basic Books, 1988.

Hobson, J. A., "Sleeping and Dreaming," *Neuroscience* 10, 1990, pp. 371–382.

Hufford, D. J., *The Terror that Comes in the Night: An Experience-Centred Study of Supernatural Assault Traditions*, University of Pennsylvania Press, 1989.

Jung, C. G., *The Development of Personality*, Coll. Wks Vol. 17, Routledge, 1953.

Krippner, S., "A Pilot Study in ESP, Dreams and Purported OBEs," *Journal of the Society of Psychical Research*, April 1996, Vol. 61 No. 843.

Krippner, S., and Persinger, M., "Enhanced Congruence between Dreams and Distant Target Material During Periods of Decreased Geomagnetic Activity," *Journal of Scientific Exploration*, 1996, Vol. 10 No. 4.

LaBerge, S., *Lucid Dreaming*, Ballantine Books, 1985.

Laing, R. D., *The Divided Self*, Pelican, 1965.

Lorimer, D., *Survival? Body Mind and Death in the Light of Psychic Experience*, Routledge and Kegan Paul, 1984.

Mathieson, A., *The Healing Power of Dreams*, abstract of paper for 5th European Congress of Hypnosis, 1990.

Maury, L.F.A. *Le Sommeil et les Rêves*, Didier, 1876.

Mavromatis, Andreas, *Hypnagogia*, Routledge and Kegan Paul, 1987.

Myers, F., Gurney, E., and Podmore, F. *Phantasms of the Living*, Society for Psychical Research, London, 1886.

Oswald, I., and Evans, J., "On Serious Violence during Sleepwalking," *British Journal of Psychiatry*, December 1985, Vol. 147.

Ouspensky, P. D., *A New Model of the Universe*, Kegan Paul, Trench, 1938, Trubner & Co. Ltd.

Paulos, J. A., *Innumeracy: Mathematical Illiteracy and Its Consequences*, Penguin, 1988.

Persinger, M. A., and Krippner, S., "Dream ESP Experiments and Geomagnetic Activity," *Journal of the American Society for Psychical Research*, April 1989, Vol. 83 No. 2.

Priestley, J. B., *Rain upon Godshill*, Heinemann, 1939.

Rivers, W.H.R., *Conflict and Dreams*, Kegan Paul, Trench, 1923, Trubner & Co. Ltd.

Roydon, R., *Dreams and Physical Illness* (in press).

Rudofsky, S., and Wotiz, J., "Psychologists and the Dream

Accounts of August Kekulé, *Journal of Human Behaviour and Learning*, 1988, 5, 1–11.

Sacks, Oliver, *Awakenings*, Picador, 1982.

Sacks, Oliver, *A Leg to Stand On*, Picardo, 1991.

Saint-Denys, Hervey de, *Dreams and How to Guide Them*, edited with an introduction by Morton Schatzman, Duckworth, 1982.

Schatzman, M., "Dreams and Problem Solving," *International Medicine* 4, 1984, pp. 6–9.

Schatzman, M., "The Meaning of Dreaming," *New Scientist*, Christmas 1986, pp. 36–9.

Schatzman, M., and Fenwick, P., "Dreams and Dreaming," in *Sleep*, ed. Cooper, R., Chapman and Hall, 1994.

Schatzman, M., Fenwick, P., and Worsley, A., "Correspondence During Lucid Dreaming Between Dreamed and Actual Events," in Gackenbach and LaBerge (eds) *Conscious Mind, Sleeping Brain*, Plenum, 1988, pp. 155–79.

Sondow, N., "The Decline of Precognised Events with the Passage of Time," *Journal of the American Society of Psychical Research* 8, 1988.

Stowell, M., "Researching Precognitive Dreams. A Review of Past Methods, Emerging Scientific Paradigms and Future Approaches," *Journal of the American Society for Psychical Research*, April 1995, Vol. 89 No. 2.

Taylor, J., "Precognition and Intuitive Decisions: An Answer to the Problems of Free Will and Causality," *Journal of the Society for Psychical Research*, October 1995, Vol. 60, No. 841.

van de Castle, R., *Our Dreaming Mind*, Aquarian, 1994.

Vieira, Waldo, *Projections of the Consciousness*, Rio de Janeiro, Instituto Internacional de Projeciologia, 1995.

Wood-Trost, L., "Possible Precognition of the Teton Dam Disaster in Idaho," *Journal of the Society for Psychical Research*, June 1981, Vol. 51 No. 788.

Index